Culture and Cognition

Cultural Sociology series

Culture and Cognition: Patterns in the Social Construction of Reality,
  Wayne H. Brekhus
Protest: A Cultural Introduction to Social Movements, James M. Jasper
The Culture of Markets, Frederick F. Wherry

Culture and Cognition

Patterns in the Social Construction of Reality

Wayne H. Brekhus

polity

First published in 2015 by Polity Press

Polity Press
65 Bridge Street
Cambridge CB2 1UR, UK

Polity Press
350 Main Street
Malden, MA 02148, USA

ISBN-13: 978-0-7456-7176-5
ISBN-13: 978-0-7456-7177-2 (pb)

A catalogue record for this book is available from the British Library.

Library of Congress Cataloging-in-Publication Data

Brekhus, Wayne,
   Culture and cognition : patterns in the social construction of reality / Wayne H. Brekhus.
      pages cm
   Includes bibliographical references and index.
   ISBN 978-0-7456-7176-5 (hardback : alk. paper) -- ISBN 978-0-7456-7177-2 (pbk. : alk. paper) 1. Cognition and culture. 2. Social psychology. I. Title.
   BF311.B7224 2015
   306.4'2--dc23
                                      2015004488

Typeset in 11 on 13 pt Sabon by
Servis Filmsetting Ltd, Stockport, Cheshire
Printed and bound in the UK by CPI Group (UK) Ltd, Croydon, CR0 4YY

For further information on Polity, visit our website: www.politybooks.com

Contents

Acknowledgments

I am indebted to several people who have contributed greatly to my thinking during the writing of this book. Eviatar Zerubavel introduced me to the exciting analytic possibilities of studying culture and cognition many years ago when I was a graduate student at Rutgers University in the 1990s. Eviatar's intellectual passion and ongoing support and friendship continue to inspire me. I have benefitted tremendously from our many stimulating conversations about cognitive sociology. My thinking about culture and cognition has been sharpened by the valuable insights of Karen Danna, Tom DeGloma, Asia Friedman, Daina Cheyenne Harvey, Kyle Puetz, and J. T. Thomas, who all read and commented on an early draft. Each of them guided me to consider new angles that have expanded the breadth and depth of this book. I am grateful for the steady encouragement and enthusiasm of Jonathan Skerrett, my editor at Polity. He has advised me well throughout the process. I am also indebted to Fiona Sewell at Polity for her very thorough, efficient, and attentive copy-editing. Finally, I thank my wife, Rachel Brekhus, who provided an extra set of eyes and a full measure of moral support whenever they were needed.

Introduction:
Culture and Cognition in Sociology

This book explores the cultural sociology of cognition. Despite the quite common feeling that our thoughts are individualistic in nature – private and uniquely our own – thinking is a distinctly social phenomenon. Our thoughts are co-produced within the cultures, subcultures, social networks, communities, and organizations that we belong to. The social construction of reality, an idea first defined and popularized by Peter Berger and Thomas Luckmann (1966), is widely discussed in introductory sociology courses and is an operating ground assumption for sociologists, though often taken for granted as background rather than explicitly outlined. Cognitive sociologists, in studying the cultural and social aspects of cognition, engage with the task of demonstrating variations and patterns in the social construction of reality. In recent years there has been growing scholarly interest in studying the nature of the relationship between culture and cognition. Within sociology, this interest cuts across many topical subfields, including cultural sociology, the sociology of race, social control and deviance, inequalities, economic sociology, social organizations, social movements, environmental sociology, urban sociology, and the sociology of identity. Sociologists of culture and cognition are contributing to a rapidly expanding body of work on how thought and action are intricately linked to cultural and social life.

The approach I take in this book is to discuss sociological research on culture and cognition across a range of cultural, subcultural, identity affiliational, and organizational settings and across varying levels of culture from macrocultures to microcultures. In doing so, I intend to illustrate both *cognitive variation* and *general social patterns* in sociocultural cognition. Here I take the social pattern analysis approach of Eviatar Zerubavel (2007), who recommends using multi-contextual evidence both to display cultural variation and diversity, and to locate general social patterns in that diversity. I organize the main body of this book around key cognitive processes (perception, classification, meaning and metaphor, identity, memory, and time construction) rather than around theoretical camps, and bring contributions from the different theoretical and methodological traditions together in order to better illuminate and understand these processes. In this introductory chapter, however, I provide a little background on sociological traditions in culture and cognition as a way of illustrating some of the key methodological and theoretical debates in the field. I will then draw from these varying approaches throughout the book to move across levels of scale, traverse both the quotidian and the morally salient, and demonstrate how culture and cognition can motivate social action and produce and sustain inequalities and simultaneously be produced by inequalities. Before I turn to these traditions, and then to the cognitive processes they study, I offer an illustrative case for why social scientists should study culture and cognition in the first place.

Why culture and cognition?

Why study culture and cognition? What does a cultural approach offer to the study of human thought and the human mind? To address this question it is worth noting that we do not think as "generic" rational human actors, but rather, we interpret the world from specific social standpoints based on the societies we live in, the communities we inhabit, and the social networks we belong to.

For fun, I begin with revelations about a peculiar group that demonstrates a unique, culturally specific thought style and view of social perception. In 2010 three social scientists (Joe Henrich, an anthropologist, and Steven Heine and Ara Norenzyan, two psychologists) published an article in *Behavioral and Brain Sciences* entitled "The Weirdest People in the World?" In this article, the authors looked at a number of classical social psychological experiments thought to explain human social behavior and discovered that the findings of these studies were not replicable in many other cultures. Years of established scholarly wisdom had assumed that these experimental studies revealed evolved psychological traits common to universal human perception and cognitive processes, when in fact the subjects for the experiments came almost exclusively from industrialized Western cultures. These studies, presumed to be measuring human cognition, were actually measuring the unique cognition of a specific cultural group. By compiling cross-cultural research on common experiments such as the prisoner's-dilemma-style ultimatum game, and visual perceptions of optical illusions, the authors demonstrated that significant elements of human thought are as much cultural and social as they are neurological.

The culture in which one is raised, these authors showed, heavily influences how one responds to a bargaining experiment or even how one perceives optical images. For example, in a well-known optical illusion showing two equal length lines where one line ends in fins that point diagonally forward to create a tail and the other line ends in fins that point diagonally backward to create an arrow tip, Americans (Illinois college undergraduates) judge the line with the tail as being significantly longer. When the test was replicated across 14 small-scale, non-Western societies, however, some cultures saw no difference in size of the main line and none saw the significant degree of difference that Americans saw. The lines are not an optical illusion to the biological human brain; they are an optical illusion to the cultural minds of Westerners. Similarly, in economic bargaining experiments that behavioral economists had considered evidence for evolved universal motivations, findings drawn from Western undergraduates, when compared against findings from 23 other societies from Africa, Amazonia, Oceania, Siberia, and New Guinea, again turned out to be outliers at the extreme end of the distribution. Ara Norenzayan, one of the experimental psychologists who revealed the group-specific cognition of the WEIRD (Western, Educated, Industrialized, Rich, and Democratic) observes that experimental psychologists and economists were so focused on finding underlying universal hardware at work that they missed the central role of culture in cognition (Watters 2013).

The fact that culture shapes the human mind is as instructive to sociology as it is to experimental psychology. The idea that we think not as generic humans, but as socially and culturally located humans, informs sociological approaches to studying culture and cognition.

Sociological approaches to culture and cognition: Durkheimian (cultural), Goffmanian (social), and Bourdieusian (individual practical actor) foundations

Sociological interest in the relationship between the mental and the social can be traced as far back as Émile Durkheim's critiques of universalist and individualist approaches to perception and thought. Durkheim ([1912] 1965) positioned himself against Immanuel Kant's universalist model of innate categories of reason, suggesting instead that the processes of the mind are socially formed and that they therefore vary by cultural location. Treating the mind as social, Durkheim rejected the idea of a universal, single, "rational" way of thinking. Society and "social facts," for Durkheim, were formed in "enacted [social] practices that give rise to real social forces that participants in the assembled group experience jointly" (Rawls 1996: 434). Durkheim also positioned himself against the individualist position of William James' pragmatism. While Durkheim ([1913–14] 1983) agreed with James that there was a dynamic relationship between thought and reality, he warned that James and the pragmatists proceed from a purely individualist position, because James linked individual thought to individual action as the only reality and therefore could not escape the individual as a unit of analysis. Durkheim argued that the relationship pragmatists posit is the action relation between the biological being and the natural world, not the action relation among social beings engaged in enacting social practices (see also Rawls 1997: 9). For Durkheim, the self and mind are socially constructed in a dynamic relationship with the social world rather than constituted only in an individual human–object relationship with the natural environment. Durkheim's collectivist, social constructionist position examines cognition beyond the individual as its primary unit of analysis.

The foundations of Durkheim's sociological approach emphasizing the cultural and social over the universal human or the autonomous individual remain influential in cultural sociological approaches to cognition. Cultural sociologist Jeffrey Alexander (2003a), for instance, uses a "strong culture" program that merges Durkheim's collectivist cultural approach with the structuralist ideas of anthropologist Claude Lévi-Strauss. Lévi-Strauss (1963) noted, for instance, that myths have similar general motifs, yet show considerable variation in specific content because of the different social worlds people inhabit. Eviatar Zerubavel (1997) emphasizes the importance of the "social mind" in his positioning of cognitive sociology as the intermediate domain between the poles of cognitive universalism and cognitive individualism. He emphasizes sociocultural variation as an important element in the study of thought as distinct from attempts to distill universal foundations of human cognition.

In contrast to the Durkheimian cultural and social orientations evident in much of cultural sociology, there is also a growing school of interdisciplinary cognitive sociologists who engage with cognitive neuroscience and developmental psychology to apply models of the human brain to cognition. They resurrect some of the pragmatist interest in the relationship between individual thought and practical action. They identify the individual, bodily responding to sensory input through largely unconscious dispositions, as the central element linking culture to social action. This school of cognitive sociology breaks from Durkheim's idea of collective representations located in the social realm and emphasizes an embodied neuropsychological view of culture and cognition that centers the individual's cognitive processing on embodied experiences. This tradition draws from the anthropology of Maurice Bloch (1998), who challenged the views of Lévi-Strauss that myths (a form of thinking) followed the same logic as language. This school in interdisciplinary cognitive sociology develops many of its sociological ideas from the foundations of Pierre Bourdieu.

Current scholarship in the sociology of culture and cognition is sometimes divided between the more cultural and social traditions inspired by Durkheim and other sociologists such as Erving Goffman and George Herbert Mead, and a more individual practical actor and neuropsychological tradition that draws inspiration from Pierre Bourdieu. After a discussion of cultural, social, and individual practical actor approaches to cognition and some of their foundational underpinnings in Durkheim, Goffman, and Bourdieu, five contemporary traditions in cognitive sociology that draw from these foundations will be presented.

Cultural approaches to cognition observe thought collectively through visible social forces or social facts such as cultural codes, discourses, or narratives. Consistent with Durkheim's vision, they tend to emphasize collective representations such as language and symbols and enacted practices such as social rituals that influence members to see and experience the world as cultural and social beings. I refer to approaches as "cultural" if they focus on macrocultural settings such as societies and "social" if they refer to more local settings such as subcultures, social networks, workplaces, or peer groups. The distinction between cultural and social is therefore heuristic rather than literal. Social approaches are closely related to cultural approaches in that they locate social life in the collective but they do so at the group level. As a result, analysts using social approaches often focus on group-level interactions, studying social life in interactional settings. These approaches focus on culture as transmitted through group-level interactions such as imitation and role modeling of the styles, moral boundary categorizations, and identity performances of peer groups, occupational colleagues, or other categories of social belonging. Practical actor, neuropsychological, or embodied individual approaches locate culture in the practical culture of individuals' largely unconscious thought processes as they respond to repeated sensory simulations within their environments. These approaches borrow from cognitive psychology and neuroscience to emphasize the mechanisms of individual thought in cognition. Each of these heuristic orientations – the cultural, the social, and the individual – may be seen as having a foundational sociologist in Émile Durkheim, Erving Goffman, and Pierre Bourdieu respectively.

Erving Goffman's influence on the sociology of culture and cognition relates to his interests in interactional social attention, social framing, and strategic identity. Goffman, like Durkheim, views the self as socially constituted but his focus is drawn toward culture in interactional and organizational forms. Goffman also expands upon sociologist George Herbert Mead's ([1934] 1967) interest in selves as emergent from social interactions and experience. Goffman's focus on the social organization of attention and inattention in social interaction, frames of interpretation, and personal and social identity management all share an interest in the social nature of attention. This broad interest, studied across different domains and across different processes of framing, interactional attention, and identity, has influenced researchers in collective representations (frames as collective representations), symbolic interactionist, and social mindscapes traditions of cognitive sociology. Goffman's analysis of attention and inattention in social interactions (1963) has influenced research on the sociology of perception; his analyses of identity in the presentation of self in everyday life (1959) and the management of social stigma ([1963] 1986) have influenced studies on the strategic presentation of identity; and his analysis of frames (1974) has inspired a range of cognitive approaches to attention, meaning-making, and classification, including David Snow and Robert Benford's research on social movement frames (e.g. Snow and Benford 1988; Benford and Snow 2000) and frame alignment processes (e.g. Snow et al. 1986). In his cartography of contemporary cognitive sociology, Piet Strydom (2007: 350) asserts that "given his wide-ranging impact on later developments [Goffman] must surely count as the most central and influential figure in cognitive sociology." Goffman's wide-ranging influence has been strongest with respect to traditions that emphasize cognition at the social and interactional levels.

Parallel to Goffman's influence on researchers emphasizing social and interactional elements of cognition, Pierre Bourdieu's influence on research traditions focused on the habitual unconscious elements of cognition is strong. In *The Logic of Practice*, Bourdieu (1990) argues that "practice" has a logic that is organized by unconscious schemas and instantaneous intuitive judgments rather than conscious reasoned deliberation. For Bourdieu (1977; 1990) culture is located less in conscious ideas or shared cultural symbols than in the routines of institutions and individuals. As such, culture is inconsistent and fragmented in its uses. Bourdieu's view of culture as located in everyday practice and lacking consistency within individuals and across collectives informs cultural sociologist Ann Swidler's (1986; 2001) theoretical approach that conceives of culture as a toolkit that people use inconsistently. Bourdieu's (1977) interest in the use of "habitus" in unconscious action has significantly influenced contemporary scholars of culture and cognition who advance an interdisciplinary, neuroscience informed cognitive sociology. Omar Lizardo (2004) argues that while many cultural sociologists are interested in Bourdieu's concept of cultural capital or his field theory of cultural production (the meso-level aspects of his work), his more psychological, cognitive-practical-level analysis of the habitus has particular relevance for cognitive sociologists. For Bourdieu, people develop unconscious schemas through life experience, and while experience can change these schemas, the habitus allows us to function in the everyday without always questioning and closely analyzing what we do. Most of our decisions, then, are not made with conscious deliberation and explicit acknowledgment of making a choice between multiple actions, but rather become part of our routines and a piece of the everyday structure through which we operate. Scholars interested in connecting sociology to findings from neuroscience are exploring the ways that we put culture into action through the habitus of unconscious schemas and intuitive dispositions.

Contemporary traditions in the sociological study of culture and cognition draw variously from these more foundational interests in the relationship between culture, thought, and action.

Five contemporary traditions in the sociology of culture and cognition

One challenge in characterizing the current sociological study of culture and cognition is that this growing area of research has several different theoretical strands and traditions, often with different goals and sometimes with competing theoretical assumptions and methodological orientations. While it is not possible in this short text to cover every theoretical approach to culture and cognition in sociology, I briefly outline five important contemporary theoretical orientations that help to illuminate some of the key foundations, analytic and methodological perspectives, and debates. Although these five schools and their theoretical influences are not mutually exclusive they are here roughly organized from more Durkheimian cultural, through Goffmanian social, to more Bourdieusian embodied individual approaches. These orientations are (1) a discourse, iconic, and neo-Durkheimian collective representations tradition; (2) symbolic interactionism; (3) Eviatar Zerubavel's social mindscapes tradition; (4) Ann Swidler's cultural toolkit tradition; and (5) an intersections with cognitive neuroscience and cognitive psychology tradition. These five orientations are not exhaustive of the sociological study of cognition, but they are important ones for representing active schools of thought and the big theoretical and methodological debates in the field. The traditions range in their primary units of analysis, from the cultural, to the social, to the embodied neurological individual, as well as in their methodological approaches for accessing the role of culture in cognition.

Discourse, iconic, and neo-Durkheimian collective representations tradition

The first tradition is a collective representations approach to understanding cultural meaning-making and cultural performance that traces its classical roots back to Émile Durkheim's interest in collective representations of social life. Researchers in this tradition locate their unit of analysis not in the individual but in cultural discourses, or meaning structures, or codes, or other collective representations of culture. Jeffrey Alexander and Philip Smith (2003), for instance, emphasize a strong autonomy of culture approach that views culture as a set of codes that guide understanding and that are reproduced through social performance and practice. They argue for a "thick description" (Geertz [1973] 2000) of the codes, narratives, and symbols that create textured social meaning, and the use of these details to look for deeper principles of social life. They view cultural structures such as codes, symbols, narrative forms, discourses, and other collective representations as durable, underlying, motivating foundations of meaning in social life. Narrative forms such as the morality play, or tragedy, or irony, for instance are general types that carry particular implications for meaning and social life (Alexander and Smith 2003: 25). Donileen Loseke (2009) draws upon Alexander's idea of symbolic codes to show how United States President George W. Bush's speeches in the immediate aftermath of the September 11 terrorist attacks linked symbolic codes of "victim," "hero," and "villain" to emotion codes of sympathy, of pride and patriotism, and of hate, fear, anger, and nationalism respectively. She argues that emotion codes are sets of socially circulating ideas about what emotional feelings it is appropriate to experience and to express outwardly when, where, and toward whom or what. She examines the president's nationally televised speeches justifying war as melodramatic tales that contained multiple emotion codes that encouraged audiences to feel in certain ways about the primary characters in the drama: the Good American victim and hero and the evil terrorist villain.

Researchers in this tradition concern themselves both with how cultural discourses shape thought and with how this further motivates social action. Lyn Spillman (1995) suggests, for instance, that the "discursive field" is the mediating link between structure and action. In *Discourse and Destruction: The City of Philadelphia versus MOVE*, Robin Wagner-Pacifici (1994) demonstrates how discourses shaped meaning in a standoff between Philadelphia city officials and the radical black separatist group MOVE that ultimately ended in the Philadelphia police dropping explosives from a helicopter onto the MOVE compound, killing 11 people and destroying an entire urban block in the process. Wagner-Pacifici shows how a discourse of sentimental domesticity constructed the Philadelphia neighborhood as an orderly community threatened by disorder brought on by MOVE and how the bureaucratic, means-oriented discourses of government and law officials contributed to the city addressing disorder as a tactical problem to be solved militarily. Using discourse, narratives, cultural codes, and other observable manifestations of cultural thought, researchers in this discursive and iconic orientation use an interpretive approach to understand meaning-making, classification, and other cognitive processes.

Symbolic interactionism

Related to and sometimes intersecting with the discourse, iconic, and collective representations tradition represented in the cultural sociologies of Jeffrey Alexander, Lyn Spillman, and Robin Wagner-Pacifici is a symbolic interactionist approach to cognitive sociology. Symbolic interactionism has its classical roots in George Herbert Mead ([1934] 1967), who emphasized that the self is constructed in interaction with society and its symbols. The approach also draws from Goffman's interest in social interaction as an important location for studying culture. The symbolic interactionist tradition highlights a concern with how our meanings are built up and negotiated through interactions with others in society and how these meanings are assembled in symbols and discourse. Symbolic interactionism, like neo-Durkheimian iconic approaches, examines collective representations, but typically analyzes them at the social group level rather than at the macro-cultural level of a whole society.

In an influential work connecting the analysis of cultural codes from the collective representations tradition with symbolic interactionism, Nina Eliasoph and Paul Lichterman (2003) link culture to action by demonstrating the ways groups put culture into use in everyday life. They use two cases – (1) an exurban activist group operating in a community where activism is muted and (2) bar patrons at a local civic space such as an Elks club – to analyze three dimensions of group style: group boundaries, group bonds, and speech norms. The group styles they highlight in relation to the default cultural style of excessive individualism include timid affiliation in the activist group and active disaffili-ation in the civic bar space group. The activist group used the language of individualism in a way that complemented the group style of timid affiliation, choosing not to confront the implied selfishness or hedonism of individualism, but instead to signify that it is desirable to give everyone room to speak out as sincere individuals (Eliasoph and Lichterman 2003: 756). The civic bar group affirmed the code of civil society by systematically and deftly inverting it to avoid the difficult burden of serious conversa tion; they avoided direct discussion of political issues, persuasive speech, serious conversation, idealist talk, and good manners, and emphasized teasing and offensive jokes as ways to appear not to take things too seriously (Eliasoph and Lichterman 2003: 761–2). Group styles, these authors argue, filter collective repre-sentations and use common collective representations and shared symbols, vocabularies, and codes in different ways. Eliasoph and Lichterman's idea of "group styles" highlights cognitive variation between groups and offers general understandings of the ways groups employ shared vocabularies and codes to filter collective representations from the larger culture. Eliasoph and Lichterman inform sociological work on local cognitive cultures (discussed in chapter 1) and group-level approaches to studying culture and cognition.

The methodological approach of symbolic interactionism emphasizes empirical investigations of social life grounded in observable social interactions. Its focus on the interactional level makes it an influential approach for studying group-level cognitive processes in peer groups, identity communities, and other reference groups. In his study of social interaction among little league baseball teams, ethnographer Gary Alan Fine (1979: 734) employs this tradition to develop the idea of an "idioculture" to refer to the system of knowledge, understandings, beliefs, and customs shared by members of an interacting group, which members can refer to and use as the basis for further interaction. Symbolic interactionism often shares with discourse and iconic perspectives an interest in cultural codes, but does so in the context of social groups in everyday interaction.

Eviatar Zerubavel's social mindscapes tradition

Eviatar Zerubavel's social mindscapes tradition of cognitive sociology draws influences from social constructionism and from Erving Goffman's social attention and inattention and social framing perspectives to emphasize cognitive pluralism and the sociocultural mind (Brekhus 2007). In *Social Mindscapes: An Invitation to Cognitive Sociology*, Eviatar Zerubavel (1997) advances a comparative approach to studying thinking. This approach draws upon classical "social standpoint" theories in the sociology of knowledge such as that of Ludwik Fleck ([1935] 1979), who proposed the idea of "thought collectives" or "thought communities" that come to see the world from a particular institutional or subcultural paradigm, and that of Karl Mannheim ([1936] 1985: 79–81), who further advanced the idea that humans think as members of collectives, located in a particular social location, and that their mental structures are shaped by social structures; their worldviews result from affiliations such as professions, generations, social classes, and status groups. Researchers in the Zerubavelian tradition focus on how perceptions of reality are shaped, filtered, and influenced by culture and social location.

Like the collective representations tradition of Jeffrey Alexander, this tradition includes Durkheim as an intellectual predecessor, but it also traces classical roots back to Georg Simmel. Whereas

Durkheim analyzed collectives as largely coherent units, Simmel focused on intersectionality as a potential source for considerable variation between individuals in the same society. In his analysis of the web of group affiliations, Simmel ([1955] 1964: 140–3) advances the idea that individuals are made up of a pluralistic mix of multiple affiliations that shape who they are and how they think. This observation represents an early sociological interest in the multidimensional and intersectional character of personal identities, and one that informs researchers in this tradition to explore the multidimensionality of identity (e.g. Brekhus 2003).

Simmel and Goffman's influences on the social mindscapes approach are methodological as well as theoretical and substantive. Studying patterns of cognition, in this tradition, involves analyzing themes and concepts across different substantive cases, and across different levels of cases (Zerubavel 2007). Important to this method is adopting a formal sociological imagination that allows us to see the generic elements of the specific as well as variation between cases. Generic concepts about how we socially construct reality come in cross-case examples and the power of a sociological concept, Zerubavel argues, comes in its applicability across cases. Erving Goffman's studies of substantively different but analytically similar "total institutions" (1961) and "stigmatized identities" ([1963] 1986) are classic examples of using multi-contextual substantive data to develop a theoretically focused analysis (Zerubavel 2007: 135). In this tradition, Jamie Mullaney (2006) analyzes abstinences from sex, drugs, meat, alcohol, television, and consumption to develop general concepts about abstinence maintenance strategies such as "fence building" and "fire walking" and to distinguish between different temporal kinds of abstinences. The breadth of levels of analysis in using a multi-contextual approach to explore a cognitive process can be witnessed in Zerubavel's (2006) general sociology of collective denial, where he explores the single theme of collective denial in small groups such as a family, medium-sized groups such as an organization, and large groups such as a nation. Although a family's denial of alcoholism and a nation's denial of genocide are substantively different in content and scale, the formal sociological patterns and general principles of social denial and social inattention are quite similar. Zerubavel's methodology emphasizes the sociocognitive dimensions of thought with a strong interest in highlighting generic social patterns from specific cases.

Ann Swidler's cultural toolkit tradition

Ann Swidler's cultural toolkit approach to understanding culture in action may be seen as a blend between cultural- and individual-level analysis. This approach is cultural in that it analyzes a common pool of cultural resources, such as Americans' culture of love (Swidler 2001), but also individual in that it focuses on individuals' contextual and fragmented uses of these cultural resources. Swidler (1986; 2001) views culture as an oddly assorted toolkit or a repertoire of symbols, rituals, stories, worldviews, and ideas that we select from in partial ways, picking up and setting aside different cultural themes at different times and under varying circumstances. In contrast to the relatively coherent view of culture found in Durkheim, Swidler views culture as too fragmented and contradictory to allow individuals to simply internalize cultural symbols, rules, or codes wholesale. When middle-class Americans talk about love, for instance, their views are often fragmented and self-contradictory (Swidler 2001: 181). They draw from cultural ideas but they often do so in a haphazard way. Because she observes culture as inconsistently deployed, Swidler locates culture less in the conscious statements of values or in the shared cultural symbols of a society, and more in the routines and habits of institutions and actors. She draws from Bourdieu's idea of "practice," which refers to action that is immediate, strategically oriented to practical outcomes, and largely organized by unconscious schemas, so that it operates intuitively, to understand the ways that culture is used in habitual everyday life. Swidler is interested in variations in the way culture is mobilized, appropriated, deployed, and linked to experience, and in the relationship of these variations to structural conditions in the culture. Specific cultural patterns shape the circumstances of action and determine what tools are most available. People are therefore constrained from freely choosing how to convert their beliefs into action.

For Swidler, culture shapes action not by providing the ultimate values that orient action, but by shaping strategies of action such as habits, styles, skills, and vocabularies of action.

Swidler's toolkit approach is more often defined as a theory of culture in action than a theory of cognition, but her interest in which kinds of culture enter one's repertoire and which kinds of strategies of action come out of the toolkit at which times is implicitly cognitive. Her cultural toolkit perspective is also important because of its central role in cultural sociology, and because its model of individuals deploying culture serves as an important debating point among cultural and cognitive sociologists about the role of culture in action.

Intersections with cognitive neuroscience and cognitive psychology tradition

A growing number of cognitive sociologists have begun to focus on the intersections between cognitive sociology and cognitive psychology and neuroscience. Broadly conceived, this tradition includes several strands such as experimental social psychology in social cognition, Stephen Turner's (2007) call for social theory to become a cognitive neuroscience, Karen Cerulo's (2010) efforts to identify bridges between sociology and cognitive neuroscience, and an increasingly influential Bourdieusian interdisciplinary cognitive sociology advanced by cognitive scholars such as Steven Vaisey, Omar Lizardo, John Levi Martin, and Gabriel Ignatow. I primarily emphasize this wing because of the recent and growing influence its scholars have on key debates in cultural and cognitive sociology. The perspectives they offer help to illustrate key differences between neuropsychological approaches and other approaches to culture and cognition. Before turning specifically to the Bourdieusian wing, it is worth noting that there has been a relatively longstanding tradition of experimental social psychology in social cognition that examines the individual social thinker and his or her thinking or brain activity in experiments. Researchers in this tradition have developed important insights about individual cognition including ideas about dual modes of automatic and controlled processes of cognition, and various models of social thinkers as cognitive misers, motivated tacticians, or activated actors. I address some ideas and concepts from important experimental studies as they shine light on the cultural sociology of cognition, but my primary focus will be sociological studies of cognition conducted outside of laboratory settings. Readers interested in the large body of research on experimental social psychology in social cognition should see Fiske and Taylor (2013).

Sociologists practicing a Bourdieusian interdisciplinary cognitive sociology combine Bourdieu's view of habitus and his theory of practical action with insights from developmental psychology and cognitive neuroscience to advance an embodied view of cognition and a view of culture as located in practical action. This perspective draws from Bourdieu's interest in Piaget's developmental psychology and Piaget's view of bodily schemas in cognitive development. Gabriel Ignatow (2007: 129) argues that these basic bodily operations can structure discourses through processes endogenous to culture itself. At the center of this tradition is the idea that culture in action is found not on the surface level but deep and embodied within the individual's subconscious. This idea is expressed in Steven Vaisey's (2008; 2009) "dual-process model" of cognition, in which the self is cognitively divided between a fast, hot, automatic, and unconscious cognitive system deep in the consciousness, and a slow, cool, reflexive, and conscious cognitive system on the surface. The dual-process model combines Bourdieu's and anthropologist Maurice Bloch's notions of culture as embodied schemas with recent cultural theory that regards culture and social structure as analytically separate (Vaisey and Lizardo 2010: 7). Scholars in this tradition emphasize that there is an inconsistency between the cultural beliefs and ideas that people talk about to explain their behavior and what they actually do. These authors propose therefore that we need to look beyond the surface to the deep intuitive level of unconscious dispositions, snap judgments, and bodily responses to find culture in action.

To demonstrate the greater coherence of culture at the subconscious level, Steven Vaisey (2009) uses a quantitative analysis from the National Study of Youth and Religion to demonstrate that fixed-response choices from a list of moral scripts on a survey question in 2002 more strongly predict youths' later behavior in 2005 on a range of issues, from using alcohol and other drugs, cheating in school, and cutting class to keeping secrets from parents, than do parents' education, peer networks, church attendance, or other sociologically established correlations. Moreover the youths showed this consistency over time even when their answers to narrative questions showed that at the discursive level they could not clearly articulate their moral decision-making or do so without contradictions.

Scholars in this tradition challenge sociological conceptions that imply a high degree of shared culture or that culture is stored consciously as ideology or values. John Levi Martin (2010) argues, for instance, that culture is largely not shared because we have different experiences and the vast majority of culture goes unused (most books sit in libraries unread, most of our memories are not shared, etc.), so that culture takes the form of haphazard chunks and a set of potentials for experiences. These scholars emphasize embodied habits in largely unconscious responses to one's environment rather than socialization and language as the primary way that culture is internalized. Omar Lizardo (2007) associates Bourdieu's habitus with the neuroscience of mirror neurons. Lizardo argues that direct instructions and socialization are not required because practices can be transmitted and largely picked up unconsciously through mirroring others. Lizardo (2007: 336) suggests, for example, that Bourdieu's (1969) metaphor of a "feel for the game," wherein social actors read off goals and purposes from other actors without ever resorting to conscious deliberation of goals and purposes, is instructive in understanding the role of unconscious strategizing and mirroring in guiding embodied cognitive behavior; that is, we can pick up practical knowledge through unconscious enculturation without direct, explicit transmission. Bourdieusian interdisciplinary sociologists attempt to blend cultural sociology and cognitive neuroscience by looking at the relationship between internalized schemas, neurology, and embodied practice. They are interested in the mechanics of cognition and in the physical and embodied processes that individuals use in cognition and social action.

Theoretical and methodological pluralism: integrating multi-contextual evidence to understand culture and cognition

What do sociologists and aspiring sociologists make of the broad range of theoretical and methodological traditions within the sociology of culture and cognition? Should we study cognition at the cultural, the social, or the individual level? Should we use the individual social actor as a unit of analysis, or must we strive for other units of analysis? Should cultural sociologists methodo- logically search for culture in discourse, in social interaction, in individual actors' narrative accounts, in comparative historical methods, in formal sociology, or in individuals' recall on fixed- response surveys?

I take a pluralistic approach to these questions. Each kind of tra- dition, the cultural, the social, and the practical actor or embodied neurological, provides fascinating insights into the ways we think as sociocultural beings. Different units of analysis, from cultural codes and discourses, to interactional settings, to the individual, give us unique analytic vantage points for exploring culture and cognition. Similarly the wide range of methods, from discourse analysis, to ethnography, to interviews, to surveys, to com- parative methods, gives us multiple ways to study culture. I also employ a pluralistic approach to the kinds of substantive topics that sociologists of culture and cognition study. In chapter 1, for instance, looking at such disparate examples as how residents of an Argentinian shantytown are encouraged to rely on automatic cognition and to avoid deliberate cognition about hazards in their environment (Auyero and Swistun 2008), and how culinary fields and sexual fields are organized to elicit deliberate cognition at some stages of one's culinary or sexual career and automatic cognition at other stages (Leschziner and Green 2013), provides uniquely different empirical sites for understanding under what conditions people are more likely to use deliberate or automatic cognition.

The range of theories, levels of analysis, methods, and types of empirical sites employed to study culture and cognition represents, itself, the kind of multi-contextual evidence that Zerubavel considers important to generating theoretical insights about culture and cognition. I portray a pluralistic range of methods, theories, and substantive sociological subfields to highlight widely varying research findings in the sociology of culture and cognition, because much of what is analytically interesting comes not only from these individual studies, but from the cumulative knowledge that examining a specific cognitive process such as classification, meaning, or identity from multiple vantage points affords us. With this playful movement across a wide range of examples, I hope to convey the breadth of cognitive sociology and its analytic observations about the social construction of cognitive processes and to demonstrate the social complexities and multidimensionality of social reality. I cast a wide net not only for analytic reasons, but also to inspire sociology students and scholars to consider the many ways that one can employ a culture and cognition analysis to their own topical, moral, theoretical, and methodological interests.

The organization of the chapters

Within each chapter on a cognitive process, I demonstrate the substantive breadth of the sociology of culture and cognition by using a range of examples. I use this range both to show cognitive sociocultural variation and to highlight general analytic insights and sensitizing concepts that cut across specific sociocultural constructions and empirical sites. Also, while much of the research cited is explicitly cognitive sociology, the work of scholars with only implicit affinities to cognitive sociology is integrated, where instructive, to demonstrate generalizable comparisons and to identify similar or contrasting social patterns in culture and cognition across research sites.

The chapters are organized around several of the most prominent sociocognitive processes covered in the sociology of culture and cognition. They include perception and attention, classification, meaning-making, identity construction, and memory and time. These processes are staples of cognitive sociological work, similar to the key thought processes that Paul DiMaggio (1997), Eviatar Zerubavel (1997), and Karen Cerulo (2002a) have outlined in their respective mappings of the field of culture and cognition. Chapter 1 looks at perception, attention, and framing, focusing on what is culturally perceived as relevant and what is ignored as irrelevant. Chapter 2 analyzes the ways people classify and categorize reality. Chapter 3 examines meaning-making, metaphor, and frames of meaning. Chapter 4 explores identity construction, looking at key aspects of identity such as identity authenticity, identity multidimensionality, and identity mobility. Chapter 5 looks at memory and time, analyzing how we construct the past and how we "do time" in the present. The concluding chapter explores ongoing debates about the direction and future of sociological research in culture and cognition and suggests ways to employ culture and cognition research to explore issues of primary concern to sociologists, such as social action, power, and social inequalities. The reader is invited to think further about the sociocognitive nature of perception, classification, meaning-making, identity, memory, and time and to explore these cognitive processes in their own research and in their everyday lives and communities of identity and belonging.

Now let us begin our journey into the sociocultural mind.

1

Perception, Attention, and Framing:
The Sociology of Relevance and
Irrelevance

How can two people look at the same thing and see something very different? What do we foreground as especially socially relevant and what do we ignore as irrelevant background? What are we socially or culturally primed to see automatically and what requires deliberation? How can one observer view something as routine and be unconcerned while another detects imminent danger? What is in frame and what is out of frame? How do cultures, subcultures, and organizations shape our expectations of what to look for and to be perceptually ready to attend? These are some of the many questions that a cognitive sociology of perception attempts to answer.

Perception is one of the broadest, most fundamental processes of cognition, and one that relates to the processes that follow. The general concepts discussed in this chapter, such as marked and unmarked, deliberate and automatic cognition, cognitive variation, framing, and priming, will reappear as guiding concepts as they relate to other cognitive processes. Perception and attention are central elements in the social construction of reality. Scholars have employed a broad array of concepts to describe the social construction of reality (perspectives, thought styles, paradigms, mental maps, frames, filters, habitus, schemes, and models), and these seemingly disparate concepts are united in that each addresses the important role of social expectations in shaping patterns of thought and perception (Friedman 2013: 20–1). Our cognitive processes of attention and perception are tied to specific cultures of seeing and framing reality.

Sociologist Émile Durkheim's ([1912] 1965) early, classic distinction between the sacred (that which a collective sets apart as remarkable and exceptional) and the profane (the mundane and everyday) represents an early sociological foundation for considering the cultural and collective elements of attention and perception. In Durkheim's view the most important contrasts for religions and cultures were not between good and evil, but rather between the sacred (which can be set apart as either good or evil) and the profane (ordinary). Setting apart and marking something as sacred and distinct from the everyday is a way of selectively guiding attention and moral interest toward that item or practice. Interest in the socially coordinated practices of attention and inattention in constructing taken-for-granted social realities has continued through both the more social-focused traditions of cognitive sociology rooted in the works of Erving Goffman and the more neuro-focused traditions of cognitive sociology expanding the work of Pierre Bourdieu.

Erving Goffman focused on attention and inattention with respect to rules of irrelevance (1961), civil inattention (1963), and framing (1974). According to Goffman, the meaning of any encounter depends on "rules of irrelevance":

> [t]he character of an encounter is based in part upon rulings as to properties of the situation that should be considered irrelevant, out of frame, or not happening. To adhere to these rules is to play fair. Irrelevant visible events will not be attended; irrelevant private concerns will be kept out of mind. An effortless unawareness will be involved, and if this is not possible then an active turning-away or suppression of attention will occur. (Goffman 1961: 25)

For Goffman our attention, and as importantly our *inattention*, are carefully organized and focused so as to produce particular, socially expected meanings. Goffman focuses both on tacit inattention (the unseen) and on active inattention or "tactful blindness" (Goffman 1955: 219) (the seen but unacknowledged). In the former, inattention is automatic and passive, whereas in the latter it is strategic and active. Pierre Bourdieu analyzed schemes of perception and appreciation and how habitus contributes to selective attention within such schemes. In discussing perceptions of art, for instance, he argues that there is a "pertinence principle" or "principle of selection" that is socially constituted and acquired, which allows the viewer to select and retain from among the elements offered to the eye those that are assumed to be relevant to the mode of perception, thought, and style of the period of art or class of artists being examined (Bourdieu 1984: 50). He focuses especially on the unconscious aspects of attention and inattention, noting that habitus allows for an "unconscious deciphering of the countless signs which at every moment say what is to be loved and what is not, what is or is not to be seen" (Bourdieu 1984: 86; see also Friedman 2013: 24). Goffman emphasized the sociocultural framing of irrelevance and the tactical inattention or active "not seeing" that social actors deploy, while Bourdieu focused largely on the unconscious selective attention (and inattention) to relevant (and irrelevant) details that individuals develop in culturally acquired schemas of perception, classification, judgment, and interpretation. These two foundational approaches to the sociology of perception and attention have influenced the development of many ideas in the sociology of culture and cognition.

Two conceptual contributions that draw from other disciplines and that build upon Goffmanian and Bourdieusian sociological traditions, which allow analysts to make general theoretical observations about perception and cognition across a range of substantive areas, are (1) social markedness and unmarkedness and (2) deliberate and automatic cognition. I first introduce these orienting concepts, before employing a range of examples and multiple contexts to show both cognitive variation and general analytic patterns in how the social and cultural realm guides our attention and perception.

Marked and unmarked: social figure and ground

Cultural sociologists observe a key perceptual distinction between the socially marked and the socially unmarked. The concepts of the marked and the unmarked, prior to their further development in the social sciences, originated in linguistics, where Nikolaj Trubetzkoy and Roman Jakobson (Jakobson 1975: 162) noted that one item of a phoneme pair is always actively highlighted with a mark or accent, while the other side of the pair is passively defined by its absence of a mark. Linguists have since expanded the concepts to also apply to grammar and lexicon. In lexical pairs, the unmarked item has the ambiguous position of representing either the specific opposite of the marked category, or the generic category as a whole (Greenberg 1966: 26). The asymmetry between the marked and the unmarked is not only linguistic, however; it is also social (Waugh 1982; Brekhus 1996; 1998). There are many binary social contrasts where cultures or subcultures notice and actively highlight one side of a contrast as *socially specialized* while ignoring the other side as *socially generic* (Brekhus 1996). Man, for instance, is the unmarked sex category that can refer to the opposite of the marked sex category (woman) or to generic humans as a whole. Similarly there are many social continua where we perceive the poles of the continuum as socially specialized while ignoring the middle as socially generic (Brekhus 1996). This distinction between the marked and "socially specialized" and the unmarked and "socially generic" is important in understanding how people attend to and perceive social contrasts. We observe the world in an uneven fashion, cognitively attending to socially marked features, while virtually ignoring and taking for granted unmarked features (Brekhus 1998). The cognitive asymmetry between how we attend to the socially marked and ignore the socially unmarked is important to the entire range of cognitive processes including perception.

The marked and the unmarked are important to the sociology of perception, because they highlight what is perceived as socially relevant and socially irrelevant and what is attended to as social figure and what is ignored as social ground. While Goffman focused on the interactional norms of attention and inattention, the concepts of the marked and the unmarked draw us to the even deeper cognitive dimensions of attention and inattention that guide our everyday interactions. Our cognitive inattention to the unmarked can be either a deliberate disciplining of the mind to ignore the irrelevant (a focus similar to Goffman's theoretical interests) or a deeply ingrained unconscious pattern of cultural or subcultural selective attention and bias (a focus related to Bourdieu's theoretical interests).

The marked and the unmarked share a similarity with Durkheim's sacred and profane in that the important analytic contrast is between the actively highlighted, set apart, and specialized (the marked) and the ordinary, generic, and taken-for-granted (the unmarked), rather than between the good and the bad. The contrast between the marked and the unmarked differs from Durkheim's, however, in that it emphasizes the tremendous normative power of the unmarked. The key cognitive perceptual element in social marking is that the most notable positive social value is not that which is explicitly highlighted and celebrated (the sacred), but rather that which is disattended, unarticulated, regarded as generic (the profane and mundane), and therefore normalized without direct acknowledgment (Brekhus 1996; Brekhus et al. 2010: 70). In the case of race, for example, the social marking of minorities and the unmarking of whiteness has its power not in the explicit valuing of whiteness but in the unreflexive, implicit construction of whiteness as the generic, un raced, default racial norm.

Even sociological researchers often reproduce cognitive asymmetry between the marked and the unmarked by making category-specific generalizations about social processes when studying people in socially marked minority categories, such as gays and African-Americans, while making generic observations about human social processes when studying people in unmarked social categories (Brekhus 1998: 38–41). A parallel can be seen in anthropology, where the practices of distant tribes are regarded as exotic and culturally specific, but practices of Westerners are perceived as generalizable and universal (as we saw in the introduction with the WEIRD). The power of the unmarked is that it is often unacknowledged or unnoticed, even sometimes by experts, and thus people are often blind to its cognitive importance in organizing our social inattention.

Nancy DiTomaso (2013) captures the hidden power of the unmarked well in analyzing the unconscious reproduction of racial privilege that occurs in mundane socially networked hiring processes. Although the public perception is that racial minorities are under-hired because they are the marked category and thus *discriminated against* by prospective employers, the more pernicious problem is that the unmarked racial majority is *discriminated for* by prospective employers. Since white employers typically have more whites in their social networks to begin with, the routine, seemingly generic and racially neutral practice of hiring people through the trusted referrals of one's social network and selecting candidates who are within one's extended social network pool has the hidden consequence of reproducing racial bias in hiring practices. Hiring based on social networks does not appear racially discriminatory because we focus on the social problem of racial discrimination by attending to instances where whites intentionally discriminate against a marked racial group, not situations where whites habitually, but unintentionally, favor members of their own unmarked racial group. Eduardo Bonilla-Silva and David Embrick (2007) similarly demonstrate the unreflexive discursive worldviews of whites when it comes to white residential racial segregation, noting that while whites see blacks living together as racial self-segregation, they do not interpret their own segregation as a racial issue; they simply see it as natural and non-racial. Whites see their own mostly race-exclusive social networks and self-segregated neighborhoods as normal, neutral, and unrelated to the social problem of racial segregation that affects black neighborhoods.

Although race is an obvious issue where social marking and unmarking occurs, the relational distinction between the marked and the unmarked is found across a variety of contexts. Increasingly sociologists are beginning to examine unmarked categories in a number of ways including racial studies that examine whiteness, queer theories that interrogate heterosexuality, gender studies that analyze men and masculinities, deviance studies that examine social privilege as well as social stigma, health studies that examine wellness as much as illness, and social problems studies that examine social solutions as well as problems. Melanie Heath (2013), for example, employs content analysis of archival data to demonstrate how the socially and culturally unmarked are used in the discourses of "marriage advocates." She draws on a cognitive sociology of the unmarked to illustrate that in the cultural battles over defining marriage and its significance, marriage advocates use a neoliberal discourse focused on individual responsibility and self-reliant family life that incorporates unmarked assumptions about heterosexuality and produces marked knowledge about single motherhood and same-sex marriage. Marriage advocates mark single mothers as sexually problematic producers of poverty whose moral failing is the failure to enter heterosexual marriage. In their attention to single mothers, marriage advocates attend to single mothers' lack of marriage rather than to the presence of heterosexuality. By contrast, in attending to same-sex marriage they focus on the presence of same-sex desires in couples, rather than the presence of the desire to marry. Advocates of heterosexual-only marriage advance their cause under generic neoliberal language about marriage that hides an unmarked, specifically heterosexual agenda.

Sociologists have imported the concepts of social markedness and the marked and the unmarked from linguistics and applied them to social rather than purely linguistic contrasts. A related conceptual contrast relevant to the sociology of attention that sociologists of cognition have imported from other disciplines is the contrast between automatic and deliberate cognition.

Automatic and deliberate cognition

Two thought styles that cognitive neuroscientists examine, which are drawing greater interest from cognitive sociologists, are automatic and deliberate cognition. Automatic cognition is effortless, immediate, subconscious thought wherein we efficiently process information without much thought or review. Automatic cognition allows us to immediately generalize, to make snap judgments, and to act more or less on automatic pilot. Deliberate cognition involves a slow, deliberate, conscious thought process. Sociologists of culture and cognition examine these two processes of cognition, often employing or testing a dual-process model of cognition that sees deliberative cognition as our surface-level cognition, but our automatic cognition as the intuitive level that is often in charge (Vaisey 2008; 2009). In a study of collaborative networks in organizations that emphasize and encourage cross-boundary collaborations, Sameer Srivastava and Mahzarin Banaji (2011) explore the roles of deliberate and automatic cognition in network formations. These authors combine a laboratory study using Implicit Association Test (IAT) and field data from a biotechnology firm to examine people's views of themselves as collaborative actors, comparing their deliberative cognition self-view with their automatic implicit self-view, to see which view is more closely associated with a person's actual choice to collaborate with organizationally distant colleagues. These researchers find that people's explicit (consciously reported) collaborative self-concept is not associated with their choice to enlist organizationally distant colleagues in collaboration, while their implicit (less conscious) self-concept is. In organizational settings, Srivastava and Banaji argue that social desirability biases can induce a disparity between our deliberative and our automatic cognition.

Cognitive neuroscientists have explored individual-level conditions that shape whether automatic or deliberate cognition dominates, showing, for instance, that deliberate cognition can be triggered by the disruption of well-established routines; these different styles of cognition and the conditions that affect them can also be applied to larger social levels of culture and cognition (Cerulo 2010) such as the aggregate disruption of routines of a community or a society. Snow, Cress, Downey, and Jones (1998) have shown, for instance, how a breakdown in the quotidian – the taken-for-granted routines, activities, habits, and attitudes of everyday life – leads to deliberative social action and the emergence of social movements. Kai Erikson's (1976) classic work on disaster and its effects on a community also explores the disruption of well-established routines at the social level. Disruptions at the social level may also alter the balance between automatic cognition and deliberate cognition as the dominant thought style within a group or society. In her call to mine the intersections between cognitive sociology and neuroscience, Karen Cerulo (2010: 117) argues that sociology is well equipped to study the structural conditions and the aggregate-, social-, and cultural-level conditions that constrain and enable these two styles of cognition.

Does societal-level rapid social change during unsettled times, for instance, enlist deliberate cognition? Ann Swidler (1986) argues that during settled times we rely primarily on routine, while during unsettled times we encounter disruptions that require us to deliberate extensively about our values and think more about remaining consistent with our ideology or changing it to account for the challenge to our worldview. During settled times we rely more on automatic thought, while we are more deliberate during unsettled times. Benjamin Snyder (2013) distinguishes between two kinds of unsettledness: epochal or gradual forms and eventful or abrupt forms. Eventful forms of unsettledness fit into Swidler's model and invoke deliberate thought, Snyder suggests, but epochal forms of unsettledness are more gradual and consistent with practical, embodied, and automatic cognition. Omar Lizardo and Michael Strand (2010: 216) modify Swidler's formulation to a contrast between contexts in which actors can rely on stable cultural scaffoldings, and thus employ cognitively efficient thought processes, and contexts in which such external cultural scaffoldings are absent, such as during periods of change or transformation, when reliance on less efficient, more reflective thought is needed. John Levi Martin and Matt Desmond (2010) explore automatic and deliberate cognition in politics, arguing that people with strong ideologies pre-organize the world for efficiency and are more likely to use automatic cognition, while those with weak ideologies seek information in developing political positions and are thus more likely to engage in deliberate cognition.

Unintentional disruptions to routine such as the changing conditions in a sexual field as men get older and lose sexual capital, or such as culinary chefs having to adapt to dramatic alterations in working conditions, as Vanina Leschziner and Adam Green (2013) demonstrate, also trigger deliberate rather than automatic forms of cognition and action. In a comparative analysis of two cognitive cultures (high cuisine chefs and gay enclave men), these authors demonstrate that shifts in the occupational or sexual field lead to changes in cognitive styles. Leschziner focuses on cognitive cultures at the institutional and occupational level of high cuisine chefs, while Green focuses on cognitive cultures at the subcultural and identity community level of gay enclave inhabitants. By lumping together high cuisine chefs and gay enclave residents, the researchers illustrate the flexibility of cognitive sociology to move between different substantive empirical foci to attend to analytic patterns and structural similarities and variations in cognition. Leschziner and Green use these two disparate fields as a case study to analyze the various structural conditions and triggers that bring out deliberate cognition in attention and perception.

In culinary fields, those in the early stages of their career encounter structural conditions that encourage deliberate cognition and attention because they have yet to internalize culinary conventions and actions as part of their daily habitus to the point of experiencing them as institutions (Leschziner and Green 2013: 132). Even more experienced chefs regularly face changing conditions that make automatic thinking and habitual practices ineffective and that thus encourage deliberate cognition; for instance, a chef running a restaurant with a successful formula may encounter an economic recession and then be required to consciously reconsider the formula (Leschziner and Green 2013: 133–4). Whereas in the culinary field a young chef is more likely to be deliberate in their cognition, for men in the sexual field of the gay enclave, age often leads to a shift from automatic to deliberate cognition. Aging erodes sexual capital and thus older men become far more deliberate about their strategies for maintaining high sexual capital and much more conscious to attending every detail, rather than adopting and then internalizing as habit most of the practices of maintaining sexual capital without consciously attending to it (Leschziner and Green 2013: 127–8). Using the culinary and sexual fields as two cases, Leschziner and Green illustrate that fields are changing configurations that encourage both deliberate and automatic cognition, which combine in complex and nuanced ways. Combining different cognitive sociology traditions, their analysis integrates ideas from cognitive sociologists, using Bourdieu's ideas to intersect sociology and neuroscience to understand automatic cognition and dual-process cognition, with the kind of cross-contextual evidence between two substantively different social fields that Zerubavel (2007) recommends as a method for generating analytic insights. In highlighting the role deliberate cognition plays, these authors suggest that dual-process models of cognition have overemphasized the automatic nature of cognition and under-theorized its active, reflective dimensions and the fluid interplay between deliberate and automatic cognition that shape social practice. While dual-process theory is an important corrective to the rational instrumentalist action theories that dominate the sociology of culture, Leschziner and Green see it as an over-corrective that can be improved by recognizing that field pressures create moments that privilege deliberate cognition. These field pressures, they argue, happen in a consequential social context that is not captured in the laboratory setting where more rigid dual-process models of cognition have originated.

The relationship between automatic and deliberate cognition and the marked and the unmarked is also worth further explora-tion. Does the unmarked routinely fall under automatic cognition? Does the introduction of markedness into an unmarked setting produce more deliberate cognition about the unmarked? The unnoticed, unseen, taken-for-grantedness of unmarked catego-ries and realities makes it likely that they are tied to cognitive efficiency and automatic cognition. People rarely deliberate or explicitly think about unmarked social categories unless these are placed in a context with the marked that causes people to reflect upon the taken-for-grantedness of the unmarked. To actively highlight the unmarked requires a disruption of routine (Garfinkel 1967) and thus may require more deliberative cogni-tion. The recent trend in the social sciences to actively foreground and study "whiteness" or to problematize heterosexual identities is an attempt to disrupt the routine cultural ways of looking at race and sexuality and to trigger more deliberative thought to analyze these topics. Similarly, reverse-marking humor, wherein comedians and satirists reverse conventional marking patterns to provocatively highlight unmarked populations as subculturally specific, deviant, and exotic, is a form of humor designed to get people to think more deliberately and consciously about privilege, stigma, and identity (Brekhus 1998). Humor and art can disrupt routines and the disruption they create is often designed to take an audience outside of their routine, automatic ways of attending to patterns of reality, which the humorist or artist wishes to challenge.

People who code-switch or attempt to pass in specific settings, while highlighting a different identity in other settings, employ more deliberate cognition as they make abrupt transitions in between different environments with different routines and demands on their presentation of self. Those who pass and code-switch are often consciously aware of and keenly attentive to elements and rules of a social setting that others do not need to consciously recognize. Sara Crawley (2002) notes, for instance, that the ability to shift codes for an audience is a "crafted sensitivity" that non-mundane individuals develop and deploy as a strategic resource to negotiate social settings (see also Force 2010). Transgender individuals, for example, pay conscious and deliberate attention to gendered cues and performances that others have embodied and embedded as "natural" and "inevitable." For folks who have to pass as ordinary, the socially mundane is vigilantly attended to as something marked and extraordinary. They are therefore likely to employ deliberative cognition to embark upon what others do with automatic cognition.

The cognitive processes of perception and attention, as well as imperception and inattention, are tied to specific cultures of seeing. We are socialized within "optical thought communities" to observe some features of reality, while leaving other aspects of reality unnoticed and in the background or "hidden in plain sight" (Zerubavel 2015). Our cultures of perception are shaped by the groups and social networks we belong to and the structural and social conditions under which we operate. Cognitive variation in perception and attention at the social level can be observed through studying local cognitive cultures of attention.

Local cognitive cultures of attention: institutional, subcultural, and socially networked norms of focusing

Our cognitive perceptions, what we "see" and foreground in our mind and what we ignore as irrelevant background, are socially organized in the communities, cultures, subcultures, and organizations we belong to. Ludwik Fleck ([1935] 1979: 38–51), in discussing scientific knowledge, refers to the "thought collective" or the "thought community" as the collective thinking of an interactive community with similar thought styles and norms of focusing. He argues that truth in science was developed by the thinking styles of particular thought collectives who exchanged ideas, interacted within a social network, and co-developed similar thought styles and worldviews that shaped the ways they apprehended and understood reality. Tamotsu Shibutani (1955) similarly argues that reference groups and social networks shape worldviews as we check our perceptions by comparing them to the perspectives of others around us. These social theorists highlight in different ways how our foci of attention are shaped by the communities we belong to and the social networks in which we interact. Different occupations, communities, subcultures, and group cultures have different ways of seeing and different rules for filtering and framing information as relevant or irrelevant. Organizations and professions, for instance, develop specialized cultures of attention that allow them to see what is relevant in their organizational culture and to filter out other information that is visible, but considered unimportant.

As an example of cognitive variation in the attention styles of two science fields, Karin Knorr-Cetina (1999) analyzes the different epistemic cultures of high energy physics and molecular biology, showing that the knowledge culture of high energy physics is organized around negative knowledge (trying to eliminate factors that could go wrong in an experiment) while molecular biology focuses on positive experiential knowledge (experimenting with and manipulating different variations of problematic factors).

Thus in high energy physics the problematic is bracketed and eliminated, while in molecular biology it is foregrounded. The two fields develop almost entirely different attention styles. Similarly, in *How Professors Think* Michèle Lamont (2009) finds cognitive variation in the attention styles of academic fields. In evaluation proposals, professors in the humanities focused on how interesting a proposal was rather than on validity, while social scientists often attended to validity and parsimony and focused little on interestingness. Lamont shows (2009: 54) that disciplinary cultures develop "epistemological styles" (preferences for particular ways of understanding how to build knowledge) that strongly channel what the discipline's members look for and therefore notice. Further demonstrating contrasting styles of attention, one of her research panelists, for instance, notes that people in English appear to value the ability to scrutinize a literary text for what is not there and absent, while philosophers rigorously focus entirely on what is there, regarding the English focus on absence as absurd. Different disciplinary cultures also form cross-culturally within the same fields.

Professional vision and organizational rules of the game collectively organize norms of focusing. William Ocasio (1997) looks at the attention structures of firm cultures, showing how they channel and distribute the attention of their decision-makers. What a firm focuses on depends on how the firm's rules, resources, and relationships distribute issues, answers, and decision-makers in specific communications and procedures. Important to the vision and focus of a firm are the rules of the game – a set of norms, values, and incentives, usually implicit – about how to interpret organization reality, which shape perception and the logic of social action. The rules of the game define what must be attended to and on what basis decisions should be evaluated (e.g. price, customer service, low costs, quality, technological innovation) (Ocasio 1997: 196). The rules of the game also help to shape what is organizationally in focus and what is organizationally out of frame.

Analyzing the attention structure of meteorologists, Phaedra Daipha (2010) illustrates how weather forecasters at a National

Weather Service office learn to do "screenwork" and visually sift and apprehend important weather information. While there is individual variation in specific repertoires of visual perception and a folk ideology within the weather forecasting center that "everyone does it differently," everyone creatively adapts small differences within widely shared, situated practices of looking and decision-making. Among the shared practices are seasonal norms of focusing and attention, requiring flexibility in one's pattern recognition muscles and strategies. In the winter forecasters are trained to focus on large-scale meteorological conditions and look at a big holistic picture, while in the summer they are trained to have the laser focus of a skilled marksman or sniper looking for the telltale target of a "hook echo" or "bell echo" radar signature and to act decisively in issuing a warning: "the spatiotemporal elusiveness of summer weather promotes a 'one shot, one kill' mentality, and forecasters have been primed to quickly identify their target before it has had a chance to do any damage" (Daipha 2010: 156). Meteorologists develop a professional vision by learning how to focus on the wealth of visual screen data available to them and how to transform that overload of visual stimuli into recognizable, meaningful information. While meteorologists emphasize their creativity and individuality, their vision is mostly a collaborative effort formed in an organizational culture and through professional socialization and interaction with others.

Similar to this research showing meteorologists' individual creativity happens within a collaborative environment of other experts with similarly trained visions, Michael Farrell's (2001) study of influential artists, writers, and intellectuals found that these individuals developed their creative visions in collaboration with others. They formed collaborative circles – a set of peers in the same discipline who through mutual collaboration and support became interdependent and developed a common vision that guided their creative work. Farrell demonstrates the socially networked and sociological nature of creativity. Rather than the lone artist using his or her individual imagination to create art, creativity is collectively cultivated and produced; extraordinary creativity is the result of collaboration and collective focus on the same problem. Farrell describes some collaboration as so "fully networked" and sharing ideas so openly and so much on the same wavelength that ownership of ideas is not clearly separable (Phillips 2007). Whether in writing cultures, meteorology cultures, or cooking cultures, individual creativity and originality are often collaboratively social rather than the product of a strictly individually creative mind. In her study of elite chefs in New York and San Francisco, Vanina Leschziner (2007: 86–8), for instance, shows how high-end chefs walk the line between originality and conforming to the norms of their niche and how they pay attention to what their competitors are doing to stay current with the latest trends in their field, while also disattending to the fact that they are paying attention to what others do. In cuisine and other fields where creation is individualized and where personal reputation is a form of capital, authorship becomes important; yet creations must still generally conform to the collective style of the field even as they appear partially original (Leschziner 2007: 80–1). Thus even in fields where originality is highly valued, the norms of attention and focusing are highly collectivist.

Locating cognitive variation affords us opportunities to make cross-context comparisons and contrasts to generate comparative analytic insights across sites. We can see, for instance, that while meteorologists, artists, and chefs have different professional interests, their desire and ability to be original within collaboratively and organizationally structured bounds of originality are quite similar.

To further illustrate the potential for analytic insights based on cross-context comparisons of cognitive variation, one can focus on local cognitive cultures of moral attention in social interactions. Here I integrate Mary Pat Baumgartner's (1988) ethnographic study on the moral attention of suburbanites and Elijah Anderson's (1999) quite different study on the "code of the street," along with other studies focused on what I will term "moral interactional attention" or "moral attention styles," to discuss neighborhood, regional, and local cultural variations in interactional norms of moral attention, social control, and social help. Although Baumgartner's approach is more explicitly cognitive in its analytic, formal, concept-generating style than Anderson's more traditional, in-depth, descriptive ethnographic approach, both highlight significant observations relevant to culture and cognition.

Baumgartner (1988) focuses on the "moral minimalism" of conflict avoidance used by members of an upper middle-class suburban community she studied, which leads the majority of suburban residents to ignore and remain silent in the face of most forms of deviance and moral offense. Suburbanites, she argues, take an active inattention and conflict avoidance approach to conflict and respond with apparent moral indifference to avoid contention. In their moral minimalist worldview, conflict is a contaminant to be avoided at almost all costs and the exercise of social control is dirty and unpleasant work. She suggests that moral minimalism arises as a consequence of the socio-demographic status of the residents; their suburban environment with its high emphasis on privacy and individuality contributed to a fluidity of social relations, a lack of social integration, and relative indifference between people.

Moral minimalism is a moral attention style found in other environments with fluid social relations, lack of social integration, and relative indifference between people, as well. This style of moral attention closely resembles Goffman's (1963) concept of civil inattention in public places, where social actors deliberately disattend to and actively pretend not to see acts of deviance out of politeness. The private setting of suburbia and the most highly public settings, such as mass transit, appear to share a similar interactional moral disattention and avoidance. Esther Kim (2012) demonstrates, for example, that civil inattention and avoidance strategies on a Greyhound bus produce comparable morally minimalist strategies of inattention. She argues that such public spaces are increasingly treated cognitively as private space and that privacy is encroaching into more and more of the public social realm. There is, of course, a dimension of power in who feels and is entitled to private space in public. Thus the interactional strategy of moral minimalism and moral inattention is closely tied to expectations of entitlement to privacy connected to social class and social privilege.

The morally minimalist use of social space is also reflected in the moral privacy of the gated community. Gated communities that wall themselves off from the rest of the world create, for instance, not only a physical barrier insulating themselves from the broader world but often a moral barrier as well (Lang and Danielsen 1997). Kim (2012) shows that even in tightly packed public spaces where there are no physical gates the relatively privileged can still develop mental and interactional gates to maintain social distance between strangers, deviants, the homeless, and others they do not want to invade "their space." Baumgartner argues that just as the moral minimalist cannot be bothered to engage in conflicts, neither can they be bothered to help those in need. Conflict and helping are opposite sides of the same coin, and conflict avoidance and helping avoidance are likewise opposite sides of the same coin. Moral minimalism is a peaceful and non-confrontational moral order, but it is an anomic peace founded on fragmentation, atomization, isolation, and moral indifference among people (Baumgartner 1988).

In contrast to Baumgartner's analysis of moral minimalism in the suburbs, Elijah Anderson (1999) argues that in the urban residential streets of West Philadelphia there exists an unwritten but interactionally visible "code of the streets" wherein one must appear hypervigilant and willing to respond to any moral affront or slight, in order to command respect and avoid being harassed as an "easy mark" in public. Respect in this context, Anderson argues, is a zero-sum game. In order to gain respect after being disrespected, one must balance the interactional ledger by responding to a moral affront of disrespect with a retaliatory disrespect of equal (or greater) value. Respect is paramount and disrespect is a major moral offense that requires a "moral self-help" (Black 1983) response. Because this moral attention style involves "incivil attention" and a direct confrontational moral response to moral affronts, it represents a "moral maximalism" or "moral vigilance" attention style that is in stark contrast to civil inattention or moral minimalism.

Putting a more collectivist twist on moral vigilance, Andrew Papachristos (2009) uses a mixed method social network analysis to study the collective social order of moral hypervigilance located in the pattern of Chicago gang homicides, showing that homicide patterns appear like epidemics and have a collective life and social pattern to them that are greater than the net of any individual's participation or motivation. Gang homicides, he argues, are socially networked and governed by moral norms of reciprocity. He provocatively likens murder in these highly contentious moral economies to a reciprocal "gift exchange" in that murders are traded between groups in a collective exchange that maintains status boundaries and in-group cohesion. Papachristos locates Anderson's code of the streets in a collective and socially networked context, showing how a single murder can spread to create multiple murders. As with other social contagions, social networks deeply affect one's risk.

Danielle Raudenbush (2012) highlights the interesting variation in moral attention styles between Red Line interactions on Chicago trains in majority middle-class white areas and Green Line interactions in largely lower-income black areas. In predominantly white areas avoidance behavior, self-involvement, civil inattention, lack of helping behavior or reluctance to help, and concealed visual interactions were the overwhelming behavioral norm. For example, when a young woman struggles down the aisle with a suitcase people glance at her quickly but then look away, avoiding involvement; when one woman does finally help she avoids eye contact and maintains a flat affect, dissuading potential conversation (Raudenbush 2012: 466). By contrast, in the lower-income majority black area, open and sustained visual interaction and verbal exchange are the norm and helping behavior is immediate, open, and widely practiced. Raudenbush identifies similar cognitive moral styles and interactional responses to those of Baumgartner's moral minimalists in more affluent white areas, while seeing a high degree of social cohesion and moral maximalism in poor black areas.

Moral attention styles have not only a spatial dimension but a temporal dimension. Murray Melbin (1978; 1987) shows that moral attention and civility between strangers increase at night. He illustrates that while the night's reputation for negative moral attention is high, nighttime interaction also shows increased civility. The night is both more dangerous and more civil as both moral extremes of hurting and helping behavior increase.

These different kinds of moral attention, from moral minimalism to moral vigilance, suggest neighborhood, network, region, and even temporal variation in moral interactional attention. The difference between a vigilant response to moral slights and to helping others and an avoidance response to conflict and to helping others reflects different styles of moral attention. Using morally minimalist styles of attention, social actors filter out much of what happens around them as they respond with avoidance to moral disruptions, while the vigilance of morally attentive styles involves social actors taking in everything around them and being finely tuned and primed to respond to moral affronts and moral situations. This cognitive variation in moral attention is located in different residential social networks and thought communities with different interactional norms of attention, as well as in their spatial, temporal, and interactional environments.

An exploration of local cognitive cultures of perception and attention begins to illustrate the ways that perception is influenced by socially networked frames for viewing reality. To further highlight cognitive variability in perception and attention across different levels of culture and between different cultural and organizational settings, perceptions of danger and safety and risk and routine also provide interesting insights.

Cognitive variation in perceptions of danger and safety, risk and routine

Perceptions of safety and danger, and routine and risk, provide interesting cases of how culture shapes what we attend to and disattend to. What do we recognize and fear as dangerous? What do we take for granted as routine or ignore altogether as not dangerous? What frameworks and schemas do we use to detect danger? When are we unnecessarily fearful and when are we overconfident? What is socially marked as dangerous and what is unmarked as a part of routine?

Whether danger is perceptually foregrounded and vigilantly attended to or perceptually eclipsed and disattended to is not simply a product of objective risk but shaped by cultural and institutional thought styles and frameworks for marking and unmarking one's environment. Some frameworks and rules of relevance are vigilant and finely attuned (and in some cases overstimulated) for detecting signs of danger, while others rely on routine and the ordinary, ignoring dangers, and requiring disruption to signify danger. What risks we attend to as relevant within these frameworks is also variable. Are we relaxed about the dangers of bad diet and automobiles, while vigilant and concerned about violent crime? Are we more concerned about climate change or terrorism? What we fear and what we feel confident around are socially organized and culturally and organizationally variable. Our visions of danger and safety, as well as risk and routine, are also shaped by power relations and who has the power to influence "collective vision."

Ruth Simpson (1996) identifies three frameworks and marking strategies for interpreting danger. The confident framework assumes safety until something is proven dangerous and marks as specialized only those things that should be approached with caution or avoided as dangerous. Because the confident framework regards safety as the default, it draws specific attention to dangers, explicitly marking them through symbolic action and signals (Simpson 1996: 556). Drivers, Simpson argues, are usually confident under unmarked routine road conditions and are only symbolically signaled and primed to think of driving as risky when temporary danger zones (e.g. "dangerous curve," "slippery when wet," "watch for ice on bridge") mark potential hazards. A less confident framework, Simpson suggests, might mark road entrances with "DANGER: heavy objects travelling at high speeds." The cautious framework by contrast assumes danger until something is proven safe. The psychological equivalent of this framework is paranoia, but she argues that group fears and phobias (such as Americans' strong collective fear of crime) are often not diagnosed as pathological since they are widely shared cultural phobias. This framework assumes danger as the default setting and marks safety as the exception from routine. In wartime, for instance, white flags and cease-fire zones symbolically mark those rare environments where one can expect to let down one's guard and feel temporarily safe (Simpson 1996: 554). The neutral framework, Simpson proposes, is an in-between framework that is neither overly confident nor overly cautious, leaving the routine unmarked but marking both danger and safety. Similarly, different occupations and thought communities use either a casual framework (which assumes non-deviance by default unless there is an ocean of evidence to suggest otherwise) or a vigilant framework (which vigilantly attends to even the slightest hint of deviance until it is proven "safe") to identify "social deviants" (Brekhus 1996: 515–17); police, for instance, are occupationally socialized to be more vigilantly attentive to the smallest evidence of criminality than civilians and rarely write off even slightly suspicious behavior as "nothing out of the ordinary" or "nothing to see."

An interesting example of a thought community's perceptions of safety and danger appears in Dan Baum's (2010) journalistic account of joining the concealed weapons carrier community and being socialized into their ways of seeing the world. Concealed weapon carriers take a cautious or vigilant approach to observing the world, treating most of it as dangerous and considering safety the exception rather than the rule. Baum notes that he was repeatedly reminded that the world is a dangerous place and that as a concealed weapon carrier he was obligated to always be on the alert and vigilant for any possible threat. Gun owners divided the world into wolves (bad people), sheep (good but naive people who are oblivious to the dangers that lurk everywhere), and sheep dogs (good people who are vigilant and on constant alert), and into threat-level conditions: condition white (a condition of being relaxed and oblivious to one's surroundings that one should avoid), condition yellow (vigilant and alert), condition orange (hyper-alert and ready to respond to danger), and condition red (responding to the threat) (Baum 2010). For this subcultural community, a minimum of condition yellow and maintaining constant vigilance to detect danger wherever it may lurk are mandatory obligations of moral citizenship anywhere outside one's home, and folks who fail to employ this level of caution and who walk the streets in condition white, blissfully unaware of the dangers, are considered weak and morally suspect. Many people outside the conceal-and-carry community, however, view danger as a highly unusual exception to routine rather than a dominant feature of social interaction. They do not assume danger as a constant in need of vigilant attention. The distinction between a vigilant, cautious framework that assumes the world is inherently danger-ous, and a relaxed, confident framework that assumes the world is usually safe, shows two very different marking systems for organizing one's world around the potential risk of crime.

Sociologists interested in media (Glassner 1999; Altheide 1997; 2002) have focused on how media in the United States emphasize extremely unusual events and thus prime viewers to be fearful and cautious of dramatic and unlikely events, while leaving hidden the routine, everyday, highly probable dangers we actually face, yet casually ignore with confidence. Media, they note, exert a pow-erful influence on cultural perceptions of fear and danger. Our attentional focus on the marked, dramatic, and rare, as media consumers, makes us poor judges of probability. Barry Glassner (1999) shows, for instance, how news coverage in the United States highlights extreme and dramatic, but rare, dangers while failing to emphasize far more objectively probable dangers. Residents of the United States, he argues, fear crime from strangers, plane crashes, terrorist attacks, rare but dramatic news-making dis-eases, and a host of other unusual events while generally ignoring more common risks to personal safety such as heart disease, auto accidents, and household guns.

David Altheide (1997; 2002) argues that the entertainment format of news media facilitates this kind of cultural attention as it emphasizes the evocation of emotions and reduces complex social problems to compelling stories with clear victims and villains. News media, he argues, develop a "problem frame" approach to entertainment that provides a narrative structure that is culturally resonant and that emphasizes morally unambiguous elements to a story on a problem such as crime, and provides moral meanings. The majority of topics presented as news involve issues framed as "problems," and the problem characteristics are organized around "a narrative that begins with a general conclusion that 'something is wrong' and we know what it is!"; the most unambiguous aspects of a complex problem are presented, such as "evil causes evil" or "corrupt officials," in a way that irons out complexity, nuance, and moral ambiguity (Altheide 1997: 654–5). In news formats the morally unambiguous is socially marked and highlighted, shaping our social attention. Media coverage of "missing children," for instance, distorts public perceptions and contributes to fears of "stranger danger" by focusing on stranger kidnappings while ignoring the frequent ambiguities of runaways and parental abductions (Best and Horiuchi 1985; Best 1987; Altheide 1997: 554).

Cognitive variation in frameworks for assessing danger and risk also organize around the distinction between using a "probabilistic" lens or a "possibilistic" lens to interpret risk. Lee Clarke (2006) argues that our fears of the dramatic may be warranted after all. He distinguishes probabilistic risk assessment (based on statistical likelihood) from possibilistic risk assessment (based on the consequences if it does happen), suggesting two contrasting thought styles about risk. These frameworks are often organizationally and culturally located. They even vary within different communities within sociology; sociologists of media and criminologists, for instance, are likely to emphasize the irrationality of American fears of rare, dramatic, consequential events on the basis of probablism (see Glassner 1999), while sociologists of risk are likely to interpret those same fears as reasonable on the basis of the possibility of large-scale disasters. Political elites and organizations, Clarke suggests, often emphasize probabilistic risks of nuclear power or toxic chemicals, while lay publics may be far more concerned with the possibilities than just the probabilities.

While Glassner and Altheide focus on how we are optically socialized to overemphasize the dangerous and extraordinary, Karen Cerulo (2006) and Diane Vaughan (1996; 2002) focus on how we can also be cognitively socialized to overemphasize the safe, the routine, and the mundane, even in the face of risk. Cerulo (2006) argues that there is a cognitive "positive asymmetry" in American cultural thinking that makes it much easier for Americans to envision "best-case scenarios" than "worst-case scenarios." She argues that we have three patterned ways of hiding worst cases from our individual and collective imaginations: eclipsing, clouding, and recasting. In eclipsing we obscure or hide the worst; in clouding we keep the worst vague, distant, and undefined; and in recasting we transform the negative into something positive. Although the general cultural pattern is one of positive asymmetry, Cerulo employs a comparative case study method to show how different optical communities perceive routine and risk differently. She presents the successful containments of the 2003 SARS disease outbreak, which originated in China and became an international health threat, and the Y2K (year 2000) computer bug threat as examples where health professionals and IT professionals responded effectively to potential disasters because they were moored in occupational settings where imagining bad or worst-case possibilities was part of the structure of the profession. By contrast, she argues, the 2001 FBI Phoenix memo, warning of the potential for a terrorist attack on the United States using airplanes, and the 1986 *Challenger* launch decision, which ended in a space-shuttle explosion and disaster, are two instances where professionals failed to respond adequately to threats and were guided by the perceptual patterns of positive asymmetry.

Diane Vaughan focuses on how institutionalized ways of seeing shaped the ways engineers could attend to the routine, while ignoring danger signals, prior to the shuttle launch decision that ended in the *Challenger* disaster. Using a method called analogical theorizing Vaughan compares different units of analysis for formal similarities, looking at decision-making in different organizational contexts such as the *Challenger* launch decision and air traffic controller decisions. The organizational and environmental influences on cognition in the first context caused participants to foreground the routine and ignore warning signals, while in the air traffic controller context, participants were finely attuned to think in worst-case scenarios and to recognize subtle signals that foretell a problem. In the organizational context of the *Challenger* launch decision, technological uncertainty was taken for granted so that problems and anomalies were routinized as normal, and the agency's culture of production set a frame by which such concerns were secondary to the primary goal of production (Vaughan 2002). By contrast, air traffic controllers are trained into a cultural common sense and formal rules and scripts that minimize choice and provide a "standardized frame of reference against which even small anomalies (what in other decision contexts might appear as weak signals that [do] not attract attention) stand out as strong signals, enabling controllers to recognize early warning signals and take corrective action, thereby preventing small deviations and errors from turning into mistakes with harmful outcomes" (Vaughan 2002: 45). Vaughan's work builds upon Bourdieu's idea of habitus by showing that it is a product of social location not only in terms of class or larger cultures, but also in terms of organizational cultures. The organizational attention style for the *Challenger* launch decision led engineers to overlook warning signals while focused on the frame of production, while the organizational attention of air traffic controllers created a situation where disaster avoidance became a primary focus.

Whereas disruptions to routine can trigger deliberate cognition, a lack of disruption can maintain automatic cognition as a dominant thought process and contribute to social inaction. Javier Auyero and Debora Swistun (2008; 2009) show how chemical companies operating in Flammable (an Argentinian shantytown) encouraged residents to rely on automatic cognition to apprehend their environment as routine rather than use deliberate cognition to recognize toxic danger. The maintenance of the mundane and commonplace in ordinary routines served as blinders to extraordinary dangers, allowing residents to screen out or suspend thoughts of the unpleasant. The chemical companies capitalized on "relational anchoring" and the domination of everyday life and ordinary social networks in the lives of Flammable residents to encourage social inaction against the companies' practices. Because residents were anchored in everyday reality and experienced a gradual shift from a pristine environment to a toxic landscape without abrupt discontinuities, there was a lack of deliberate cognition about pollution. As residents' environment was slowly changing for the worse they were building families, working, and enjoying friendships; they were thoroughly embedded in the routine organization of daily life (Auyero and Swistin 2008: 369; also see Bourdieu 1998; 2000 on groups embedded in history and routine organization), and as such their perceptions of environmental hazards were relationally anchored in the mundane, unmarked reality of everyday routines. As the contamination process was gradual and no major accidents or obvious abrupt transitions from safe to toxic occurred, Flammable residents' schemas of perception obscured dangers (Auyero and Swistun 2008: 369). Rather than marking toxic pollution as an outside observer might, their mundane activities of everyday life and the epochal rather than eventful nature (Snyder 2013) of the pollution led to it being primarily unmarked and often ignored as a background feature of everyday reality. Organizational actors exerted their institutional power to produce ambiguity and uncertainty about the dangers and to focus residents on the everyday, to further maintain this collective restricted vision among residents. Daina Cheyenne Harvey (2012) demonstrates a similar cognitive denial of danger in the responses of residents of New Orleans to the environmental hazards caused by the British Petroleum oil spill in the nearby gulf.

Robert Wuthnow (2010) asserts that denying peril is not instinctive but something we learn culturally. The conscious suppression of worst-case scenarios of environmental catastrophes, pandemics, and nuclear annihilation, he argues, is shaped by culture and power. Our basic schemas for understanding them are influenced by our family and friendship networks, neighborhoods, businesses, religious organizations, government, and mass media, and the meanings of peril are shaped by influential institutions. Moreover, he suggests that peril today is largely transferred to hope in experts because only large-scale organizations are capable of managing it. We are not unaware of large-scale disasters but the abbreviated scripts we use to deny their importance (e.g. "scientists will figure it out," "the risks of this happening are way too small to worry about") are rationalizations we have picked up from others, and we minimize discussions of perils not because we fail to see them at all but "because power arrangements encourage [us] to talk about other things" (Wuthnow 2010: 11). Power arrangements encourage us to not discuss these things and to therefore leave them seen and unacknowledged rather than unseen.

The social guiding of attention and disattention can be explored furthered by comparing Asia Friedman's (2013) cognitive analysis of perceptual inattention to sex similarities with Mica Pollock's (2004) analysis of verbal inattention to race differences, then extending this to a broader discussion of social inattention and aggregate forms of cultural and social blindness and muteness.

Seeing sex and talking race: sensory and social attention and inattention

In her book *Blind to Sameness*, Asia Friedman (2013) provides an interesting case comparison of how two different communities attend to and disattend to different features of reality. She interviews 41 transgender people, who tend to be sex/gender "experts" acutely aware of how sex and gender are constructed, and 27 blind people, who are "outsiders" to visual sex attribution. Friedman's methodological choice to theoretically sample two substantively very different populations (blind people and transgender people), in order to develop analytic similarities, highlights the multi-contextual approach that sociologists of culture and cognition can employ to study patterns in social processes across different empirical foci. She selects the blind because they must rely on non-visual perception, and transgender people because their social standpoint gives them a sort of expert knowledge on male and female bodies and an "elevated awareness of which body parts are the most important to sex cues" (Friedman 2013: 59). Both groups, she finds, experience sex perception through subcultural filters that get layered on top of the hegemonic filter of "sex difference" in ways that both partially accept the dominant filter and also challenge the taken-for-grantedness of sex differences in the dominant filter. Transgender respondents who found it easy to pass as their chosen gender and to shift in appearance from one sex to another, for instance, developed a heightened awareness of sex similarities. The blind, Friedman finds, sometimes do not attribute sex and often do not consider it among the most relevant factors to attend to in people because it is often ambiguous and hard to determine. She notes that the sighted perceive sex differences as obvious, natural, and unambiguous but that they are able to do so by emphasizing the most obvious visual cues, while disattending to more ambiguous cues. Showing that both the blind and the sighted are members of communities who perceive some things while ignoring others, she notes that the sighted often emphasize the most visible cues that support the idea of sex difference and often do not see the many ways that male and female bodies are proportionately similar to one another. In short, the sighted are blind to sex similarities.

While Friedman focuses on what we are socialized to see and not to see with respect to sex, Mica Pollock (2004), in her book *Colormute: Race Talk Dilemmas in an American School*, examines what high school students are socialized to say and not to say with respect to race. While Americans are socialized to be blind to sex similarities, they are socialized to be mute (and to feign colorblindness) with respect to racial differences. Pollock emphasizes that *not* talking about race is often a tactical inattention involving deliberately avoiding mentioning race in relation to many issues, especially those involving power relations. While students in Pollock's high school spoke matter-of-factly about race in broad brush terms when talking about everyday interactions between students, they routinely denied that race mattered and referenced its absolute irrelevance, in their mind, to most situations. Some topics were scripted in the minds of students to be matter-of-factly racial (questions about social networks directed at students such as "who do you hang out with?") while other topics were scripted so that race labels were conspicuously absent (questions directed at adults about student–faculty relations and discipline). In discussing student–adult conflicts and the allocation of discipline, race was conspicuously absent from adult accounts of these issues (Pollock 2004: 45).

Further demonstrating the "color muteness" associated with

our desire to be "colorblind," Nina Eliasoph (1999: 479) notes that well-meaning white Americans try hard not to talk about race in many situations. In a way that is reminiscent of Goffman's idea of civil inattention, whites in the United States work hard to pretend that race is not there and to not acknowledge it, even as it is a socially constructed reality around which much of social life is organized. Phillip Goff and his co-authors (2013) provide a cognitive experimental social psychological perspective on this same issue, looking at the avoidance of race talk and the use of "strategic colorblindness" in both inter-racial and intra-racial settings. They found that white respondents were more likely in mixed-race interactions than in intra-racial interactions to (1) indicate that paying attention to race was negative, (2) state that they were uncomfortable categorizing people by race, and (3) state that racial categorization or acknowledgment causes harm (Goff et al. 2013: 337). Only white participants used these colorblind arguments in any context; black participants made no such colorblind comments (Goff et al. 2013). Whites employed strategic colorblindness and avoided talking about race for both self-protective and egalitarian reasons.

Blindness to sex similarities and muteness on race differences provide an interesting comparative case between how people's perceptions about important social categories are organized. Sex difference is a dominant cultural frame for understanding the sexes and it is often expressed openly and taken for granted. Although race differences are also assumed, whites, in particular, assert that they are "colorblind" and prefer not to openly acknowledge race difference, suggesting that paying attention to race and stating its presence itself causes harm. In the dominant cultural filter of sex perception people do not share the same aversion to seeing and acknowledging difference. In fact difference is assumed and optical communities who do not "see" difference or who find sex differences hard to detect through sensory ambiguity have to chart a perceptual path that either dismisses or makes new sense of these ambiguities.

Although sighted people claim to be "colorblind" about race, Osagie Obasogie (2013) challenges this metaphor in finding that even blind people themselves are not "colorblind" to race. He demonstrates that through the continual processing and filing of small pieces of information, blind people learn to "see" and experience race using their other sensory perceptions and to attach meaning to race. Through their social networks, interactional experiences, and cultural cues they are trained and socialized to perceive race. Race then becomes an issue that is just as much a part of their sensory perception as it is for the sighted. Actual physical eye vision is far less important to seeing race than social vision.

Perception: framing and priming relevance

In *Frame Analysis*, Erving Goffman (1974) focuses on what social actors attend to as in frame and what they ignore as out of frame, and how the frames and definitions of the situation that we use shape our perceptions. He highlights a number of concepts important to the sociology of attention. These include the frame itself (a general meaning context within which social actors interpret action), breaking frame (acts or events that break down or redefine a frame), bracketing (instances where one maintains the frame even when it is disrupted by bracketing the disruption and disattending to it as socially irrelevant, through either passive or orchestrated inattention), and in frame and out of frame. Goffman also focuses on subtle verbal and interactional strategies such as keying that signal to others how something is to be interpreted (e.g. as serious or a joke, as official or "off the record," as in frame or out of frame).

Goffman's concept of framing and his analysis of the ways that we signal entering or exiting a particular frame are ideas that apply across a wide range of frames and units of analysis. Goffman primarily covered how individuals adopt and use frames to order and make sense of reality, but more recent uses of frame analysis have shifted the focus from how individuals employ frames to how social movements and media devise frames that shape our interpretations of reality. In social movements theory, for instance, Robert Benford and David Snow (2000) demonstrate that movements foreground and highlight some issues and events as salient, thus also simultaneously submerging other issues and events by omission or lack of accenting, to frame perceptions of an issue. Diana Kendall (2005) similarly shows how in news stories about social class, media highlight certain items, thereby elevating them in salience and making them more noticeable than other items – for instance, where bits of information are placed in a text, how they are introduced, how often the information is repeated, and the extent to which the information is associated with other symbols familiar to the media consumers all shape how social class (and other issues) are attended to. Murray Davis (1983) analyzes framing in an erotic context, examining how people slide into and out of erotic and everyday frames with transition rituals, upkeying and downkeying, and other strategies to mark the transition. While in erotic reality, they attempt to disattend to out-of-frame, everyday interruptions such as phone calls and doorbells ringing. If they are unable to, these events break the erotic frame of reality. Individuals devise a number of strategies to slide into and out of such frames.

Charles Goodwin (1994) shows how framing shaped perception and interpretation in the 1992 trial of four Los Angeles police officers who were acquitted of beating black motorist Rodney King in a high-profile police brutality case whose verdict sparked the Los Angeles riots on April 29, 1992. The defense and its witnesses framed the situation not as a single prolonged beating of a suspect by four officers, but rather as multiple administrative responses to subduing a potential threat. Goodwin shows that they framed the situation *organizationally* to portray the officers as acting dispassionately and professionally to subdue a suspect who ultimately controlled the situation. Lawyers defending the officers argued that the beating tape could only be understood by framing the events within the work life of the police profession. The defense framed the beating as "an example of careful police work and a form of professional discourse with the victim in which he was a very active coparticipant – indeed, the party who controlled the interaction" (Goodwin 1994: 616). In order to make this claim the defense provided the jury with a specific organizational or professional coding scheme to analyze the events on tape. A coding scheme was applied to the tape wherein "1) if a suspect is aggressive, the proper police response is escalation of force in order to subdue him; 2) when the suspect cooperates, then force is de-escalated" (Goodwin 1994: 616). The power of coding schemes to shape perception and attention was central to the defense strategy. The use of this coding scheme radically transformed the images visible on tape by putting them into an organizational expert frame of reference where what appeared to be continuously beating a suspect into submission was recast as several separate demonstrations that a period of de-escalation has ceased (Goodwin 1994: 617). The ability of the defense to quickly cognitively orient the jurors to interpret events and images through a specific organizational frame of reference allowed the defendants' acts to be reinterpreted, from an everyday frame to an organizationally specific frame favorable to the officers. Attention was redirected to Rodney King's movements and away from the officer's movements except in how they responded to movements of King's individual body parts. Goodwin shows how the "professional vision" of police work changed the perception of the assault on Rodney King from a brutal beating to careful, dispassionate administrative procedure.

Consistent with Goodwin's frame of organizational vision, Zygmunt Bauman (1989) illustrates how organizational framing of issues tends to focus on "technological morality" (are the most efficient technologies and procedures being used and are the most efficient means used to achieve the organization's desired ends?) at the expense of substantive moral concerns that remain outside the organizational frame of vision. He argues that the technological morality of organizations moves moral concerns from the plight of the objects of action to the procedural efficiency with which the targets of action are handled. In a bureaucratic organization, moral attention is shifted away from the plight of the objects of action and onto technical matters of procedural efficiency and effectiveness in performing one's assigned role (Bauman 1989: 159). Organizations often play an active role in framing our moral attention and vision.

Eviatar Zerubavel (2006) analyzes how silence and denial are practices that take events that could be at the center of the frame and move them out of the frame entirely. Learning what to ignore and what to not notice is as important to what we see as learning what to focus on and what to notice. Conspiracies of silence are collaborative acts of collective social, cultural, or organizational muteness that remove the proverbial "elephant in the room" from the center of the frame and place it entirely outside the frame. The social organization of attention necessarily also involves the social organization of disattention. In instances of denial and avoidance it is actually the organization of disattention that takes the lead in organizing our attention. Zerubavel demonstrates that the general social patterns of organizing disattention hold across multiple types of silences and scandals, and that they are applicable and comparable across different scales of analysis including the micro, meso, and macro levels of social life. By deliberately ignoring a family open secret at the micro level, a political scandal at the meso level, or genocide at the macro level, and by bracketing such things out of our vision as things not to be acknowledged or discussed, we channel and frame perception (Zerubavel 2006).

In their study of media representations of looting in the wake of Hurricane Katrina, Kirk Johnson, Mark Dolan, and John Sonnett (2011) illustrate how news media framed the response of residents who took items from stores in the wake of disaster and thus organized viewers' social attention and moral interpretations. News scenes overwhelmingly used white speakers to frame narratives around looting by black residents, and the newscasters editorialized motive without asking the looters why they were doing it in all but 3 of the 104 looting cases analyzed (Johnson et al. 2011). These authors show that newscasters decontextualized the looting and provided their etic (outsiders') perspectives on the acts without getting the emic (insiders') explanations. The newscasters portrayed looting as wanton opportunism perpetrated by anti-social criminals, whereas residents often saw it is a rational response to a disaster landscape where one needed to provide food and shoes for one's family when social order was disrupted and everyday rules could not be taken for granted (Johnson et al.

2011). Newscasters framed the looting in ways that encouraged their audience to bracket context and focus on the act of stealing (it was framed as stealing rather than as taking) in and of itself, while residents, when given an opportunity to explain their actions, tried to foreground context. News organizations favored established norms and observed events from a white middle-class standpoint. For instance, when one newscaster reported that "some National Guard troops have arrived, 300 out of Arkansas *with 'shoot to kill' orders*. They are working the streets trying to take them back. *That's a bit of good news we can report tonight*" (Johnson et al. 2011: 314), the framing of the issue of law enforcement being authorized to use lethal force to defend property (a controversial tactic) as good news presents the issue through a specific cultural lens. In a similar manner, much news coverage critical of why poor, black residents did not just pick up and leave during Hurricane Katrina was presented devoid of context. While upper middle-class residents with resources and widely geographically dispersed social networks could leave relatively easily, Elizabeth Fussell (2006) shows how long-term poor residents of New Orleans not only often lacked transportation and resources to leave easily, but more importantly had a number of strong network ties in the area that effectively anchored them in place. News media framed leaving New Orleans as the obvious response to a hurricane, but this assumed the subculturally specific perspective of mobile middle-class people with geographically diffuse social networks and fewer anchoring ties. How an issue is framed and whose implicit social standpoint is used to interpret and contextualize or decontextualize events shapes social and moral perceptions of the issue and the actors involved.

With the growing interest in implicit cognition, sociologists have begun to look at priming as another way to conceptualize the role of culture in affecting cognition and shaping social action. Whereas framing emphasizes moving an issue into frame so it is thought about, priming focuses on influencing how we think about an issue when messages cue, renew, and activate implicit associations we already hold in memory. When a particular concept is primed in our social environment, associations with the primed item in our memory are activated. For example, in a psychological experiment, John Bargh, Mark Chen, and Lara Burrows (1996) show that when non-elderly participants were primed with stereotypes about the elderly they took longer to walk down a hallway than those who were not primed. The study of implicit prejudice and implicit bias and the ways they are primed is an area of psychological studies in cognition that has potential interest for sociologists. Hana Shepherd (2011) calls for sociologists to build upon implicit association research in psychology to understand how cultural environments, including symbols and media, place, situations, and networks, prime and activate cognitive associations. Such research can be particularly instructive in understanding how latent stereotypes and associations such as implicit racial associations and biases influence cognition and social action.

Conclusion

Sociologists of culture and cognition explore perception, attention, and the social organization of relevance as well as their opposites: imperception, inattention, and the social organization of irrelevance. Human perception and attention are organized socially and show significant cognitive variation across settings. Local cognitive cultures shape what people think and how they think. Even in situations where social actors are rewarded for originality, their creativity is collaboratively created rather than individually generated. As conceptual tools for understanding general patterns of social perception across cognitive variation, the concepts of the marked and the unmarked and deliberate and automatic cognition can be employed.

As part of an exploration of cognitive variation in this chapter we looked at different frameworks for evaluating danger and risk. People perceive risk and routine, danger and safety, and a host of other perceptual elements in culturally and organizationally channeled ways. Looking at sensory perception, as well as sensory perception metaphors, such as "blindness" and "seeing," this chapter examined how what people see (and what they say) is socially and culturally organized. What is in frame and out of frame and how people are influenced to attend to some associations and not others are also culturally organized. Our attention and inattention are culturally guided on quotidian matters, such as acknowledging or not acknowledging transit interactions or sliding into and out of erotic reality, and they are also culturally influenced on morally salient issues more explicitly tied to social power and inequalities, such as how we interpret race and class-based realities. Next I turn to classification and categorization, cognitive processes that relate to and further build on sociological understandings of perception and attention.

2

***

Classification, Categorization, and Boundary Work

Classification and categorization are central ways that we sort, make sense of, and construct social reality from the stimuli we attend to. Not only do we perceive things socially (as we saw in the last chapter) but we categorize and classify what we perceive socially. Classification as a process, like perception, relates to meaning, identity, and memory and time (issues discussed in later chapters). Classification at the cultural level has long been an interest of sociologists and anthropologists, dating back to Émile Durkheim and Marcel Mauss' (1963) work on symbolic classifications of a religious and moral nature. These authors argued that systems of classification and the categories we construct are emergent collective representations. Anthropologist Mary Douglas (1966) demonstrates how classifications and boundaries separating the sacred and the profane are maintained by social and cultural taboos and by symbolic metaphors of purity and pollution. Sociologist Barry Schwartz (1981) has emphasized that across many different classifications the vertically higher is given greater moral weight, that which is above or up is perceived and classified as morally superior, while that which is below or lower is seen as morally inferior. Arnold Van Gennep (1960) specifically analyzed boundary work, studying "rites of passage" that mark socially significant events, such as coming of age, marriage, birth, and death, that signify abrupt transitional passages across social categories and classification boundaries. He observed deliberative, conscious markings of boundary transitions, cross-culturally exploring transitional rituals marking significant life events, while reflecting on the patterned, formal similarities across contexts, for example by analytically highlighting rites of separation, transition rites, and rites of incorporation as three general stages in the process of passage. Victor Turner (1967) builds upon Van Gennep's analysis, focusing on the "liminal period" of transition in rites of passage as a temporal moment where individuals are ambiguously positioned and potentially threatening and polluting, but also freer to break out of convention, because of their unclear, disordered status. These foundational works have inspired a range of scholarship on the social foundations of classification, categorization, and the maintenance as well as symbolic negotiation and transgression of social boundaries.

While Durkheim and Mauss focused primarily on broad, sweeping classification systems, contemporary sociologists also analyze classification and categorization at subcultural and group levels. The sociology of classification and categorization asks what similarities and differences we establish between phenomena and what differences and distinctions we assign social weight to as things that matter. How do we maintain classificatory boundaries and how do we cross categorical divides? What rules do we use to classify and order social reality? We engage in a number of classification conventions to order and classify reality and we employ strategies to define and maintain categories. In classifying and categorizing reality, we think categorically rather than continuously, and we create distinct categories of meaning out of continuums and gradations (Zerubavel 1991). We classify reality in quotidian ways on things that appear to have little substantive significance but are nonetheless imbued with localized subcultural meanings that matter. We also classify reality and make distinctions on highly consequential matters that have important and wide-ranging social and moral implications. The sociology of classification focuses on how we identify and lump together similarities and split differences; how we exaggerate distinctions between categories; how we maintain symbolic boundaries to keep categories separate, maintain purity, and avoid cross-contamination between categories; how we cross boundaries; and how we use rites of passage to mark transitions between categories.

In this chapter, I focus on cognitive variation in classifications of race, classifications of nature and civilization, uses of
dirt/cleanliness and purity/impurity metaphors to polarize boundaries, and styles of boundary maintenance and border crossings.
I highlight general social patterns such as how marked attributes
weigh heavier in classifications than unmarked ones, how similar
impurity metaphors and pollution rituals maintain boundaries
across widely disparate types and levels of social categories, and
how different kinds of boundaries are maintained as well as
bridged and transformed through formally similar strategies.
Before addressing cognitive variation on these dimensions I discuss
the process of social differentiation and categorization through
the broad, general, sensitizing concepts of rigid, fuzzy, and flexible
classification mindsets and of lumping and splitting developed by
Eviatar Zerubavel (1991), and examine classification and categorization disputes and shifts of classificatory boundaries that change
over time, using Sylvia Fuller's (2003) work on boundary disputes
among rock climbers.

Lumping and splitting: thinking categorically

Eviatar Zerubavel (1991) develops broad sensitizing analytic
concepts for thinking about social classification across different
contexts. He identifies three classification mindsets for ordering
social reality: the rigid, the fuzzy, and the flexible. These mindsets
represent ideal-type strategies for classification. They are sensitizing analytic concepts for understanding strategies of boundary
maintenance, boundary transgression, boundary flexibility, and
social change. The rigid mind, he shows is committed to keeping
categories separated, to purity and order, and to avoiding overlap
between categories. Ambiguities and anomalies, from this mindset,
are disturbing instances of disorder that are out of place. Such
mindsets are common in orthodox religious communities, minority communities in danger of disappearing, and institutions such
as law (Zerubavel 1991: 51–60). The fuzzy mind, by contrast is
fluid in blending categories together, playful in engaging in ritual

fluidity, and socially promiscuous in transgressing boundaries. Whereas the rigid mind is committed to order and purity, the fluid mind upends social order and has its own moral dimension: an objection to social divisions (Zerubavel 1991: 103). Such mindsets are more often found in transgressive institutions such as art and humor. The flexible mind, he proposes, represents a middle ground between the other two classification mindsets.

Zerubavel (1991; 1996) highlights "lumping" and "splitting" as two categorization processes that people use within their various classification mindsets to group together some things as essentially the same and interchangeable and to separate other things as distinctly different categories. The concepts of lumping and splitting originated in taxonomy, a field concerned with identifying species, subspecies, and races in the animal kingdom. One might think of lumping and splitting of social categories as a kind of social taxonomy or architecture of meaning. In lumping, we, as social actors, establish social clusters by giving weight to a social similarity within a cluster, while ignoring differences within the cluster (Zerubavel 1991: 17). In splitting we carve a line between categories, creating a separation that also involves implicitly ignoring or downplaying between category similarities (Zerubavel 1996: 27). For instance, we may accentuate the difference between sexes and ignore across-category similarities, seeing gendered traits belonging to men and women as two discrete categories while ignoring overlapping bell curves of gendered attributes. We also assign weight to social categories (Mullaney 1999), wherein the act of categorization itself implies that whatever common experience or attribute the category has should be weighted more importantly than attributes not used to assign members to the common category. For example, people often see members of a race, sex, social class, or occupation as sharing something in common as members of a social category, and thus may assume a common experience that has weight. People engage in a variety of cognitive practices and rituals to polarize different clusters and keep them distinct from one another, as well as in practices that can shift or change symbolic boundaries over time.

Sylvia Fuller (2003) applies a Zerubavelian framework to

boundary disputes and categorization within a rock-climbing subculture. As an example both of classification disputes over orthodoxy and heresy and of how symbolic boundaries change over time from such disputes, she examines the creation and contestation of boundaries in the subculture of mountain/rock climbers. Two climbing innovations, "hangdogging" and "rap-bolting," made climbs easier and safer and thus altered the mix of skills and dispositions necessary for the climbing capital of first ascents (Fuller 2003: 9). Elite climbers felt their subcultural capital was threatened by these new practices because they sensed that the first ascents they made without such technologies would be cheapened and degraded. In order to maintain status and create a symbolic boundary and classification between their climbs and climbs using the innovations, elite climbers classified climbs as "free" or "aided," which created a categorical gap between all climbs that did not use these techniques and all climbs that did (Fuller 2003). All free climbs were lumped together and all aided climbs were split and marked as an inferior, altogether different kind of climb. The key in the first stage of the conflict over these new techniques was differentiation (Fuller 2003). Climbers opposed to the innovations created boundaries that marked the strategies as inferior deviations from standard ascents, thus eliminating them from the category of "pure" climbs, and they did so in two separate ways: by employing a hierarchical spectrum of ethics to downgrade ascents using these techniques as less ethical and by segregating them as an entirely different category – an "aided" climb (Fuller 2003: 6).

Practitioners of these techniques first accepted the hierarchical logic of these distinctions but downplayed their significance, attempting to minimize the differentiation. But as the conflict over climbing styles intensified, critics developed ideas of orthodoxy and heresy and of purity and contamination to counter the growing practice and legitimation of these strategies. Critics framed the issue as one where the new practices did not simply aid individual climbers but threatened the integrity of the climbing experience and of the rocks being climbed themselves; this distinction did not simply put such climbs in a less prestigious category but defined them as polluting and threatening to the integrity of climbing in general (Fuller 2003: 13). In such a symbolic system it simply was not possible for the two climbing practices to exist simultaneously. As purists defined these boundaries more rigidly, Fuller notes that innovators opted for a reciprocal segregation strategy, agreeing with a hierarchical distinction, but inverting the values for the two sides of the distinction to value the marked rather than the unmarked side of climbing. While innovators originally chose to defy the logic of making distinctions or emphasized how their practices were continuous with them, they eventually embraced the hierarchy and reversed the values.

Although Fuller looks at a specific, seemingly idiosyncratic subculture, the processes of classification, boundary construction, and boundary maintenance she uncovers are general ones that, while revealed in a specific case, shed light upon larger social patterns of classification disputes, differentiation, and shifts in boundary strategies. Attempts at the preservation of purity and orthodoxy in the face of things that purists consider contamination or heresy occur across a range of classification practices. Similarly, the pattern of differentiation, reciprocal segregation, and boundary shifts over time is one that can apply to a variety of contexts. Outcasts defined as heretics may eventually develop counter-identities that reverse the valuation of the hierarchy.

Having looked at lumping and splitting within rock-climbing subcultures as a very specific context that affords interesting general observations, we now turn to cognitive variation and patterned similarities in the broader, more salient issue of racial classifications.

Classification conventions, categorization, and weight assignment: race as an example

Perhaps one of the most interesting places to begin looking at classification conventions and mental weighting of categories is in the classification and categorization of race. While many cultural weighting rules are implicit and unstated, race has often involved legal definitions that make classification and weighting rules explicit. Scientists, anthropologists, and sociologists have demonstrated that race is one continuum with no discrete breaks or categories, yet cultures create distinct racial categories out of this continuum. These are then perceived as real and treated as real in practice. Richard Williams (1990) notes that race is also an especially important arena for examining cultural classification because it involves placing natural marks (skin pigmentation) onto social marks (culture). There is considerable variation in specific examples of how race is classified and assigned, yet, at the same time, one can observe patterned similarities in what counts when it comes to weighing racial classifications. The insights uncovered about classification from looking at how race is categorized and how racialized attributes are weighted have broader implications for the sociology of categorization and weight assignment.

F. James Davis (1991) shows that in the United States, black ancestors weigh more heavily than white ancestors in one's racial classification. Anthropologists refer to this form of weighting, where mixed black/white children are assigned the status position of the parent group with lower racial status (blacks), as the hypodescent rule of racial classification (see Davis 1991; 2006: 17). Davis explores in depth a specific manifestation of the hypodescent rule known as the one-drop rule; in much of the United States South the one-drop rule, whereby any trace of black ancestry classified one racially as black, emerged as early as the mid-1600s in the colonies of the upper South (Davis 1991: 33; 2006: 17), later spreading through the United States, where it has existed as the dominant classification convention. There were periodic challenges to this classification convention but it has dominated most of the United States history of racial classification and was strengthened in the early twentieth century through Jim Crow segregation laws in the United States South (Davis 1991: 54–8). Various courts have ruled different amounts of black ancestry count but the fractions one-thirty-second, one-sixteenth, one-eighth, and one-fourth have reinforced hypodescent rules and the greater weight of black ancestry. As late as 1983 the rule was upheld in a lawsuit brought by Susie Phipps, whose application for a passport was denied because she checked "white" as her race; Phipps looks white, has always lived as white, and thought she was white, but the state of Louisiana produced evidence that she was three-thirty-seconds black, and by a 1970 state statute, being one thirty-second black qualifies one as black (prior to the 1970 statute any "traceable amount" was enough in the state of Louisiana) (Davis 2006: 18). Davis contrasts the hypodescent rule with other rules of classification. Another classification convention assigns mixed-ancestry children to a classification status in between the two parent racial classifications. Rather than the children being assigned to the lower of two racial groups they fall into a separate, in-between category. In apartheid South Africa, for instance, any "mixed-blood" person was assigned a Coloured racial category, which was accorded a status between whites at the top of the racial hierarchy and blacks at the bottom. Whites, Asians, Coloureds, and blacks represented four racial categories and the offspring of any mixed union of any combination (e.g. black/Asian, Coloured/black, white/Asian, or black/white) were classified as Coloured (see Davis 2006: 21). Yet another rule, he shows, places persons of mixed ancestry at the bottom of the ladder, as being of lower status than either parent group. And in some places such as Latin America mixed-race persons are assigned a racial status that may vary from very low to very high, depending as much on education and wealth as on skin color alone; that is, as individuals of mixed racial ancestry experience educational or economic success their racial designations within the society change (Davis 1991: 99–100; 2006: 23–5).

Rogers Brubaker, Mara Loveman, and Peter Stamatov (2004: 35) note that while studies of official categorization may have profound consequences for the self-understandings of the classified, the categories and classifications used by individuals in everyday life can differ substantially from official ones. These authors show that categorization and classification can be highly variable, as in the context of Brazil, where a large number of racial categories are used and accomplished in social interactions. A common theme in research on the production and reproduction of racial and ethnic distinctions and boundaries in everyday life is that ordinary social actors maneuver within the constraints imposed by official definitions and can sometimes deploy such categories strategically, or infuse official categories with alternative, unofficial, everyday meanings (Brubaker et al. 2004: 35).

The notion of doing things to count toward a racial or ethnic classification is also present in American Indian racial classifications in the United States. While the common view in the United States is that ethnicity and race are biological, people's conceptions of themselves along these lines are situational and changing (Nagel 1994: 154). Joane Nagel shows, for instance, how Native Americans may choose from various levels of ethnic identification depending on context, so that their classification can move from, for example, mixed-blood on their reservation, to "Pine Ridge" when on another reservation, to "Native American" when interacting with non-Indians, to "Sioux" when answering the US Census (Nagel 1994: 155). Although these examples show some choice in ethnic and racial identification, these choices are also constrained by larger structural and cultural definitions.

Eva Garroutte (2003) analyzes the complicated questions about what the proper framework for making a racial or ethnic determination of American Indian identity is. She highlights the broad range of factors that enter into such a designation, including cultural association, blood quantum, and self-identification. Garroutte draws attention to "doing Indianness," as reflected by living in Indian communities and participating in Indian cultural practices, as an example of how one can add social weight to the claim of an American Indian classification. In this regard American Indian identity bears some resemblance to Latin American racial classification schemes that allow practices to shape racial and ethnic identity. The possibility of "doing Indianness" points to race and ethnicity as social accomplishments and not inherent, unambiguous, biological classifications (Garroutte 2003).

Aliya Saperstein and Andrew Penner (2012) highlight the fluidity of racial classifications in the United States, demonstrating that micro-level racial fluidity reinforces racialized social inequalities by redefining successful people as more white, and unsuccessful people as more black. Using data from the National Longitudinal Survey of Youth from 1979 to 1998, they show not only that some individuals change their own racial classifications over time, but that how these people are classified by others changes, and that this classification is not random but socially patterned and reliant on cultural stereotypes. Because the survey is longitudinal and includes interviewers' classifications of the survey respondents' race each year, the authors are able to observe changes in the racial classification of subjects over time. That is, they measured changes in how interviewers classified the race of their survey respondents. Interestingly, because interviewers had to choose a fixed race (e.g. white, black, other) for classifying their survey respondents, Saperstein and Penner's research design utilizes the advantages of capturing the intuition and cognitive efficiency of automatic cognition, which Vaisey (2009: 1688–9) highlights as a methodological virtue of fixed-response surveys, with the added twist of analyzing the fixed racial category responses that the survey interviewers themselves used to classify their subjects.

Saperstein and Penner (2012) found that changes in racial categorization are correlated with key status variables. For instance, having been unemployed for a long period of time, experienced poverty, been incarcerated, or been on welfare all had statistically significant effects such that individuals were more likely to be classified as black. The odds ratio for having ever been in poverty indicated, for instance, that net of all other measured variables (including if the person had been classified as white the previous year), having been in poverty reduced the odds of being classified as white by 30 percent (Saperstein and Penner 2012: 698–700). Likewise, net of all other variables including if the respondent had been classified as white the previous year, the odds of being classified as black were 1.7 times greater for interviewees who lived in the inner city (p. 700). To illustrate with cases from the sample where unemployment affects racial classification, these authors provide some examples of their data strings, where W = white, B = black, O = other, and a period = missing data. These strings help to demonstrate shifts in classification; for example, before unemployment WOWW, after unemployment BOBOWOBBOBO; before unemployment OOO, after unemployment BBBBBBBBBBBOBB; before unemployment WWWWWWWWWW, after unemployment

WWOOOO). Positive life-course variables showed trends in the opposite direction and toward greater classification as white. Highlighting social psychological research that shows that research subjects take longer and make more errors in racially categorizing admired blacks (e.g. Martin Luther King, Jr.) and disliked whites (e.g. Jeffrey Dahmer) (Richeson and Trawalter 2005), Saperstein and Penner suggest that interviewers faced with ambiguity in racial cues used preconceived schemas or stereotypes about race to tip the scales toward the racial category that best "fit." Saperstein and Penner demonstrate race classification to be a flexible and mutable propensity influenced by social factors. Negative factors tip one's weight toward the marked racial classification, while positive ones push one's categorization to the unmarked. These findings may have general implications for how stereotypes combine with negative and positive life events to shape ethnic and other kinds of classifications beyond race as well.

Brubaker, Loveman, and Stamatov (2004: 47–9) argue that we should not consider the empirical domains of race, ethnicity, and nationalism as analytically separate. For a long time these were treated as separate analytical domains with largely non-overlapping literatures. This conceptual bracketing – sometimes informed by political concerns – Brubaker et al. argue is misplaced because it loses the advantages of comparing differentiation and classification across different domains. Among the issues that cut across each domain are membership criteria, the fixedness and fluidity of membership, and the degree and form of naturalization (Brubaker et al. 2004: 48). They go on to explain:

> Cognitive perspectives suggest further reasons for treating race, ethnicity and nation together, as one integrated domain rather than several distinct domains of study . . . race, ethnicity, and nation are fundamentally ways of seeing. The cognitive processes and mechanisms underlying these ways of seeing are identical throughout the larger domain. If nation, for example, is famously treated as an "imagined community" or a "conceived order," this is no less true of ethnicity or race. If race . . . involves folk sociologies that divide people into intrinsically, putatively natural human kinds, this is no less true for ethnicity and nation. If ethnic boundaries . . . are sustained by

processes of categorical self- and other-description, then this is no less true for racial and national boundaries. The processes of classification and categorization, formal and informal, that divide "us" from "them"; the forms of social closure that depend on categorizing and excluding certain potential competitors as "outsiders"; the categories and frames in terms of which social comparison and social explanation are organized; the schemas, scripts, and cultural models that allow one to perceive, experience or interpret situations and sequences of action in standardized racial, ethnic, or national terms; the cognitive biases in the retrieval and processing of information that lead us to evaluate evidence in selective ways that tend to confirm prior expectations and strengthen stereotypes – all of these and many more cognitive and socio-cognitive mechanisms and processes are involved in essentially similar forms in phenomena coded as belonging to distinct domains of race, ethnicity, and nationalism. Of course there are great variations in the content of patterns of classification and closure, social comparison and explanation, schemas and cultural models, but these cut across conventional distinctions of domain. (Brubaker et al. 2004: 48–9)

Brubaker and his co-authors emphasize the importance of looking at classification and categorization and these ways of seeing around classification orders as generic social processes around which to build analysis that cuts across the domains of race, ethnicity, and nation. This statement embodies the spirit of a formal cognitive sociology that cuts across domains and units of analysis and avoids analyzing categories only within their specific, morally and politically salient, analytic or "epistemological ghettos" (Brekhus 1998). Analyzing race, ethnicity, and nation as formally similar domains allows us to better understand these processes.

The sociomental weighing of acts and attributes in categorization and classification

Brubaker and co-authors' point can be taken even a step further. Classification rules in the domains of race, ethnicity, and nation can inform understanding of categorization in other empirical contexts. For example, the use of hypodescent rules that assign greater social weight to the subordinate category also shines a focus on the variability of cultural and sociocognitive weight in making classifications generally. In classification and categorization, some attributes and some actions weigh heavier than others and weigh more in some contexts than others.

Jamie Mullaney (1999) develops the concept of "mental weighing" to illustrate that how much a given action counts toward an identity is highly dependent on the social, cultural, subcultural, and contextual weight an action is given. This concept applies not only to acts and identities but to attributes, characteristics, and classification assignments more generally. When people make classification and categorization decisions they give some attributes and actions considerable weight and others very little or no weight. Sociocultural weighting norms influence what counts, what does not count, and how much something counts. In a close parallel to the hypodescent rule, Mullaney notes that highly marked acts earn a categorization or classification based on a "one-time rule" (a single act, much like a single drop, is enough), while unmarked acts earn categorizations based on a "maximum-capacity rule" (they have to be repeated regularly to count toward one's identity). Employing these concepts, for instance, one can suggest that an individual need only commit a highly marked act such as homicide once to be classified as a murderer for the rest of their life, or at least for a very long time, while smoking a single cigarette will not likely classify someone as a smoker, nor will a single incident of gambling define one as a gambler.

The weight of attributes and acts is also tied to social context (Mullaney 1999), such that the same attribute or act can have great weight in one setting and very little in another (bracketing something as play, vacation, holiday, or humor may reduce its weight, for example). The famous tourist marketing slogan "what happens in Vegas stays in Vegas" is a call to aspiring gamblers and sinners to bracket "Sin City" as a space where they can sin on vacation, without the sin attaching to their everyday, non-Vegas identities. Their sin is tied to the bracketed context and the marked space, not the person. Similarly, acts conducted as part of one's profession, such as a police officer or military soldier killing in the line of duty, carry less weight toward one's classification than the same acts conducted without a professional rationale (Mullaney 1999: 279). The bracketing of weight by context allows for some acts and attributes to socially and morally count and others to not count. A successful bracketing will allow a marked act to be committed that does not count toward the moral labeling of an individual. The idea of cultural weighting systems in classification and categorization allows us to examine formal rules of what counts and what does not count in classification and categorization processes. One can look at categorization in all manner of cases and look for what types of things hold weight and what contexts add to or subtract from weight.

Social markedness of identities also carries classificatory social weight. In Saperstein and Penner's study of racial classification discussed in the previous section, we saw that negatively marked life events such as unemployment, poverty, or incarceration tipped the weight of racial classification toward a black racial identity. This relates to the social marking and mental coloring of identity; marked categories are "mentally colored" by their negative examples or extremes, leading to an asymmetrical classification process whereby marked and unmarked identity categories are prevented from overlap (Brekhus 1996). By cognitively "coloring" subjects with negative life events as more black, the coders reproduced a mental gap between the marked and the unmarked. The perception of coders that unemployed people are "more black" and employed people are "more white" actually eliminated from the data the empirical overlap between blacks with positive life events and whites, and between whites with negative life events and blacks, thus unintentionally reproducing socially constructed racial category stereotypes.

Exploring classification and boundaries in another context, we turn to classifications of nature and civilization, starting with local cognitive subcultures and then moving into analytic observations about purity, contamination, and symbolic boundary maintenance through metaphors related to nature/civilization and dirt/purity.

Local cognitive subcultures and nature/civilization classifications

Gary Alan Fine (1998) explores classification within different local cognitive subcultures of amateur mushroomers, demonstrating how mushrooming subcultures are socialized to classify mushrooms, sharing common rules of perception, attention, interpretation, classification, and valuation. One of the first tasks is to identify their discoveries and to differentiate them from others of that class so that a mushroom is not simply a mushroom (Fine 1998: 58). He shows that mushroomers learn to classify some mushrooms as elite and good (morel mushrooms) and others as trivial and bad (LBMs or little brown mushrooms). Morels, as elite mushrooms, are given special subcultural capital and weight. Mushroomers are not only classifying mushrooms; they are categorizing nature and civilization. Fine identifies three different ideal-type worldviews for how mushroomers categorize and classify nature: a protectionist view, an organic view, and a humanist view. In the protectionist view, nature is a pure and sacred environment, uncontaminated and completely distinct from the built environment. Nature is distinct from civilization and must be preserved and protected. It has special moral weight. In the organic view, humankind and its activities are also a part of nature and there is no clear boundary between nature and civilization. Human activities are a part of nature. In the humanist view, there is a sharp divide between culture and nature, and nature is to be used for human purposes. Humans have a vested interest in nature (through agriculture, hunting, fishing, mining, recreation) and protect what benefits them. Nature has no special moral weight and humans use it where it suits their interest. These three different views of nature provide interpretive frameworks through which mushroomers understand and explain their activities (Fine 1998).

Rik Scarce (2000) examines the construction of nature in the organizational worldviews of salmon biologists in the United States and Canada. He examines the worldviews of fisheries

73

biologists, who use salmon as resources, apply many of the same technologies used in agriculture (genetic modification, spatial and temporal control and domination, etc.), and treat salmon largely as an industry to be controlled for economic and political interests. This view aligns closely with Fine's humanist framework of nature. By contrast, conservation biologists view salmon as having intrinsic worth as part of a natural ecosystem and emphasize the need for special protection to preserve "natural" salmon (Scarce 2000) – a view close to Fine's protectionist worldview of nature. The local and organizational subcultures of categorizing nature and of classifying and attributing meaning to it reflect different modes of thought around nature and civilization, tied to different occupational and recreational social networks and reference groups. Whether salmon and mushrooms should be collected and used for human purposes or preserved also reflects a contrast between worldviews committed to prioritizing human use and ones committed to preserving the "purity" of a pristine and separate "nature."

Purity and impurity concerns arise in the attitudes of many urban and suburban denizens who want to keep nature in its proper place apart from human civilization. Intense controversies about wild animals in urban landscapes, for instance, are about the border between "nature" and "civilization" and when "nature" transgresses the borders without permission (Jerolmack 2008: 74). When nature crosses into the metaphorical container of civilization it is perceived as out of place and threatening to social order. Maintaining purity apart from contamination is an issue that arises often in classification. The classification of nature and civilization and the metaphors we associate with the disruption of order, such as "weeds" and "rats," are issues of symbolic boundary maintenance and categorization associated with polarizing a moral divide between the in place and the out of place. Classifications of nature and civilization shed light on larger issues of categorization and moral meaning.

Purity and contamination: categorization, polarization, and symbolic boundary maintenance

Michèle Lamont and Virág Molnár (2002) highlight the symbolic nature of boundaries in discussing their role across a range of areas where we make boundary distinctions, including social and collective identity; class, ethnic/racial, and gender/sex inequalities; professions; knowledge and science; and spatial boundaries of community and nation. These authors highlight the need to study properties of boundaries such as their durability, salience, and permeability, as well as the need to look at mechanisms for boundary maintenance, bridging, and crossing. As mechanisms of boundary maintenance, representations of purity and contamination arise as significant symbolic notions that enforce symbolic boundaries and categorization. Concerns about purity and contamination underlie many classifications. The climbing controversy that Fuller (2003) studied was not just expressed in terms of innovators adopting new techniques; it was also about heretics who polluted the purity of the sport, threatened the environment, and contaminated the pastime. Intense controversies over the racial integration of swimming pools reflect a segregationist view of social order that desires to maintain the "purity" of races and that is deeply concerned with the "contamination" of racial integration (Wiltse 2007). People often maintain categorization schemes by invoking notions of purity and contamination (Douglas 1966). Purity and contamination metaphors help to keep categories separate and to provide moral meaning to social objects. Moral meanings that arise out of classification and frames of meaning are issues to explore in greater detail in the next chapter, but their relationship to classification and boundary maintenance through "purity" and "impurity" distinctions is discussed here as these relate to mentally splitting and polarizing categories.

Colin Jerolmack (2008) analyzes the modern construction of pigeons in United States urban areas as problem animals or "rats with wings" to understand the cultural-spatial logic and moral meanings of problem animals. The problematization of the pigeon, according to Jerolmack, is a symptom of a larger cultural logic wherein pigeons symbolically represent a greater perceived threat of disorder and impurity (Jerolmack 2008: 87–8). He relates the fear of the epidemiological dangers of pigeons (which are actually low though perceived as high) to the metaphorical deviance and immorality of the pigeon, showing that language around pigeons is similar to language around criminals, vandals, vagrants, and other "deviant" human social actors.

> While the epidemiological danger may be low, the unchecked presence of these "dirty birds" signals a cityscape that is not subdued. The logic here is analogous to "broken windows theory" (Kelling and Wilson 1982), which argues that the presence of minor disorder such as broken windows or litter signals a lack of social control that, if left alone, will bring greater disorder. While controversial, former New York Mayor Giuliani used this framework in his "quality of life" campaign of the late 1990s that saw people fined and jailed for minor infractions. Vulnerable populations, such as the homeless, were easy targets in efforts to "clean up" the city (Duneier 1999). Hoving (*New York Times* 1966) explicitly linked pigeons to the homeless and to disorder ("vandals"), as did other articles that called pigeons "bums" and "squatters." In "cleaning up" cities, certain objects and human and animal groups are bound to be perceived as "out of place," and their removal signals the restoration of order. (Jerolmack 2008: 88)

Pigeons disrupt the compartmentalization of "urban civilization" from "wild nature" and as such are metaphorically perceived as deviants that disturb the social order. They defy the modern urban metropolis, which is orderly and sanitized and where nature is subdued and kept apart. While the problem animal frame is the dominant one for observing pigeons in urban areas of the United States, Colin Jerolmack's (2013) book *The Global Pigeon* shows that there are many different cultural frames in which to see pigeons and the analogies, metaphors, and meanings for what they represent, and many of these frames are positive.

The use of classificatory out-of-place metaphors to reflect disorder cuts both ways. Not only are "out-of-place" animals such as pigeons compared to social deviants, but "out-of-place" human deviants are metaphorically compared to "vermin" or "weeds." Zygmunt Bauman (1991) notes that "weeds" are a metaphorical language we use to suggest contamination or invasion. He discusses, for instance, how the modern state uses gardening metaphors to split populations into useful "plants" to be encouraged and carefully propagated and "weeds" to be discouraged, removed, or systematically rooted out. He argues that moral classification systems separating good plants from bad weeds are endemic in rational bureaucratic societies: "Weeds are the waste of gardening, mean streets the waste of town planning, dissidence the waste of ideological unity, heresy the waste of orthodoxy, strangerhood the waste of nation-state building. They are waste as they defy classification and explode the tidiness of the grid. They are disallowed categories that must not mix" (Bauman 1991: 16). Waste and weeds are the social detritus and the imperfections that symbolically pollute a setting. Such metaphors are sometimes explicitly used in political discourse, as Mike Davis (1992) points out in noting how President George Bush's "weed and seed" initiative to rebuild inner cities involved rooting out, arresting, and segregating society's human "weeds" before "seeding" social policy with enterprise zones and tax breaks. The connection between gardening, neatness, and moral order can also be embodied in practice. Maria Kefalas (2003) shows how a community of white working-class Chicago residents define their morality and symbolically differentiate and defend themselves against a perceived threat from African-Americans by cultivating their gardens, maintaining and guarding their property, and keeping their homes clean. Gardening and maintaining a clean, orderly environment are important aspects of their symbolic moral boundary work.

Like Bauman in his analysis of weeds and social order, Mary Douglas (1966) examines purity and danger in an anthropological context, noting that what constitutes "dirt" is socially constructed and that rituals associated with avoiding dirt and maintaining taboo are largely designed to maintain order. Our pollution rituals are reactions intended to condemn any object or idea likely to confuse or contradict cherished classifications (Douglas 1966: 36). Rituals of purity and impurity are centered on cultural classifications, and dirt is basically matter out of place. Space and context are, in fact, central to the matter of pollution – an item in its proper space is not contaminating but it becomes so when not thus socially ordered. Jerolmack's (2008) analysis of how pigeons are classified and metaphorically equated with rats in some urban metropolises explores a deeper logic of order, classification, and cultural frames of purity and impurity that has implications for human inequalities and control as well as pigeon control. The problem animal frame he discusses looks much like other problem frames, including the problem human frame that Bauman and Davis allude to.

Omar Lizardo (2012: 367) argues that dirt and cleanliness frames to "conceptualize moral propriety or impropriety emerge from metaphorical extensions into various realms of experience (e.g. sports, governance, introspection) grounded in an idealized cognitive model in which dirt is conceptualized as matter out of place and clean is conceptualized as ordered arrangement." Dirt metaphors, he suggests, brand an ambiguous action or agent as violating the rules of order of a setting. Cleanliness metaphors reflect an ordered arrangement wherein dirt is matter that does not belong, has no place in the setting, and should be excluded, expelled, or eliminated. In sport, game, and contest frames, for instance, he indicates that the contest is usually conceptualized as a container with rules that govern what actions and agents are morally permissible and which ones are out of place. When disallowed actions enter the frame, they are defined as out of place and conceptualized as "dirty" because they bring an action from a region where it "belongs" into a contest frame where it "has no place." Similarly in government politicians, judges, and police who engage in actions that are disallowed within the rule-governed realm are described as dirty. Even the mind, Lizardo (2012: 380) argues, as a rule-governed setting in Judeo-Christian tradition is conceptualized as a container where some thoughts are allowed and others are considered matter out of place (e.g. "you have a dirty mind" or "impure thoughts"); the symbolic ritual of confession can be seen as a purity ritual that restores order by linguistically expelling the thought from the mind back to the outside. Lizardo suggests that the dirty/clean metaphorical distinction is useful for understanding a wide range of cultural issues including the metaphors we use to discuss moral panics regarding media, immigration, and disease.

Barrie Thorne (1993) analyzes pollution and contamination rituals in the everyday play of school children, maintaining gender boundaries and classifications. When girls chase boys in schoolyard games, boys engage in pollution rituals in which girls are said to have "cooties," which are highly contagious and easily spread from contact with a girl. These pollution rituals suggest that girls are symbolically contaminating as a group, and serve to maintain a symbolic boundary and gender divide between the higher-status boys and lower-status girls. Pollution rituals maintain symbolic boundaries and preserve the purity of classificatory boundaries.

Metaphors of dirt and cleanliness and of purity and impurity linguistically reinforce social categories and classificatory boundaries and help to define what actions, objects, and persons are in and out of place in a setting. Rituals associated with pollution and contamination highlight social boundaries and socially and symbolically reinforce them.

Understanding classification and categorization involves looking not only at boundary maintenance through keeping categories physically or symbolically separated, however, but also at how boundaries and borders are transitionally crossed and changed.

Transitional boundary work: crossing boundaries, bridging realms, boundary shifts, and liminality

In "Border Crossing: Bricolage and the Erosion of Categorical Boundaries in French Gastronomy" Hayagreeva Rao, Phillippe Monin, and Rodolphe Duran (2005) analyze how categorical boundaries change through innovation and emulation. Working within a tradition in organizational cultural sociology that examines how people use systems of categories to identify genres and organizational forms and to assess their categorical fit and authenticity, these authors explore how boundaries erode when high-status actors blend boundaries and trigger emulation. This tradition recognizes that "audiences rely on category boundaries to identify and make sense of producers," and much research in the tradition has demonstrated that producers who participate in multiple categories are either ignored or explicitly devalued because their category-spanning transgresses cultural codes where categories are seen as distinct or oppositional (see Hsu et al. 2009: 151). Although there are penalties for transgressing cultural codes of categorization, Rao and co-authors explore how some violations spanning rival categories get emulated and accepted when enacted by high-status actors. These researchers argue that when categorical boundaries are strong because of segregating pressures, borrowing elements across genres is low while variance in the number of elements borrowed is high, but that borrowing by high-status actors can jump-start a process of imitation that increases the mean number of elements borrowed and decreases the variance (Rao et al. 2005: 969). To test this they studied French gastronomy from 1970 to 1997 when two rival categories, classical and nouvelle cuisine, competed for the allegiance of chefs and their customers. Rao et al. employed a regression analysis testing several hypotheses about borrowing elements from rival cuisine traditions:

> Our analyses of French haute cuisine show that those who borrowed techniques received penalties in the form of a downgrade by external evaluators. We show that the penalties diminished as the fraction of chefs who borrowed increased and borrowing became prevalent in the social system. Thus, changes in the blueprint diminish the symbolic potency of boundaries and deactivate penalties for boundary crossing. (Rao et al. 2005: 988)

They draw general observations about the relationship between producers, critics, and social boundary maintenance and transgression, noting that critics police category authenticity and the borders of categories, but that high-status producers who can champion emulators redefine boundaries for critics to recognize; thus critics are "midwives of boundary changes" more than zealous guardians of genres (Rao et al. 2005: 989).

Like categorical boundaries between genres, temporal boundaries and mental boundaries between realms such as home and work can invoke different kinds of boundary maintenance and border crossings. While boundary work often involves building fences and erecting barriers between categories to prevent contamination, boundaries can also be segregated and maintained or integrated and blurred through different kinds of transitions and transition rituals. Using ethnographic interviews about people's home and work lives, Christena Nippert-Eng (1996) shows how home and work are rival categories often maintained by drawing physical and mental boundaries between the two realms. She follows Goffman's (1974) frame analysis in noting that individuals who segment home and work use transitions to bracket the one from the other. Focusing on cognition in the quotidian matters of everyday life, she illustrates that the mundane practices people use to cognitively mark home and work realms and to move in between them include their calendar, their keys, their clothing, and their commutes. Individuals engage in different practices to either keep the two realms rigidly segregated from one another or integrate and bridge the two realms. Those who integrated their home and work lives and moved fluidly between the two realms without segregating, fence-like boundary transitions, she shows, tended to have one all-purpose pocket calendar, while those who kept the two realms distinct maintained separate, realm-specific wall calendars for each. Like calendars, keys were similarly organized in different ways that suggested different cognitive ordering of the home/work divide. Home and work integrators maintained all keys on one ring, whereas segmenters kept their home and work keys on two separate rings with no overlap. Similarly changes in clothing indicated maintaining a cognitive boundary between home life and work life, whereas those who integrated the two realms showed little if any variation in clothing from one realm to the next. The commute from home to work and back often served as a transitional phase where individuals gradually or abruptly moved into the mindset for one realm from the other. The different styles of maintaining and classifying work were generally tied to structural conditions and their associated occupational subcultures. The lab scientists at the workplace with higher-status jobs and more work autonomy were likely to integrate home and work in significant ways and to lack a rigid boundary between the two worlds. The lab workers such as the machinists, who had less autonomy and whose jobs more closely resembled factory jobs, tended to have much clearer classificatory boundaries and rituals of separation that kept home and work separate from one another (Nippert-Eng 1996). Their cognitive styles were part of larger occupational subcultural ideas about the separateness of home and work.

Karen Danna Lynch (2009) analyzes the techniques home-based workers in suburbs of New York City, Long Island, and New Jersey use to transition from home to work. Without the physical commute that Nippert-Eng's interviewees had, Danna Lynch's interviewees made a cognitive transition. Home-based employees perform a number of rituals to transition from leisure to work roles – such as vacuuming the house or sharpening pencils before settling in to the work role (Danna Lynch 2009: 84). She shows that individuals use three general types of strategies to classify their activities in the social space of the home as work. They use techniques of (1) routinization, establishing a specific routine and repetition around time, space, and activities that make clear the distinctions between leisure time and space and work time and space; (2) goal targeting, utilizing a goal orientation to interpret surrounding objects as related to the work goal even though they have a different meaning in a leisure context, and developing emotional blinders to non-goal-specific stimuli; and (3) emotional alignment, evaluating the meaning of objects and establishing a relationship to the objects in the home according to one's current emotional state. Danna Lynch thus illustrates the micro strategies people use to transition across mental boundaries from home to work even when no physical travel to different realms occurs.

In an unconventional focus on boundary work, Iddo Tavory (2010) uses ethnographic fieldwork in an Orthodox Jewish neighborhood of Los Angeles to "chart the mundane ways in which donning the minimal mark of a religious Jew, the yarmulke, gives rise to interactions in which members are categorized as Jews by anonymous others in the street" (2010: 49). He shows that the habitual and routine wearing of the yarmulke, put on unreflexively as a matter of daily habit, becomes an interactional hook or place holder that others treat as signaling relevant categorical membership. He shows how the yarmulke functions to facilitate several different boundary-making processes in mundane space and interactions that vary on a spectrum ranging from Jewish members using the hook to construct sociality, to friendly categorizations and small talk from non-Jewish others, to rarer anti-Semitic confrontations that suddenly, aggressively mark the member as a Jew. Tavory's approach differs from much interactional research on boundary work in that it focuses less on intentional and consciously deliberative strategies of category performance than on how people anticipate categorization based on their embodied practices that include routinely placed signs. His informants came to tacitly anticipate boundary-forming interactions but with their own self-categorization operating at the margins of embodied consciousness. He argues that this shifts the analysts' emphasis from sites of performance to sites of expectation, and has implications for a range of empirically different but analytically similar cases where individuals learn to expect identification and categorization by others (for example, when and how do girls start expecting to be categorized as sexual objects, or when do African immigrants to the United States learn to expect to be constituted as racialized others in some interactions?) (Tavory 2010: 66). He suggests further that when expectations of interaction have been embodied, exploring the sites of action where marginal consciousness is more (or less) embodied adds a "phenomenological layer to questions of religious, ethnicized, gendered, and racialized identifications [that] can help develop a more nuanced account of the ways in which the lived reality of those signified identifications and boundaries are [*sic*] navigated in everyday life, with identifications assumed, forgotten, rematerialized in the acts of others, and tacitly expected" (p. 66). Tavory argues that rather than thinking about boundaries as either institutionally formed or existing primarily in conscious performance, understanding these sites of expectation allows us to better appreciate the nuances and complexities of boundary work, shifting boundaries, and categorization.

Much of our boundary work is unconscious and subtle. Stephen Vaisey and Omar Lizardo (2010) analyze the effect of cultural worldviews on network composition, and show that social networks form around shared moral-cultural worldviews over time. Like Tavory they illustrate boundary work that is embodied. While Tavory focuses on marginal consciousness, Vaisey and Lizardo show how even unconscious boundary work serves to reinforce social divisions and distinctions over time. Drawing on Bourdieu (1984: 241), these authors argue that we cluster with like-minded people and distance ourselves from others through unconsciously registered antipathies or sympathies and the "unconscious deciphering of expressive features." In contrast with theories that see social networks as largely determining culture for two or more people thrown together, Vaisey and Lizardo argue that people use fast and hot automatic cognitive-affective processes to identify and interact with like-minded people. The degree of fit between social interactional input and cultural or subcultural bias serves as an important determinant of tie persistence and tie erosion over time. That is, cultural worldviews have significant effects on the long-term composition of one's local relational environment, and these effects are not simply a spurious byproduct of the network's pre-existing characteristics. Using two waves of the National Study of Youth and Religion surveys, Vaisey and Lizardo (2010) found that worldviews are strong predictors of changes in network composition among youth; for instance, people with expressive-individualist, utilitarian-individualist, community-centered, or theistic worldviews had more enduring ties with individuals with like-minded outlooks, while ties with those with different world-views were less likely to endure. The reshaping of our network boundaries over time, through unconscious cognitive processes, to reflect our own worldviews represents a subtle yet enduring form of boundary creation.

Clustering with like-minded folks, interactional encounters with strangers, and transitional rituals from home to work are all among the mundane boundary work and boundary shifts that occur as a part of everyday practice. For individuals in a period of transition between social categories and classification boundaries, the concept of liminality is instructive. Mandy Wilson (2002) draws on Victor Turner's ideas to analyze the transitions of transgender individuals in Perth, Australia, noting that a multiplicity of gendered identities circulated in various times and spaces and that gender conventions were temporarily suspended in the support groups and transgender social networks of transgender individuals, but that this liminal period was often preparation for incorporation into a normatively gendered self as a man or woman. Wilson discusses the role power plays in a binary gender classification system, suggesting that transitioning to a "legitimate" gender position is socially enforced and that few transgender individuals in Perth therefore wish to remain outside the gender binary beyond a temporary, liminal period. She elaborates on this using Douglas' notions of purity and contamination to explain that "without a rite of aggregation through which the liminal individual rejoins society in a new (conforming) position, the individual remains threateningly 'outside' order, holding no place in society, a constant source of danger" (p. 440). Although some queer theorists and gender outlaws point to the liberatory and radical potential of living betwixt and between or outside of the gender binary (see Bornstein 1994), for Wilson's research informants, responding to coercive strictures and external pressures, "liminality" was a temporary state to move through rather than one to live in.

In an auto-ethnographic account of her own experiences negotiating her biography of poverty and a social class identity in academia, Sara Callahan (2008) notes that her performance of a middle-class identity is not part of a process of becoming "authentically" middle-class but rather a constant negotiation in the liminal space between two class identities. Each community, she argues, expects certain characteristics and performances and these expectations collide in the liminal zone of passing. The liminal zone is also a place of boundary work, where rupture and a queering or challenging of seemingly static boundaries occurs; passing, she argues, defies essentialist understandings of identity and creates the potential for destabilizing categories that work to oppress and exclude (Callahan 2008: 371). The liminal space becomes a space of resistance and challenge.

Conclusion

This chapter examined classification, categorical thinking, weighting items in categorizing, purity and impurity in classification, boundary work, and rites of passages to cross categorical divisions. The sociocognitive nature of classification and categorization is evident in local cognitive cultures, such as moral disputes among rock climbers about subculturally authentic practice, and in how different subcultures construct nature. It is also apparent in the more macro-level classifications of race across different societies and different racial identity groups.

Classification rules and the weighting of markedness within cultures of classification become especially visible in social constructions of race. Not only does one drop of marked "black blood" classify one as black (Davis 1991), but one negatively marked event such as unemployment can tip the weight of one's racial category from white or other to black (Saperstein and Penner 2012). The implications of such sociocognitive weighting and categorizing are significant for reproducing racialized social inequalities. And these implications may well extend analytically to marked categories beyond race. Extending Brubaker, Loveman, and Stamatov's (2004) suggestion that we observe categorizations of race, ethnicity, and nation as formally similar rather than analytically segregated domains, sociologists can look for general social patterns of classifying minority and majority, valued and devalued, and marked and unmarked social categories across a range of domains.

Conceptions of dirt and disorder, and contamination and impurity, and metaphors associated with these conceptions reinforce the significance of social boundaries and attach moral meaning to social divisions. Even the analysis of seemingly mundane everyday social classifications such as seeing pigeons as urban pests can shed analytic light on less mundane, morally salient issues. The metaphorical construction of pigeons as avian deviants is analytically relevant to similar metaphors for humans perceived as deviant and out of place (Jerolmack 2008) and to the study of broad cultural issues with implications for social inequality. Lizardo's (2012) suggestion that dirt/cleanliness metaphors are important for understanding a broad range of cultural issues, including immigration and moral panics, points to the general relevance of such metaphorical logics. Meaning is also constructed through maintaining social boundaries, as well as reconstructed through shifting social boundaries and blending borders. Pollution rituals and other polarizing practices maintain symbolic meanings, while rites of passage across boundaries mark their social significance and commemorate shared meanings. Yet boundaries, their dimensions, and their moral meanings can be negotiated in everyday interactional settings, transformed and reconstituted in cultural practice, and shifted over time. Moral meanings and their connection to metaphor and analogy are issues to explore in greater detail in the next chapter.

3

Meaning-Making, Metaphor, and Frames of Meaning

Classification and categorization lead to meaning. Meaning is not something that is just out there and naturally apprehended, nor is it something that we determine alone without the help of others. We have cultural frames of meaning that shape the meanings we assign to objects and practices. These meanings are tied to how we classify and categorize things, and there is often a moral component to meanings. Moral meanings can be explicit on highly contentious moral issues, or they can be merely implied where the issue does not appear on the surface to have an obvious moral component. We saw in chapter 2, for instance, how even disputes over rock-climbing practices, or the sociocultural classification of pigeons in many urban areas as pests rather than desirable birds, have moral connotations. Meanings are social and moral within a social context; they are sociomoral. In this chapter we look more closely at meaning by looking at cultural frames of meaning and meanings attached to metaphor and analogy.

Framing, discussed in relation to perception in chapter 1, also relates to meaning. Erving Goffman (1974) emphasized the importance of framing to the construction of meaning and interpretation, as well as to perception. His ideas about signaling to others how something is to be interpreted and whether it is to be considered in frame or out of frame apply to cognitive cultures such as social movements that strategically frame issues to mobilize participants. David Snow and co-authors (1986) have employed Goffman's idea of frames to show that frames function to guide action both individually and collectively, and that participation in social movements is dependent in part on alignment of individual and social movement organization's interpretive frames. Snow et al. argue that rather than seeing the success of social movements as related only to changes in opportunities and mobilization of social resources, the effective framing of the organization's definition of the situation and goals to align with individual interpretive frames is also important to a movement's success.

Meaning is culturally constructed and its construction is dependent upon discursive and narrative frames that employ metaphor, implicit comparison, categorization, and analogy. Metaphors and analogies shape our cultural understandings of everyday life and construct moral meanings through their implicit drawing of connections between different events and phenomena. Metaphors can be especially powerful because the comparisons they imply are left unmarked and not explicitly marked as a comparison, as is the case with similes, with words such as "like" and "as" (Bateson 1972; Roffman 2008: 249). The terms "like" and "as" make conscious and deliberate the comparison, whereas metaphors leave it indirect and largely automatic and unconscious. Gregory Bateson (1972: 56) illustrates this point in stating that:

> A metaphor compares things without spelling out the comparison. It takes what is true of one group of things and applies it to another. When we say a nation "decays," we are using a metaphor, suggesting that some changes in a nation are like changes which bacteria produce in fruit. But we don't stop to mention the fruit or the bacteria.

Metaphors can be constructed in ways that play into our pre-existing schema and trigger us to adopt an autopilot reaction to a new situation. Many studies of metaphors in discourse and narratives have focused on their instrumental uses. But the use of metaphor need not be as conscious as its use by social movement leaders and public figures attempting to motivate action. Metaphors often enter into language as reflections and representations of the ways cultures, organizations, and communities are living and thinking. They can become a part of our language that further reinforces our thought and action even when we may not consciously be intending to use metaphor. They can also bring with them the unstated assumptions and historical blind spots of those who have used the metaphors in the past (Bowers 2009). Analogical thinking can also be oversimplified in ways that encourage us to see events in a given way and to not see them in other ways. Research in the sociology of culture and cognition complicates understandings of meaning-making, metaphor, analogy, narrative, and discourse by showing the ways that these processes are often employed rather automatically without conscious deliberation and clear intent.

An illustrative case through which to analyze cultural frames of meaning and their cognitive variation is the social and cultural meanings attached to money. Money is something that seems on the surface to have an objective, rational meaning based on its use value, but the cultural and cognitive story behind the meaning of money is more complicated.

Cultural frames of meaning: money as a case

Sociologists of culture who study economic life have focused on the meanings tied to different classifications of money, challenging rational actor theories advanced by some economists that imply that money has a standardized meaning that is fungible across contexts. These sociologists note that the meanings and uses of money are tied to how the money is categorized, earmarked, and perceived. Only some sociologists in this tradition define themselves as studying culture and cognition, but in looking at how we perceive, classify, and morally think about money they contribute to our understanding of the sociocognitive meanings of money. I begin with their contributions as a lead in to a broader discussion of cultural frames of meaning.

Viviana Zelizer (1994; 1996; 2011) analyzes the different meanings associated with monetary payments depending on whether they come in the form of gifts, entitlement, or compensation, and the different connotations attached to bonuses and payments. Noting that economic psychologists have developed the concept of "mental accounting" to document the ways that individuals distinguish between kinds of money and thus treat a windfall income much differently, for instance, than an inheritance or a bonus even when they are quantitatively the same amount of money, Zelizer (2011: 99–100) points out that this challenge to purely rationalist economic definitions still requires a fuller "sociological accounting." She emphasizes the important roles of culture, structure, and the social in marking and defining the social meanings of money:

> Special money in the modern world may not be as easily or visibly identifiable as the shells, coins, brass rods, or stones of primitive communities, but its invisible boundaries emerge from sets of formal and informal rules that regulate the uses, allocation, sources, and quantity. How else, for instance, do we distinguish a bribe from a tribute or donation, a wage from an honorarium or an allowance from a salary? How do we identify ransom, bonuses, tips, damages, premiums? True, there are quantitative differences among these various payments. But, surely, the special vocabulary conveys much more than diverse amounts. Detached from its qualitative differences, the world of money becomes undecipherable. (Zelizer 2011: 100)

Culturally we give different kinds of money different symbolic meanings, different moral meanings, and different uses. We treat routinized payments such as salaries different than discretionary payments such as bonuses and gifts. And our earmarking and differentiation of different kinds of monies have important implications. How money is earned influences how it is spent. In households, for instance, Zelizer shows that money is generally not multi-purpose but earmarked as specialized and restricted for specific purposes. This social marking of money as specialized by how it was earned and who earned it appears to vary by social class, ethnicity, immigration status, and other communities of belonging (see also Wherry 2012: 96). Among the wealthy the distinction between higher-prestige "old money" that has been handed down generationally through inherited wealth, on the one hand, and less prestigious "new money" (Warner et al. 1949) that has been recently earned, on the other, represents another example of the social marking of money where similar quantities of money can have quite different symbolic qualities.

Frederick Wherry's (2012) *The Culture of Markets* demonstrates how people attach different cultural meanings to different kinds of payments and purchases, and that these decisions do not make economically "rational" sense but can be understood in terms of the culture and cognition of accounting. He suggests that prices and spending are not culturally neutral and that moral accounts are made about the qualities of people based on how they spend money and what they spend money on; consumers are judged as frivolous or frugal, foolish or faithful, on the basis of their evaluations of and types of items they purchase and on the social location and status of the purchaser (Wherry 2008; 2012: 100). He argues that these classifications and symbolic moral judgments reproduce durable social inequalities. For example, in understanding the United States housing crisis, he argues that how near to or how far outside the mainstream (how unmarked or how marked) a person is in terms of their social location shapes whether defaulting on a loan will be judged as foolishness (and therefore implicitly immoral) or bad luck (and therefore implicitly moral) regardless of the circumstances of the case.

In addition to variable meanings of money, consumer goods have similar contested meanings. Pierre Bourdieu (1984) argues that meanings attached to goods differ across different social classes and households. Frederick Wherry (2008), in his analysis of how Thai artisans made some products such as amulets for sacred in-group use while they sold others to tourists as economic exchange for survival, illustrates that certain products have a moral meaning that brackets them from pricing, while others are economically priced. Allison Pugh (2009) complicates understandings of the meanings of consumer items, demonstrating that the consumer behavior of children and their parents is centered on dignity, meaning, and belonging. In contrast to critics of excessive child consumerism who see this as simply conspicuous consumption to acquire status and "stay ahead of the Joneses," Pugh (2009: 55) observes that consumer goods serve as scrip enabling one to belong to and feel a part of the group; rather than striving to triumph in a status competition, child consumers were looking to use valuable tokens to forge a community and their sense of a place in that community. Children's consumer goods, she argues, are purchased not as an ostentatious display of status but as a means to group belonging. She observes meanings of consumer goods as tied to social location. Lower-income parents engaged in "symbolic indulgence," in which they made sure (often at considerable sacrifice) to provide their children with those items or events that would have the most symbolic value for their children's social world; affluent parents would sometimes practice "symbolic deprivation," limiting their children from an item to symbolically differentiate themselves from the Joneses and show that they were above consumer conformity (Pugh 2009: 9–10). These parents use symbolic moments of frugality as a moral statement of originality and lack of conformity to the frivolousness of market consumption. Pugh demonstrates the structural pushes on symbolic practices and the ways that parents use their resources to make implicit moral statements. Like Wherry in his observations about moral judgments, Pugh shows that lower-class parents who spend economically to provide their children with scrip are frequently judged as foolish when, in fact, their decisions can be understood as parenting decisions of sacrifice to promote the dignity and belonging of their children.

In *To Owe Is Not to Own: Why Russians Reject Mortgages (and Why Americans Accept Them)* Jane Zavisca (2010) analyzes the metaphors and moral meanings that Russians and United States residents apply to home mortgages (see also Zavisca 2012). For Russians the primary metaphor for a home mortgage is debt bondage. They use this metaphor as well as terms such as slavery, burden, shackle, and yoke to portray mortgages as long-term sentences of debt peonage to the bank as the true owner of the house. In addition to the primary metaphor of debt bondage they use a secondary metaphor of scam to describe mortgages. Tied to these metaphors is a pessimistic future orientation predicated on the idea of permanent crisis and on an understanding of the meaning of interest as overpayment. Zavisca argues that many Russians' objections to mortgages are partly instrumentally rational on the basis of a calculation of costs, benefits, and risks under conditions of financial uncertainty, but that the Russian aversion to mortgages goes well beyond the instrumental and is also moral. They see practical ownership as a social right and regard artificial juridical ownership under mortgage debt as a burden and a scam, rather than as a sign of independence, personal responsibility, and moral virtue, as United States residents often perceive mortgages (Zavisca 2010).

Zavisca argues that Russian metaphors about mortgages operate in stark contrast to metaphors in the United States, where consumers interpret mortgage debt as outright rather than conditional ownership. Underlying these different metaphors is the way Russians reflected a future orientation that was pessimistic and based on the idea of permanent crisis, while people in the United States had very optimistic future orientations that involved a cognitive disconnect wherein households made consumption decisions based on rosy, rather than risk aware, predictions for the future. In the United States, Zavisca shows that the primary metaphor for mortgages is homeownership and the meaning of interest is not overpayment but the price of ownership. Whereas Russians portray the primary political meaning of a mortgage as a breach of the social contract and their right to practical ownership, US residents see this meaning as personal responsibility. The moral meanings of mortgages have a negative valence in Russia and a positive one in the United States. As an interesting aside, Zavisca (2010: 17) notes that a study of British mortgage holders (see Cook et al. 2009) asked "if your mortgage were an animal, what would it be?" and noted that holders chose domestic animals that could be managed, trained, and tamed to represent mortgage arrangements that were taken for granted and entrenched in daily life. She suggests that Russians call their own variety of capitalism "wild" (*dikii*) and would likely be more inclined to see the mortgage as a wild animal than a domesticated one.

In demonstrating the cognitive variation in mortgage meanings and metaphors between a former socialist society interacting in a relatively new capitalist mortgage market on the one hand, and a society where mortgage markets are often taken for granted as part of the fabric of the American dream on the other, Zavisca highlights how different cultural conditions affect cognition. These different cognitive orientations toward mortgages also have consequences for social action. She shows that imported American-style mortgage markets and financial institutions failed to resonate with Russian conceptions of property, ownership, and rights, and that this cultural and moral view in concert with structural problems and economic uncertainty led most Russians to reject mortgages (Zavisca 2010; 2012).

Brian Steensland (2006) brings culture, cognition, morality, and meaning directly into understanding state welfare policy, demonstrating that economic decisions are also symbolic and moral decisions at the macro level of social policy. He argues that cultural categories of worthiness affect welfare policy through their contribution to cultural schemas, their deployment by social actors as discursive resources, and their institutionalization in social programs that reinforce the symbolic boundaries between categories of the deserving and undeserving poor. He suggests that while the classification of the poor as either deserving or undeserving has long been a part of American cultural classification systems and has been extensively documented, mainstream sociological perspectives largely ignore culture; instead they explain policy decisions by other factors such as the power and interests of business, social movement pressures, the role of government bureaucrats, and the institutional structure of the polity.

Borrowing from DiMaggio's (1997) suggestion that schematic cognition provides the mechanisms by which culture shapes and biases thought, Steensland analyzes how cultural categories of worth exert schematic influence on welfare policy developments by framing the range of cultural perceptions and normative evaluations that social actors imagine and find plausible. Because schemas affect cognition by providing templates for categorization, they are especially applicable to studying social policy, since policy itself often involves creating official social categories (Steensland 2006: 1282). For welfare policy development, he argues that categories of worth provide a template for program design, which then reinforces the programmatic and symbolic differentiations between different categories of deserving and undeserving poor people. Most approaches to the study of welfare policy focus on collective actors and institutional structures, bracketing out cultural explanations, but "cultural categories of worth constrain strategies of policy development by shaping cognitive perceptions and normative pre-suppositions"; the schematic template created by categories of worth made GAI (Guaranteed Annual Income) proposals that dissolved categories of poor people susceptible to symbolic pollution; discourse that presumed pollution between categories further amplified these concerns (Steensland 2006: 1315). The stigma associated with AFDC (Aid to Families with Dependent Children) benefits contaminated the social status of "deserving poor" elements of the benefits program. Even though the majority of benefits for Nixon's GAI proposal were to go to the working poor, at the schematic level it was considered a "welfare" proposal because of the moral contamination and symbolic weight of the AFDC benefits (Steensland 2006: 1315). Skilled political actors mobilized language that conjured up moral contagion between categories by arguing that the stigma of welfare would contaminate and pollute the working poor and also put them in a state of dependency, thus undermining the economy. These claims were effective because they played upon the uncertainty of erasing and destabilizing longstanding categorical boundaries (Steensland 2006: 1316). The categorization of types of poor people led to symbolic boundary work to maintain purity and avoid "contamination" between categories, consistent with other forms of classification and moral meanings around metaphors of symbolic pollution.

Jeffrey Kidder and Isaac Martin (2012) locate similar moral meanings of deserving and undeserving people in discourses over tax policy. Interviewing white Southern small business owners they show that tax discourse is morally charged and associated with symbolic boundary work and a sense of group position. Economic issues, these authors argue, are as much social and moral as are abortion, crime, sexuality, alcohol, and other issues more commonly identified as primarily social and moral. Everyday fiscal discourse, Kidder and Martin suggest, is morally charged

and tied to symbolic boundary work and a sense of group position. Their respondents discussed fiscal policy as hurting them as
members of the deserving middle class while favoring the undeserving poor and the undeserving wealthy. They created clear
moral boundaries between themselves as hard-working deserving
members of the middle class who should be afforded personal
autonomy and dignity, and undeserving poor and rich people who
benefitted unfairly from their middle-class taxpayers' labor.

The sociological study of culture and cognition related to the
moral meanings in economic and consumer exchanges in the
social world helps to paint a social picture that can inform, and be
informed by, the kinds of experimental studies in behavioral economics that explore cultural variation in responses to economic
games and problems. The meanings of money, consumer goods,
economic transactions, and fiscal policy are tied to categories and
moral classifications. Morality and meaning are also attached to
the metaphors we use.

Meaning and metaphor

Not only does cultural life move into interpretations of economic
life, as we saw in the previous section, but metaphors for economic
life move into cultural life. George Lakoff (2002) shows that we use
economic metaphors such as "interaction is exchange" and moral
accounting schemes based on monetary accounting metaphors to
interpret interactional debts and payments of debts. In metaphorical life in the United States, social interaction is a social exchange.
One who does someone a favor is "owed a debt" and the other
is in social and interactional debt until they balance the ledger by
returning a favor (Lakoff 2002). The cultural metaphors we apply
to other contexts to describe things shape how we interpret reality.
Using economic metaphors for social life has implications for how
we interact and how we perceive our interactional relationships.
George Lakoff and Mark Johnson (1980) argue that metaphor
is pervasive in everyday life, not only in our language but also in
our thought and action. Our concepts and the metaphors that we

use shape the way we think, perceive, and understand our experiences and interact with one another (Lakoff and Johnson 1980: 3). Metaphors frame cultural meanings and they often do so in ways that we do not consciously recognize.

The variable use of metaphor across different contexts illustrates how metaphor and meaning are collectively constructed within group and cultural contexts. While diverse examples across different contexts demonstrate cultural variation, one can also focus on comparative issues and general patterns, such as (1) the connection between metaphor and social action; (2) how metaphors become embodied in moral meaning-making; (3) how metaphors are reflections and representations of moral meanings, moral aversions, and symbolic boundaries; (4) the instrumental uses of metaphor; and (5) how metaphors with cultural resonance are more effective in tapping into people's pre-existing unconscious schemas. I examine each of these in what follows.

Metaphors are developed in a social context. They shape not only how we think about things but how we act. They can also become a part of what Gabriel Ignatow (2009) refers to as "embodied cognition" as metaphors themselves become embodied. Ignatow shows that findings from cognitive neuroscience can be combined with a modified version of Bourdieu's habitus to understand schemas as embodied cognitive structures that link individuals to primary-group discourses. This approach allows us to generate insights into moral culture and to understand ways that people employ culture in cognition to drive social action and to make changes in their lives (Ignatow 2009). Looking at purity and cleanliness metaphors associated with religion and morality, he analyzes primary-group discourses in two internet support groups for overeaters: one group secular and one religious. Arguing that social discourses may have very different social effects across cultures and subcultures, he finds that members of the secular overeaters' support group tended to use abstract, self-oriented metaphors and embodied metaphors focused on disgust at overeating, while members of the religious support group used abstract God references and embodied cleanliness and purity metaphors. While members of the two groups used some similar metaphors and language, the religious group used far more metaphors of cleanliness and purity than the secular group.

Ignatow links the underlying moral rhetoric of purity to action in showing that members of the religious group who used purity metaphors contributed more intensely to the group and stayed with the group longer. The embodied cleanliness and purity metaphors had more effect in bonding members to their group; Food Addicts Full of Faith (the religious group) members' use of these metaphors was associated with posting more messages as well as remaining with the group longer, while Overeaters Support Group (the secular group) members' use of embodied disgust metaphors did not predict participation. Ignatow (2009: 666) argues that culture's effects on social bonding can be more readily identified when culture's structures are conceived as embodied cognitive structures that operate both within the individual habitus and at the level of small-group discourse. In this case, cleanliness and purity are embodied cognitive structures that tie in with meaningful symbolic moral discourses and classifications of purity and dirt and danger. Use of embodied cleanliness metaphors predicted social action toward staying in a support group, bonding with others, and being more socially active within a group oriented to making moral change in one's life.

Daniel Winchester's (2008) ethnographic fieldwork, examining how Muslim converts used embodied practices of ritual prayer, fasting, and covering to construct a moral habitus as "good Muslims," similarly connects moral cultures to embodied practice and social action. Fasting Muslims, for instance, metaphorically defined their embodied practice as a kind of training or exercise in "moral discipline" and moral order (Winchester 2008: 1770). Studies of moral and religious life, he argues, tend to privilege mind over body and thought over action, but this fails to recognize the distinct moral and ethical effects of embodied practice. Ignatow and Winchester develop cognitive sociological approaches to embodied moral metaphors that emphasize the body and social action while simultaneously addressing issues of cognition and meaning-making.

Metaphors also reflect underlying worldviews. Gabriel Ignatow

(2003) demonstrates that profane metaphors related to the human body, bodily functions, and disease are especially widespread in the jargon of high tech industry and that these metaphors are thematically ordered in ways that signify threats to technological progress. These metaphors, he argues, "buttress a moral worldview in which technological advance is understood as morally benign, while the non-technological world and threats to technological progress are rendered as profane (base, foul, corporeal, mortal)" (Ignatow 2003: 2). He offers an interesting twist for neo-Durkheimian analysis by suggesting we study the profane rather than the sacred, an innovation he sees as important to understanding culture. He argues that in high tech jargon it is the profane metaphors, not the sacred symbols, that help create moral order and social meaning, an insight that reminds us that meaning-making is relational and often defined in contrast to that which is perceived as lacking authenticity, importance, or serious meaning. Profane metaphors are used for alternatives that threaten technology, and as such their use is *moral*: to reaffirm a symbolic, meaningful moral world valuing technological innovation (Ignatow 2003: 15).

Matt Cousineau's (2014) ethnographic study of an engineering robotics research lab provides another example of moral meanings produced in a high tech group. Cousineau analyzes the discourse, humor, and everyday interactions of lab workers as they discuss and allude to a range of issues from technology, to business, to spirituality, to nationality. Lab workers use body-part metaphors that anthropomorphize robots, such as referring to "elbows" and other "body parts" on robots that are not in human form. They similarly use metaphors and symbols that "technomorph" humans, including themselves and their co-workers, into quasi-machines. Their metaphors blend together distinctions between machine and human, implying human agency and sensory perception in machines and machine-like rationality in humans. When discussing spirituality, their descriptions of God appear to perceive God as behaving much like an engineer (Cousineau 2014). Their metaphors too reaffirm a meaningful world valuing technological innovation.

Cousineau also highlights how lab workers used "atrocity tales" to mark moral boundaries and construct moral meaning between themselves and their work and that of technocrats. Most notably, they told atrocity tales about the perils of working at large computer businesses, such as Microsoft, where the money was good but they would have to become technocrats, and sell out to the almighty dollar rather than practice the art of engineering and robotics in its pure form as a meaningful activity removed from profane monetary awards. These atrocity tales reaffirmed the symbolic and social value of their low-paid but creative work in technological innovation as an important source of meaning. Atrocity tales about what and who they were *not* helped to reaffirm their value and to implicitly define what and who they *were*. Their atrocity tales, metaphors, and jokes all collectively revealed moral meanings and moral selves.

Showing how metaphor reflects the worldviews and symbolic boundaries of suburban youth, Yuki Kato (2011) analyzes the extensive use of the spatial metaphor of a "bubble" that her suburban middle-class adolescent informants used to refer to their privately developed Southern California community. She shows that suburban teens used the bubble metaphor to make symbolic distinctions between their communities and others and to imply both cultural superiority and insularity. Although suburban adolescents expressed both positive and negative attitudes about the bubble, it was a meaningful metaphor by which they asserted a cultural boundary between their neighborhood and other neighborhoods. Youth associated the bubble with a unique way of life that distinguished their community from the profane world outside it (Kato 2011). The bubble metaphor became an easy way by which teens constructed a sense of place and made sense of the meaning of their community within the context of a larger culture. Within its metaphorical structure it expressed a number of symbolic boundaries, including economic boundaries (a consensus around the superior status of upper middle-classness), cultural boundaries (a consensus around the benefits of reputable public schools, ethnic diversity, and rigorous aesthetic maintenance), and moral boundaries (mixed feelings about whether the bubble reflected a motivated and informed youth community or a naive and ignorant, insular community) (Kato 2011).

Metaphors often reflect worldviews in ways that reproduce power relations and dominance hierarchies. In her study of the connections between social theory and social insects such as ants and bees, Diane Rodgers (2008) draws attention to the cultural assumptions that went into the dominant discourses, metaphors, and analogies that entomologists and social theorists have historically used to describe social insects. She argues that these metaphors and analogies derived from people located in hierarchical social systems, and they often naturalized hierarchy in their own descriptions of social insects. Descriptions of ant division of labor in early twentieth-century accounts, for example, portrayed efficient, hierarchical, class-based colonies that functioned harmoniously as a model of utopian industrial capitalism (Rodgers 2008: 122). In a similar example of imposing human culture onto insect culture, entomologists from colonial powers renamed ants that indigenous populations called "ants of visitation," because they regularly visited en masse to clear dwellings of insect pests, "army ants"; what indigenous people described as periodic visits were redescribed by colonizers as systematic colonization, complete with an "invaded region," "military maneuvers," and "strategies and tactics" (Rodgers 2008: 127–8). Her examples illustrate that how we see social insects varies culturally and is shaped by the organization and structure of the societies that we are a part of. In addition to showing cognitive cultural variation, it also demonstrates the subtle ways that cultural metaphors, analogies, and discourses can reinforce inequalities, even when describing insects.

Rebekah Massengill (2013) uses the contentious debates over retail giant Wal-Mart to analyze the moral vocabulary and social meanings that Americans rely on to evaluate the moral dilemmas of capitalism and to think about issues of individual and community, thrift and benevolence, and freedom and fairness. Massengill finds that conservative activists including Wal-Mart and its political supporters situate their moral language in gemeinschaft metaphors and meanings related to family and community, while progressive activists such as Wal-Mart's political opponents situate their metaphors and meanings in the more rationalized gesellschaft categories of modernity, such as "citizen." Massengill shows that people focus on economic issues in a moral framework that brings family, morality, and economy together. The family, she asserts, is both a social morality and an economic morality project.

In related research, Massengill (2008) demonstrates the instrumental uses of metaphor, comparing the moral metaphors used in the liturgies of right-to-life and faith-based labor movements. She demonstrates how certain communication tools combined with the right types of metaphors are more culturally resonant and trigger specific kinds of social action. Drawing from George Lakoff's (1996) analysis of family metaphors for government, wherein he argues that conservatives employ a "strict father" moral worldview centered on self-control and resisting temptation and that liberals employ a "nurturant parent" moral worldview emphasizing moral and spiritual growth, Masengill analyzes these styles of metaphor for religion. She interrogates the two key metaphorical structures of *Life is a journey* and *Moral growth is physical growth* inherent in Lakoff's construction. In the moral journey view, being moral requires one to walk a straight and narrow path, to resist temptation, dangers, and evils, and to "turn away from sin," while in the moral growth model one is a tiny seed that must blossom and grow, much like a plant in a garden (Massengill 2008: 343–4).

Within these larger moral worldviews Massengill analyzes their associated vertical and horizontal family metaphors. In the Strict Father model, for example, parents have authority over children and ties are vertical in nature, while in the Nurturant Parent model empathy is prized and horizontal ties between siblings and between family members, rather than a central authority structure, are prioritized in the raising of children. Massengill (2008: 355) shows that vertical expressions are the primary metaphors used when one's discussion with God is related to the transformation of the self, whereas horizontal metaphors tend to focus on one's religious community and one's social networks taking charge of tending the garden that was once the province of God the gardener, and helping religious believers to grow through support and working together as siblings under God. She uses these observations to highlight the instrumental aspect of metaphors used by social movement religious leaders. Some metaphors had greater potency and resonance on the basis of their fit with the sociocultural context. For instance, if individual change was needed, improving one's actions, or one's relationship with God, or one's lifestyle, vertical metaphors were far more effective and able to tap into existing cultural schemas, whereas if one needed to be inspired to care for others, or attend to the needs of others, horizontal metaphors were far more effective in driving social action (Massengill 2008: 355).

In *Brown Tide Rising: Metaphors of Latinos in Contemporary American Public Discourse*, Otto Santa Ana (2002) focuses on the use of metaphors – dangerous waters, weeds, animals – to discuss immigration policy. In particular, he notes that the employment of complementary metaphors, such as immigration as dangerous waters and nation as house, create additional resonance. In debates over California Proposition 187 to deny education and non-emergency health care benefits to undocumented immigrants, he shows that the dominant metaphor for Latino immigration was "dangerous waters" (e.g. floods, tide, waves) and that the United States was often described metaphorically as a "house." Additionally, he identifies a number of prominent secondary metaphors for Latino immigrants, including war/invasion metaphors, animal metaphors, and bodily disease/burden metaphors. The implications of metaphor for how people think about issues and social policy, he argues, are significant. In the case of "immigration as dangerous waters," associations are inherited from water, overlooked, taken for granted, and repeated. Treating immigration as dangerous waters conceals the humanity and individuality of immigrant lives: "in their place a frightening scenario of uncontrolled movements of water can be played out with devastating floods and inundating surges of brown faces" (Santa Ana 2002: 77). When connected with the nation as house it conveys the image of a flood or rapid influx of water that threatens the house with disorder, disaster, and matter out of place.

Both Santa Ana and Massengill demonstrate how metaphors that play into already existing associations have greater cultural resonance. These kinds of connections made through metaphor are more likely to motivate action than those that fail to fully resonate. Metaphors can be deployed strategically by influential social actors and institutions to achieve instrumental ends, particularly when they can be used in ways that play into the automatic cognition of others. They can also seep into everyday discursive and interactional life without connection to instrumental strategy.

Meaning, analogy, and narrative framing

Similar to metaphor, analogy is a related way that we discursively construct meaning through association, linkage, and relating one cultural object or event to another. The analogies we use to frame meanings and link items shape how we perceive and make sense of those items. And metaphors themselves contribute to analogical reasoning. The ways that events and items are narratively framed shapes how those events and items are interpreted and how we make meaning from them.

Jeffrey Alexander (2003b) analyzes narrative framing and analogy in the morally salient case of the Nazi mass murder of Jewish victims. He argues that initially the mass killings were narrated and framed inside a progressive narrative where the killings were coded as evil but not given significant weight in and of themselves. They were a part of the ordinary evil of the Nazis and not a unique evil in human history. In this initial narrative, the evil and trauma the Nazis wrought were liminal and temporary, they would be washed away by a just war and a wise and forgiving peace, and their darkness would be replaced by the powerful light of progress (Alexander 2003b: 38). They were conceived temporally as an event that would be followed by a new progressive beginning, not a tragic end of eternal return in collective memory. Alexander (2003b) argues that this narrative was eventually superseded by a tragic narrative that gave the evil significantly great symbolic weight; the evil became deepened, generalized, and weighted with extraordinary gravitas as "engorged" or "sacred evil," and it spread to enlarge the circle of perpetrators and to morally color the actions of everyone involved. The separateness of sacred evil demanded that the trauma be renamed, because generic mass murder normalized the trauma and put it too close to the banal and mundane, and "the Holocaust" emerged as the dominant linguistic representation (Alexander 2003b: 51). The new linguistic identity, Alexander argues, allowed the mass killings of the Jews to become a *bridging metaphor*: it provided the symbolic extension necessary to represent the trauma of the Jewish people not as a war crime (its earlier construction) but as a moral, universal trauma for all humankind. As a bridging metaphor, the Holocaust allows analogical bridging together of mass evils that victim groups that experience "collective cultural trauma" can appropriate.

Anne Kane (1997) explores extension by analogy in analyzing the use of symbolic structures and interpretation during the Irish Land War of 1879–82. She uses this as a case study that demonstrates how meaning was constructed in a social movement through the metaphoric nature of symbolic systems and then transformed through analogical extension. She highlights the discursive competition between farmers using a discourse of retribution and those using one of conciliation. These two discourses influenced an understanding of the nature of the situation and constructed different meanings. Kane shows that over time the retribution discourse won out by reconstructing and reshaping metaphors and transforming them by analogical extension. For instance, over time farmers were able to make rent analogous with confiscation. Rent was interpreted and metaphorically transferred from its usual meaning as a contract to mean domination, confiscation, oppression, and injustice. The meaning of rent was also transformed through a change in the meanings of conciliation and deference; tenants had long viewed deference to landlords as essential to keeping their land and conciliation was a preferred route to gaining concessions (Kane 1997: 267). But as rent and the landlord–tenant relationship itself became understood as a primary mechanism of national oppression, these concepts were no longer seen as providing potential for change or security (Kane 1997). Kane shows how the use of metaphor and analogy transforms meanings and shapes social movement goals, out-comes, and participant action. She argues against Swidler's (1995) idea that concrete situations organize and create cultural meaning, and suggests rather that the interpretation of concrete contexts by individuals using coherent cultural models and narratives creates cultural meaning.

Analyzing ethnic conflict, Jens Rydgren (2007) shows that people's inclination toward simplified inductive reasoning in the form of cultural analogies often leads them to memory biases in reflecting on past events that create a heightened perception of conflict and threat. When ethnic groups noticed elements similar to past conflict, they used analogical reasoning, seeing similarities to past outcomes and assuming such similarities would repeat themselves. Rydgren (2007: 235) uses the following example from the interethnic war in the former Yugoslavia to illustrate analogical reasoning:

1. When Croatia was a sovereign state (p) in the 1940s, Serbs were mass-murdered (q).
2. *Since Croatia is on its way to becoming a sovereign state again (p), in the 1990s,*
3. Serbs have good reasons to fear mass murder (q).

In this and comparable analogisms, Serbs compared the Croatia likely to emerge to a past Croatia governed by the proto-fascist Ustasa; similar corresponding analogisms comparing present-day Serbs with the Cetniks of the 1940s circulated among Croatians (Rydgren 2007: 235). Rydgren argues that the choice of the 1940s as a reference point was rooted in sociocognitive processes of meaning-making, categorization, attention, and memory. Pre-existing, systematized schemas of knowledge, he argues, shape not only the ways we categorize but also how we make inferences and draw analogies. Individuals are cognitive misers motivated to save time and cognitive energy, which leads them to use cognitive strategies without much reflection (automatic cognition rather than deliberate cognition) (Rydgren 2007: 228). Although this often works for us in everyday situations that are continuous and repetitive, Rydgren suggests that when we face new or black-box situations that we lack experience in handling, dubious knowledge structures including myth and rumor are more likely to be activated. This is also when we are likely to rely on the authority of those we most trust because they are in positions of authority or because they are in a similar social category of belonging to us (e.g. the same ethnicity) (Rydgren 2007).

Analogisms are often misleading because people tend to remember significant (culturally marked) events more than insignificant (culturally unmarked) ones. The effect of our selection bias is that we disproportionately notice and therefore remember and give greater analogical weight to dramatic events, while allowing common, mundane events to fade into the background or disappear. Routine events that are dull but representative of a certain period are easily ignored while dramatic but usually unrepresentative events are easily remembered (Rydgren 2007: 230). Elites often assist in directing our selection bias and tipping our analogies toward the dramatic in their speeches and propaganda to motivate supporters and action, and commemorations focusing on the most vivid, and therefore usually the most spectacular, events further socialize our cognitive attention to the extraordinary.

Rydgren argues that narrativization further orients our meaning-making, and the process of narrativization is heavily influenced by culture, especially cultural processes such as commemoration. Narrativization constructs an orderly, inevitable course of interconnected events out of what is initially a flow of relatively disorganized, unstructured events. Narrativization, Rydgren notes, leads to simplification as some events are amplified or magnified while others are disregarded as non-events. This often contributes to memory distortions and distinct cognitive biases (Rydgren 2007). Ultimately, he argues, these memory biases lead people to act on their fears and to mobilize or take pre-emptive action in ways that further conflict. They affect not only thought but action. Analogy, metaphor, and narrative work hand in hand to construct meaning and connections that shape both thought and action.

Abigail Brooks (2004) analyzes the way narratives and analogies around cosmetic surgery shaped its normalization. Two dominant narrative frames were used to discuss cosmetic surgery. One narrative frame focused on it as a new technology and the other centered on candid, first person accounts of it. Most, but not all, media coverage of cosmetic surgery fell into one of these two frames. In the first narrative frame, new cosmetic technologies were related, for instance, to scientific wonder, innovation, and progress. The narrative framing of cosmetic surgery as new technology analogous with cutting-edge scientific discovery framed the technology and those who used it as innovative, progressive, daring, and forward-thinking. As such the users of these cosmetic technologies become living symbols of scientific advancement and innovation (Brooks 2004). The narrative framing of candid accounts developed the analogical virtues of courage and candor for those who discussed openly their use of cosmetic surgery. Full disclosure admissions are associated with virtue, so admitting to their cosmetic surgery provided an ethical service to others, giving them the security to engage in the practice without fear, stigma, and mandatory secrecy. This narrative frame also turned the act of having cosmetic surgery into one of independence, struggle, and rebellion (Brooks 2004). The underlying moral structure of these narrative strategies, Brooks argues, recast cosmetic surgery in a more positive light. These narrative framing strategies, and the analogical thinking that equates cosmetic surgery with innovation and candor, oriented perceptions of cosmetic surgery away from a deviance frame to a normalization frame (Brooks 2004).

Conclusion

Meaning is culturally constructed and its construction is dependent upon discursive and narrative frames that employ metaphor, implicit comparison, categorization, and analogy. As one example of the importance of cultural frames for meaning, money has multiple and changing meanings across a wide range of contextual uses. Money is not simply money but rather has a span of meanings and moral connotations that vary culturally and socially.

Metaphors and analogies shape cultural understandings of

everyday life and construct moral meanings through their implicit drawing of connections between different events and phenomena. The metaphors people use for home mortgages or immigration have significant implications for their perception of these issues. Metaphorical and analogical thinking can be significant in perpetuating inequalities. Viewing social insects as harmonious, class-divided societies, or perceiving undocumented immigrants as an inundating flood, or as animals or invasive armies or weeds, has implications for how people think about social class divisions or undocumented immigration. Gardening metaphors to describe different kinds of human populations – those implicitly worth cultivating and those worth culling – can underlie inequitable social policy, harsh social control measures, and even genocidal policies that elevate groups in power and suppress and oppress minority groups.

Metaphors and narrative framing can, however, shift thinking and transform definitions and social value in more than one direction. The narrative framing of cosmetic surgery as technological innovation, for example, changed its meaning from negative to positive (Brooks 2004). Otto Santa Ana (2002) notes that political metaphors are not fixed, and suggests that analysts and activists can contest dominant and conventional metaphors with insurgent metaphors that seek to overcome rather than perpetuate and reproduce social inequalities.

4

Identity Construction: Identity Authenticity, Multidimensionality, and Mobility

Identity is interrelated with all of the cognitive processes discussed so far. Perception plays a role in what collective identities are assigned, what attributes have weight in defining one's identity, and what people attend to and disattend to in defining and constructing identities. Classification and categorization are essential to identity processes. People do boundary work around these classifications, particularly in terms of maintaining and policing boundaries, but also in blending and transgressing boundaries. Meaning is attached to these boundaries; doing and maintaining identities is often an implicitly moral project.

In his foundational work on the social nature of self-identity, George Herbert Mead ([1934] 1967) argues that individual selves are the products of social interaction; they emerge from social experience. Mead focused on the continuing double dialogue between internal conversation and external interaction in the forming of the temporally emergent social self. In *The Presentation of Self in Everyday Life*, Erving Goffman (1959) demonstrates that human individuals, as social actors, engage in performances of self that are adaptive and attentive to audience. The self, in this view, is dependent on context and the social situation. We present our self-identities strategically to others. In *Stigma*, Goffman ([1963] 1986) specifically analyzes how people with spoiled or discreditable identities manage their damaged self-identities in social contexts to minimize stigma and social harm. He discusses stigma management strategies of passing (hiding the

111

discrediting part of one's identity) and covering (attempting to minimize the obtrusiveness and importance of the discrediting part of one's identity, while not visibly hiding it altogether). Mead's and Goffman's observations about the relationship between personal identity and the social world are foundational to a cognitive sociology of identity.

Sociologists study identity in terms of both identities as collectives and the collective elements in individual identities. Paul DiMaggio (1997: 274) highlights this distinction in discussing how some studies of collective identities are about broad, supra-individual, shared representations of a collectivity such as a nation, an ethnicity, or a race, while other research on collective and social identities is about the complex issue of the ways social and collective identities enter the constitution of individual selves. The marked and the unmarked and issues of mental weighing and coloring are closely related to this second issue. What attributes count toward our identities? How do we incorporate salient and marked collective identities into our complex selves? What is in frame and out of frame when it comes to defining ourselves and others? How do different social and collective identities interact in our individual selves?

Building on Goffman's foundational view of identity as something that is strategically deployed and managed, contemporary scholars recognize identity as a resource that can be drawn upon in different ways across different contexts. I organize my discussion of identity as a resource around three issues related to identity construction. These are *identity authenticity* (strategies members use to assert commitment to an identity and to police claims to that identity), *identity multidimensionality* (the number of intersecting collective identities social actors balance and negotiate in their individual identities), and *identity mobility* (the ability to move between, shift, and adapt and adopt identities across contexts). This chapter analyzes identity as a form of boundary work, contestation, and distinction as it relates to these three issues.

Identity not: identity as boundary work

Identity work is simultaneously boundary work. People often create distinctions by defining themselves against a "marked other," someone or something that they want to make clear that they are not. In her analysis of how "cultural omnivores" with worldly and cosmopolitan tastes actively dislike and define themselves against low-status musical genres such as heavy metal, country, rap, and gospel, Bethany Bryson (1996) illustrates that cultural omnivores define their own musical tastes in imprecise ways, saying that they like "all kinds of music" and expressing an open, tolerant desire to be diverse in their cultural tastes. In contrast to their vague, imprecise, and fuzzy notions of what they like, omnivores are very specific about musical genres that they actively dislike and that thus fall outside even their wide boundaries of tolerance. Bryson observes that these disliked genres such as heavy metal and rap tend to attract cultural univores – listeners who are narrow in their tastes and only listen to and are only familiar with one genre. In their rejection of genres whose fans are the least educated and have the narrowest tastes, omnivores express their own identities as culturally tolerant cosmopolitanites with multicultural capital. Their cosmopolitan identities are maintained, however, as much by the musical genres they abstain from as by those they consume.

In her analysis of the boundary work of identity based on not being or doing something, Jamie Mullaney (2006) explores different kinds of abstainers who form identities based on various not-doings, including abstentions from sex, drugs, alcohol, meat, driving, television, and technology, to highlight the significant boundary work that goes into identity construction. Because abstainers define themselves by things they actively choose not to do, their identities are highly relational. A virgin, a vegan, or a member of the voluntary simplicity movement is understandable only in relation to the sexually active, the carnivore, or the consumer. Their values and who they are are defined in significant part by who they are not. Mullaney demonstrates that across very substantively different abstinences, similar general social patterns arise. Among these similarities are that abstainers develop thresholds of what counts and what does not count as abstinence, and engage in hotly contested disputes over those thresholds. In defining identities based on abstinence the metaphorical moat separating 0 and 1 is a highly significant and consequential one, whereas the lines between 1 and 2 or between 2 and 3 become less significant. General classification disputes arise between a rigid approach, where abstinence is an absolute point or threshold that cannot be crossed, and a more flexible approach, where abstinence is a gray zone in the liminal space between 0 and 1 (Mullaney 2006: 108–12). And while the threshold between 0 and 1 may seem obvious, there are often matters of what counts and what does not count as well as rules and exceptions that allow one to do something that does not count against their abstinent identity. Bracketing certain times and places or contexts so that they do not count toward one's identity is a common exception that allows one to engage in an act and not have it count. A vegan in the United States might, for example, bracket eating turkey while visiting their carnivorous family on Thanksgiving as a marked, special, holiday occasion that affords them a "time out" from practicing their identity.

Mullaney highlights two distinct and conflicting patterns of maintaining an abstinent identity. "Fire walking" involves actively exposing oneself to temptation and to the behaviors one is abstaining from as a way to test and therefore affirm one's commitment to the abstinent identity. The idea behind fire walking or "facing the fire" without getting burned is that one's ability to resist must be tested in order to prove one's integrity and the authenticity of one's ability to abstain (Mullaney 2006: 127). One who merely avoids sin for lack of opportunity is only passively innocent, not actively pure, in this formulation. The second strategy, "fence building," involves insulating oneself from temptation and demonstrating one's commitment not only by avoiding the sin, but by insulating oneself from temptation and sin in the first place. Fence building is an identity strategy based on surrounding oneself with likeminded social networks and separating oneself from the marked or deviant lifestyles and activities that one is trying to avoid. The social network approach of Alcoholics Anonymous, wherein participants are encouraged to establish social networks with other recovering alcoholics and to avoid contacts with their drinking networks, follows this approach to abstinence. The fence-building strategy of abstinence is premised on the idea that doing and sin are slippery slopes and that even nearing the abstinence threshold runs the considerable risk of crossing that threshold and tumbling down the abyss of doing (Mullaney 2006).

Similar to Mullaney's ignoring the substantive differences in types of abstinence to look at formal similarities is Jenna Howard's (2006) ignoring the substantive variation in a wide range of diagnostic labels, such as agoraphobic, alcoholic, anorexic, bulimic, co-dependent, depressive, and social phobic, to develop a general theory of identifying and de-identifying with diagnostic labels. She compares ex-labelers or people in *recovery identities* across a wide range of substantive recovery labels to illustrate how people who once defined themselves by conditions with labels now define themselves against such labels. Howard finds that ex-labelers initially desired labels such as alcoholic, addict, or co-dependent as ways to clearly define their problem and allow them to find a supportive community of people facing similar issues, but later saw defining themselves by their labels as stunting their growth, narrowing their self-perception, and limiting themselves by making the label a noun-like, central, defining attribute or master status. Howard's (2006: 317–18) description of Gretchen, who started to see her label as an all-defining, essentializing noun that had come to take over and become her lifestyle, helps to illustrate how an identity label can become omnirelevant:

> Some delabelers describe their growth as compromised by a long-term identification with the labels as essentializing nouns. This description involves the feeling that the means to recovery was becoming an end in itself. Delabeler Gretchen, who formerly identified as an "addict," expressed this sentiment in discussing the centrality of the "recovery lifestyle" to her life. She explains that she became "wrapped up in the lifestyle of recovery" by living in college dorms for recovering addicts, attending Narcotics Anonymous meetings, and using the "slogans

and mottoes all the time . . . my entire life was recovery!" Gretchen believes that over time, the label became a "hollow" identity that "took the place of the original intent."

In Gretchen's description the label has come to shape her social networks and interactions and to dominate her identity. Her identity as an "addict," even in recovery, was crowding out all other aspects of her self. Consequently she moved away from the label and redefined her identity against performing her recovering addict identity as a noun. Gretchen chose to sacrifice the definitive certainty and security of a dominant label in order to redefine herself in a more fluid manner. Howard shows a number of ex-labelers employing narratives that demonstrate a transition between defining their label as an essentializing noun and redefining themselves as more complex and in need of recognizing all the parts of themselves; this notion of seeing one's label as only one of many parts of the self connotes a switch from regarding the recovery identity as a noun to regarding the recovery aspect of one's self-identity as one of many adjectives that make up the overall self.

In looking at multicontextual examples, Mullaney and Howard analyze the formal ways that identity is used as a resource to craft symbolic boundaries against others, to define one's own self in relation to others, and to determine the relative salience and weight of acts and attributes in the constitution and construction of identity. Both also look at identities that can be fluid and flexible, thus demonstrating that identity can be used strategically as a resource.

Strategies of identity: identity as a resource

How do people think about their identities? How do they socially organize their identities? How do they use identity as resource? To explore these questions, one can look at three different general types of identity strategies. In my ethnographic and interview research analyzing as a case study how suburban gay men managed their gay identity, I developed three ideal-typical (Weber [1925]

1978) "identity strategies" that social actors use to organize their identity in relation to a meaningful or marked social attribute (in this case identifying as gay) (see Brekhus 2003). The first of these ideal types is that of gay "identity lifestylers," who organize their gay attribute as an essentializing *noun* that defines them, live in gay identity enclave space, demonstrate the "auxiliary characteristics" (expected characteristics that go along with a status role) (see Hughes 1945) associated with being authentic in the identity category, and have and value gayness as the dominant attribute in their self-identity. The second ideal type is that of gay "identity commuters," who organize their gay attribute as a mobile *verb*, who live in unmarked space and travel to gay identity spaces to activate their identities, code-switch their auxiliary characteristics, playing up and playing down different identity attributes to match their social setting in the given moment, separate their social networks by setting, and value mobility in their identity performances. The third ideal type is that of gay "identity integrators," who organize their gay attribute as a modifying *adjective*, live in integrated, unmarked identity space, challenge the idea that being authentic in an identity requires performing "auxiliary characteristics," have one large, non-identity-specific social network, and value presenting a multidimensional balance of identity attributes that comprise their organization of self. These three ideal types are visually represented in Figure 1.

Each of these ideal types demonstrates different strategies for presenting identities in space and time (identity duration) and managing auxiliary characteristics, markers, and behaviors commonly associated with an identity (identity density). Tied to these different strategies are duration disputes (contestation over when it is appropriate to perform a certain identity) and density disputes (disagreements over how many auxiliary characteristics should be displayed and how intensely they should be displayed) within identity communities (Brekhus 2003: 98–113, 157–98). In duration disputes, for instance, lifestylers are critical of commuters for being inauthentic because commuters only do the identity part-time; in density disputes, lifestylers accuse integrators of being inauthentic because they only present the

	Gay is a:	Space	Auxiliary characteristics	Social networks	We value:
Lifestylers	Noun	Live in gay enclaves	Have them and police them	All or mostly gay	identity dominance ... and those others are inauthentic.
Commuters	Verb	Travel to gay enclaves to be gay	Code–switch to match setting	Separate gay and suburban networks	identity mobility ... and those others are inflexible and limited.
Integrators	Adjective	Live in 'generic' space	Challenge the idea of them	Mixed social network	identity multidimensionality and balance ... and those others are excessive in one dimension of identity

Figure 1   Gay lifestylers, gay commuters, gay integrators

Source: Adapted from Brekhus (2012: 196)

identity in a bland, diluted form without the requisite auxiliary characteristics that lifestylers see as the markers of authenticity. Commuters, by contrast, are critical of the other categories for being too fixed in their identity duration and lacking the flexibility to move in between categories. And integrators are critical of the density of lifestylers and commuters (when they present the identity) for displaying their identity with too much stereotypical excess and too one-dimensionally as a master status (Brekhus 2003; 2012).

Consistent with a general social pattern analysis, these three ideal-typical strategies can be used to understand the organization of social identities more generally. One could substitute Latino identity, Muslim identity, sorority identity, working-class identity, vegetarian identity, or punk identity for gay identity and find similar strategic, space, auxiliary characteristic, social network, and identity value strategies across these different types of identity. There are of course some differences between these types of identities, based on social privilege, relative visibility/invisibility, and other factors, but these differences do not negate significant analytic commonalities. Central to these ideal types is the idea that identity is something that can be presented as a strategic resource across different contexts. Identity as a resource, of course, is not equally available to everyone in identical ways, and how it is enacted is constrained by power, economics, geography, and other structural and historical factors. But looking at identity as an interactional resource allows us to develop interesting general analytic insights about how people organize identities more or less as a noun, verb, or adjective. Referring back to Howard's analysis of labelers and ex-labelers, we can see, for instance, how ex-labelers shifted from organizing their identity and social networks around an attribute, as an essentializing noun or master status that centered the role, to organizing it as a modifying adjective that was just one aspect of the self, to be integrated around the edges rather than located near the core.

The concepts of identity authenticity, multidimensionality, and mobility (Brekhus 2003) have broad relevance to thinking about social identity. Each of these values can be observed and compared in a meta-analysis of research across different empirical studies in the sociology of identity. Several scholars, for instance, have observed debates and disputes over identity authenticity within communities they study. These authenticity disputes draw attention to boundary policing and category maintenance as well as speak to what attributes count and do not count toward claims to an authentic identity. Similarly, the growing interest of sociologists in studying intersectionality can be related to the issue of multidimensionality. Thinking about how collective identities enter into the constitution of selves in terms of identity multidimensionality allows us to consider the cognitive dimensions of social standpoint and intersectionality. The debate between valuing identity authenticity and dominance, as expressed by representing an identity in its most concentrated, "pure" form, and identity multidimensionality, as expressed by desiring identity balance through not letting any attributes dominate, is a persistent one in identity communities. The concept of identity mobility allows researchers to observe the boundary work, identity shifts, and fluid use of social categories that social actors employ to both maintain and transgress social divisions. Thinking of identity as something mobile and fluid that changes across contexts draws attention to the strategic deployment of identity.

Identity authenticity claims and identity disputes

Boundary work in identity construction is done not only between categories, but within categories. Maintaining a legitimate identity and membership in a collective identity depends, in part, on claims to identity authenticity. Claims to authenticity to a collective identity category often involve some of the following elements: (1) a strong commitment to the identity as evidenced by time and intensity doing the identity, (2) the accentuation of auxiliary characteristics associated with the identity, and (3) an essentialist view of the identity and the belief that it is one's calling or "true self" (Brekhus 2003: 140). Authenticity is fought over in terms of both the density of an identity (whether one performs the identity adequately) and its duration (whether one performs the identity enough of the time). We can think of the duration of identity in terms of the time one lives an identity in the present, but we can see that essentialist claims to have been born into an identity also make a very strong claim on duration by asserting that at one's core, one has always been the identity.

Claims to authenticity often use "born this way" narrative accounts to assert an identity as at the core of one's essence. These essentializing statements are asserted as identity accounts even in many instances where the identity may appear "chosen" to outsiders. In her qualitative analysis of Pagans' "rhetorics of continuity" in conversion narratives, for instance, Erin Johnston (2013) shows that individuals assert that they were born to be Pagan but had just recently discovered their true self. In narrating their identity transitions to Paganism, practitioners used a central, unifying logic of discovering an underlying true self that they had always had (Johnston 2013: 560) but just had not discovered and revealed earlier. Several of the practitioners she interviewed directly described Paganism as an essential and permanent element of their being, with one even describing it metaphorically as part of her DNA (Johnston 2013: 561). Participants, Johnston explains, did not define their transition to Paganism as a transformation of the self by adopting a new perspective and way of being, but argued instead that "exposure to Paganism prompt[ed] an uncovering of their true, authentic selves that were previously hidden, forgotten, or not fully articulated" (Johnston 2013: 561). Pagan practitioners backed up their claims of essential authenticity by citing childhood events and experiences that could be connected with their inner, Pagan, true self and by highlighting events that emphasized that they had always been this way. Being Pagan, according to their rhetorics of continuity, was something felt deeply and perhaps even innately embodied. Through the use of metaphors of natural fit and coming home to their true selves they portrayed a Pagan identity as ascribed not achieved – Pagan was something they were and always had been, not something they simply did (Johnston 2013: 564).

The theme of authenticity in an identity category is especially prevalent in subcultural identity studies. Kembrew McLeod (1999) uses discourse analysis of hip-hop magazines and interviews with hip-hop artists to analyze authenticity discourse within the genre. Authenticity claims are structured, meaningful discourse, and are, according to McLeod, particularly common in subcultures threatened with assimilation by a larger, mainstream culture. Such authenticity claims are a way of preserving the purity of an identity from being diluted by commercial, mainstream culture. In McLeod's (1999: 139) analysis, auxiliary characteristics associated with a hip-hop identity, such as "staying true to yourself," being racially "Black" (and therefore more authentic as a hip-hop artist), being part of the underground, being hard, being of the street, and being old school, are all central to claiming an authentic hip-hop identity. By contrast, following mass commercial trends, being racially "White," being commercial, being soft, being from the suburbs, and being part of the mainstream are all signs of being inauthentic to a true hip-hop identity. Identity authenticity is also about defining what is not authentic. Hip-hop artists often defined themselves against the mainstream, the commercialized, the suburban, and the corporate as ways to buttress and enhance their own authenticity and to define themselves against being watered down by commercial pressures and the need to conform to a generic, mainstream identity (McLeod 1999). In the hip-hop subculture, authenticity is policed by ensuring that a sufficient number of the associated auxiliary characteristics are present. Artists who fail to display these auxiliary characteristics are portrayed as mainstream, fakes, sellouts, and diluted or even polluted representations of what it means to be hip-hop (McLeod 1999). From the standpoint of those who police these characteristics, authenticity is about displaying one's identity appropriately with a density of auxiliary characteristics.

In his study of the fluid complexity of punk authenticity, William Force (2009) shows that subcultures use authenticity claims to first show what they are not as a way to define what they are. Force analyzes the construction of punk authenticity, noting that auxiliary characteristics such as owning records on vinyl that materially flag subcultural membership are important to authenticity claims. He also shows, however, that conforming to the entire uniform set of auxiliary characteristic demands for being punk will also call one's authenticity into question, because one then appears to be trying too hard and engaging in a conscious effort to appear punk. One of the keys to being authentically punk is to appear to be punk "naturally" without trying. It is this ability that allows one to claim punk authenticity at the essentialist level of being punk, not simply doing punk. Social actors in the subculture must therefore walk a tightrope between conforming to the practices of the subculture and creatively deviating from the script just enough to appear original.

J. Patrick Williams (2006) explores the issue of identity authenticity in his study of straightedge identities and online disputes over straightedge identity on an internet forum. He observes that subcultural youth talk about their identities in essentialist terms, making claims to *be* real and authentic, while charging others with simply *doing* subcultural things or auxiliary characteristics such as acting, speaking, or dressing in certain ways to be cool or to fit in (see also Widdicombe and Wooffitt 1990). Straightedgers, for instance, talked about always being straightedge at their core even before they knew the subculture existed, and as "discovering" their inner, essentialist, straightedge identity that was always within them, once they joined the subculture. Williams (2006: 178) argues that subcultural identifications are a cognitive and affective experience invoking positive emotions as people identify as legitimate members of a group; they construct clear and rigid boundaries setting them apart from the mainstream, yet at the same time individual claims to authenticity require demonstrating that one is not influenced by peer pressure or the desire to fit in and conform to others. Williams sees a complex definition of authenticity wherein individuals demonstrate a commitment to a subcultural value structure or lifestyle while also expressing that commitment as something that is not faked or simply done as impression management, but that is a natural and an embodied facet of who they are.

Authenticity disputes extend well beyond subcultural identities. Eva Garroutte (2003) highlights intense authenticity disputes over American Indian ethnic and racial identities. She shows, for instance, that one of the most effective ways for others to delegitimize an individual's claim to an Indian identity and to showcase the inauthenticity of others is to refer to them derogatorily as "ethnic switchers." Indian people who have maintained a stable, permanent racial identification, who have endured as visible Indians for their entire lives and paid their dues, often resent "new Indians" who have only recently begun to play up aspects of their Indian identity and heritage (Garroutte 2003: 85-6). These more established "Indian lifestylers" see the ethnic identity mobility of ethnic switchers, who have jumped from a long life of passing under non-Indian identities to suddenly flip a switch to claim high-density Indian identities, as crass opportunists, a sort of wannabe "traveler" or "migrant" to, rather than "native" to, an Indian identity.

Prudence Carter (2003) demonstrates that African-American youth gain symbolic status among their peers and maintain "authentic" black identities by using auxiliary characteristic markers of racial authenticity such as using "black talk," listening to the proper music, walking with a specific gait, and wearing the appropriate clothing. She refers to these attributes as "black cultural capital," arguing further that one of the instrumental uses of non-dominant cultural capital is to navigate ethnic and racial authenticity. Members of the racial group follow and police cultural codes and signals in navigating authenticity. She shows that African-American youth set symbolic boundaries to gain status as group members and to ward off outsiders, but also used these attributes to evaluate "which of their co-ethnics was most worthy of 'black' cultural membership based on their use of specified [identity] resources" (Carter 2003: 142). Carter adds: "respondents frequently judged each other's authenticity, or rather their legitimacy as 'real' Black persons. In these moments, my study participants revealed that they used cultural authenticity as a basis to draw boundaries not only between themselves and other ethnic groups but also to socially control the behavior of other co-ethnics" (2003: 142). Within intra-racial and intra-ethnic spaces, she argues that authenticity is achieved and policed by the degree to which one can do or act race or ethnicity. John Jackson (2001) provides a similar analysis in illustrating that black men in Harlem deploy race- and class-based auxiliary characteristics to signify authentic "blackness" with and between one another.

Natasha Warikoo (2007) notes, in analyzing how second-generation teenagers in multi-ethnic contexts in New York and London evaluate and express racial authenticity among diverse peers, that while racially authentic cultural practices vary between groups they are nonetheless important for status. Expectations of racial authenticity limit boundary crossings and some displays are regarded as more authentic than others. Peers sanctioned one another for making false claims to group identities that were not accepted as plausible or legitimate. She notes, for instance, that hip-hop was popular among nearly all youth, but non-blacks who were perceived as "trying too hard" and therefore posing were dismissed as inauthentic and trying to "act black." She shows that in multi-ethnic contexts both in-group members and outsiders work to maintain racial and ethnic boundaries, but that members of racial and ethnic groups develop hybrid practices of cultural consumption that combine interests common to all groups with specific "authentic" practices based on their own racial and ethnic identities.

Disputes over identity center on contested authenticity claims and criteria. Within identity categories it is important to be perceived as legitimate and authentic, not a fake, a wannabe, a pretender, a sellout, or a fraud. These disputes represent battles over the tensions between being and doing. In these conflicts, combatants who police authenticity emphasize depth of commitment as an important issue, and they question "doing" as a surface-level, non-essential performance that can be reduced to mere "play" or "identity tourism" and that demonstrates that one is not committed to the identity as an essential attribute at the core of who they are. Stein (1997: 162) shows, for instance, that within lesbian communities some women's lesbianism is questioned as ideological play or lesbian tourism, and they are considered less authentic than truly committed lesbians. Similarly, in a New York gay enclave and commercial district, suburban gays who travel to the city to express their gay identity are denigrated as inauthentic, part-time, "tunnel and bridge" tourists or commuters to a gay identity (see Levine 1998: 51; Brekhus 2003: 99–100). Claims to identity authenticity based on essentialist underpinnings, more permanent duration, and "being" rather than "doing" are typically afforded more social weight in identity communities and subcultures (Mullaney 1999; Brekhus 2008).

Identity authenticity claims are also advanced for organizational identities and place identities. People use cultural and subcultural meanings to attach value to "authentic" experiences, places, and products and to devalue the "inauthentic" and manufactured. Consumers seek authenticity in experiences and places and producers strive to market authenticity. In his analysis of the strategies luxury wine firms use to create an impression of authenticity, Michael Beverland (2005) shows that the public avowal of hand-crafting techniques, relationship to place, and passion for wine making, and the simultaneous disavowal of commercial motives, rational production methods, and the use of modern marketing techniques, were used to construct a notion of brand authenticity. In employing an impression management strategy that implied that they were not motivated by market concerns, these firms maintained their valued status and the high market prices, associated with authenticity, that they appeared to be above. Josée Johnston and Shyon Baumann (2007: 179) analyze authenticity as a frame, noting that qualities that lend themselves to the social construction of authenticity include creation by hand instead of industrial manufacture, the perception of genuine expression removed from conscious calculation or strategy, local flavor, anti-commercialism, closeness to nature, and distance from institutionalized power. These authors also note that authenticity is sometimes constructed through a negotiation between adherence to traditional standards and showing selective originality that departs from those standards (see also Peterson 1997: 220). This balance between adhering to the qualities and auxiliary characteristics expected of an identity, on the one hand, and selectively violating the rules just enough to demonstrate that one is original and genuine rather than calculated and manufactured, on the other, also applies to individual identities in many organizational and subcultural contexts (e.g. Force 2009).

Marie Gaytan (2008) examines the multiple ways that Mexican restaurants in New England construct and negotiate place-based, authentic ethnic identities for their businesses. Among the strategies they use, she demonstrates, are emphasizing symbols of Mexican ethnic heritage and preserving some traditional cultural elements, while at the same time adapting hybrid innovations and the strategic use of language in food descriptions that cater to New England customer demands and illusions of what Mexican food is. Offering "mesquite-grilled" salmon, for instance, emphasized traditional Mexican flavoring and blended it with the inclusion of a non-traditional Americanized entrée (Gaytan 2008: 332). The creation of authentic ethnic cuisines, cultural experiences, brands, and identity consumption opportunities based on theme and lifestyle is often co-opted and transformed by corporate producers and capitalist logics into standardized forms of authenticity that are packaged, branded, and marketed to consumers. Paul Chatterton and Robert Hollands (2002; see also Hollands and Chatterton 2003) show, for instance, that modern urban nightlife is internally segmented to offer new identity consumption niches that attract previously underrepresented marked social categories such as ethnic, racial, gender, and sexual minorities, but that these "ethnic entertainment zones" and "gay villages" are often packaged in gentrified and sanitized formats.

In ethnographic and subcultural studies, researchers often select the most visible and influential sites of collective identity construction, where the most committed cultural insiders police category membership and express the auxiliary characteristics of social and subcultural identities (Brekhus 1998; Williams 2006). While displaying auxiliary characteristics is one important way that people perform authenticity, members who are not at the center of subcultures often produce alternative definitions of authenticity that downplay the importance of manifesting auxiliary characteristics. One way they do this is to claim an authentic personal identity that trumps coherence with an authentic social identity. John Jackson (2005) distinguishes between authentic identities established by adhering to expected cultural scripts for a category and those established by being true to one's self, suggesting that authenticity be measured on the axis of personal sincerity, not culturally coded authenticity. While much identity scholarship focuses on battles over cultural or subcultural identity, where authenticity in a collective identity is established by demonstrating a strong, visible commitment to the identity, maintaining dense social networks within the community, and presenting identity-specific cultural or subcultural practices, there is growing interest in studying identity in all its complexity and multidimensionality, beyond analyzing the most subculturally dominant and visible expressions of group identity and authenticity.

Identity multidimensionality

Modernity involves people in multiple social networks, giving them a complex web of relationships and intersecting social standpoints that are rarely reduced to a single master status identity. Modern social actors navigate complexity either by bringing their many affiliations together to form one multiply influenced and socially networked self (multidimensionality) or by balancing their affiliations across time and space, shifting the salience of competing attributes and foregrounding and performing different selves across different social networks and social contexts (mobility).

In *The Saturated Self* Kenneth Gergen (1991) argues that self-identity is under siege from increasing strains and threatened by an ever-expanding multiplicity of competing demands and commitments. Saturated by a flood of meanings, messages, and criteria for social acceptability, Gergen contends, the self is diluted and dissolving with little sense of a true core identity left. In this view of the self, consistency and coherence are both desirable and increasingly fleeting and unattainable amidst the competing demands on the core self. In "The Self in a World of Going Concerns" Jaber Gubrium and James Holstein (2000) argue that we are faced with an increasingly vast and diverse range of opportunities to defend, find, make, and recreate ourselves (though these opportunities are unequally distributed) and that the increasingly deprivatized self in a fully penetrating social world offers expanding possibilities for self-identity. These competing visions of identity in the modern (or postmodern) world underlie different orientations toward complexity. Some scholars emphasize role strain and role conflict as significant issues that threaten self-coherence and reflect the growing modern assault on the self, while others emphasize individuals negotiating complexity with relatively little effort and without strong concerns for lack of coherence. Much research on identity multidimensionality is more closely tied to the latter view of how individuals negotiate the modern world.

The modern self is heavily networked and comprised of multiple category memberships and social locations, and these multiple affiliations contribute to identity being multidimensional. Gubrium and Holstein (2000: 102) describe the self and social identity as products of our multiple interactions:

> From the myriad formal organizations in which we work, study, pray, curse, play, and recover, to the countless informal associations and networks to which we otherwise attend, to our affiliations with racial, ethnic, and gendered groupings, we multiply engage in a panoply of going concerns most of our lives. The self is a product of this engagement. Many of these going concerns explicitly structure or reconfigure social identity.

How do we make sense of who we are in a world of multiple, overlapping identity demands? How do we negotiate identity through our many interactional engagements, institutional arrangements, and social affiliations? Where do we find balance in the saturated demands placed upon us? These are questions that can be explored within the context of individual and social identities.

One trend toward understanding how multiple demands shape identity in the study of social identities has been the move toward understanding intersectionality or intersectional social standpoints in standpoint theories of identity. Standpoint theories focus on the importance of one's social position to their identities, worldviews, and understandings of the world. Standpoint theorists focus on the axes of gender, class, and race as central shapers of how individuals experience, understand, and interpret the world and how one's position in these dimensions shapes one's perceptions and identities.

The cognitive sociology of identity can build upon standpoint theory's ideas that social location shapes one's perspective and worldview, and that intersecting social locations complicate one's positional understanding, by expanding the theory to suggest that membership in social categories beyond gender, class, and race that are not salient to sociologists are also significant parts of one's social standpoints and standpoint-based cognitions (Brekhus 2007). Religion, moral self-identification, occupation, and age are among attributes that also shape one's social standpoint. While social standpoint theory traces its classical roots to Karl Marx's recognition that different social classes have different interests and therefore competing worldviews, Georg Simmel's ([1955] 1964) web of group affiliations is a classical foundation for understanding social standpoints as highly complex and intricately intersectional. Simmel saw an individual's identity as produced by their overlapping ethnic, geographic, familial, religious, social, occupational, and other affiliations; the idea that one's identity is based on a combination of the entire constellation of intersecting and overlapping affiliations one has moves us into consideration of a greater range of influences on social identity.

Social standpoint theories began with defining alternative social standpoints in terms of broad social categories, such as "women" or "the working class," as a way to challenge the implied universal standpoint of dominant theories based on implicitly male or capitalist class understandings. These early standpoint theories developed the important insight that category membership and the social experiences of being a member of an identity category shape social understandings, worldviews, and a person's structural vantage point from which to view the world. Nancy Hartsock (1983) analogized from Karl Marx's observations that the class structure is more apparent from the lived vantage point of the oppressed social classes to argue similarly for a women's feminist standpoint for understanding the gendered ordering of society. Through standpoint theory, feminist scholars challenged the generic, universalizing, "everyman" perspectives of earlier sociological theories to highlight the importance of gender identity to one's perspective.

Early standpoint theories, while transcending the human universalizing of theories about "man," often assumed the primacy of a single attribute such as sex or gender in one's social vantage point. Early feminist standpoint theories, for instance, privileged women's position as women as their main social standpoint. Later scholars emphasized that women's class, race, ethnicity, and other attributes also matter. In discussing multiple jeopardy and multiple consciousness, Deborah King (1988) suggests, for instance, that many women share multiple positions of relative disadvantage, minority status, or power differentials and that each of these positions uniquely shapes their social standpoint on the world. And these varying social positions cannot simply be added together but instead have variable and fluid effects. In some situations two positions of oppression can add to each other, in others they can cancel each other out, and in still others they can have a multiplying effect on each other. The effects are complex and interactional and the salience of various standpoints can matter significantly, depending on what setting one is in and on what attributes interact with one another. In this view, a woman's standpoint and identity as a woman cannot be all-encompassing because she must also live as a raced, classed, and ethnic person. This moves analysis away from perceiving a single identity standpoint as a master status noun, and toward considering intersecting attributes that shape one's identity standpoint more as adjectives that work together or compete to form a multiply influenced self and social standpoint.

Scholars of identity have become increasingly interested in analyzing dimensions of intersectionality. Researchers look not only at intersecting elements of oppression, stigma, and minority status, but also at the intersectionality of privilege and how it interacts with stigma. They explore the interactions between the marked and the unmarked, and between disadvantage and privilege, in the collective elements within individual identities as well as within collective identities. Julie Bettie (2000; 2003), for instance, analyzes the classed, raced, and gendered identity performances of working-class and middle-class white and Mexican-American girls as they navigate the social terrain of their high school. Arguing that most studies prioritize either gender or race or class and that scholars of gender are often inattentive to class, she argues for understanding the complexity of identity by clarifying how race and gender are lived through social class, and how class, race, and gender are performed and their boundaries maintained and negotiated within subcultural styles. Girls, she argues, use subcultural styles to express class and racial/ethnic differences between themselves and others, using clothing, hairstyle, and makeup as class and ethnic as well as subcultural markers of identity and distinction. Girls, she shows, perform femininity and express group membership as embodied distinctions by choosing lipstick and nail-polish colors that set them apart from other subcultures. Bettie points to the problems of ignoring intersectionality in noting that *las chicas* (a vocationally tracked Mexican-American female subculture in the school) performed girl culture and heterosexual identity as classed and raced forms of femininity more to establish in-group membership than for instrumental reasons of attracting heterosexual interest, but that this was often misinterpreted by teachers and the higher-class prep subculture as reducible to their simple "over interest in sexuality and desire." Bettie shows how social class is often performed through categories of style and difference and that its performance never exists outside race and gender meanings. In some instances, she shows that middle-class Mexican-American girls felt the need to perform working-class identities as a marker of racial/ethnic belonging. These identity performances, she argues, are largely performances of forms of cultural capital tied to available material and cultural resources, and they often reflect unconscious learned dispositions or what Bourdieu refers to as habitus.

Amy Wilkins (2008) analyzes intersectionality in the goth subculture (as well as Christian and Puerto Rican wannabe subcultures), demonstrating that goths are subculturally stigmatized, and goth women fall into the marked sex/gender category, but that goth women also use their privileged unmarked statuses as white and middle-class to shape their uses of identity as a resource. Wilkins shows, for instance, that such women use their white and middle-class statuses to define their subculture as a "cultural taste" and protect themselves from some of the social costs of experimentation, while still stepping outside the unmarked mainstream, but in a manner that could be temporary rather than permanent. They use identity as identity politics to get recognition and sympathy as a derided group, while also maintaining racial and class privilege (Wilkins 2008: 52–3). She notes that goth women pursued sexual liberation as a form of authenticity. They evoke a cultural discourse where sexuality, especially white middle-class or elite sexuality, is perceived as in need of liberation from an unnatural, Puritanical repression, and where there is an

Identity Construction

understanding that individuals should pursue their "authentic" desires in the advance of social progress (Wilkins 2008: 64). These women defined their goth sexual practices as socially progressive and authentic. Wilkins suggests that the development of "freakish" goth identities is also a strategy for goth women, as white middle-class women, to stake a claim to a marked identity and to extend beyond the blandness of a culturally unmarked and "cultureless" white identity.

Pamela Perry (2001; 2002) similarly demonstrates the ways that privilege on one dimension of one's social standpoint relates to deploying identity as a resource. Unlike Wilkins' goths, who shape their privileged identities into culturally marked presentations of sexual and subcultural tastes and style, Perry's white youth discursively expressed their whiteness as cultureless. White high school youths implied unmarked racial superiority and privilege by describing themselves as cultureless and devoid of ethnic or racial culture. In doing so they defined themselves as the "norm" (the standard by which others should be judged as deviations) or "rational" (developmentally advanced). She observes that the notion of the unmarked as rational, developed, and superior appears in the everyday race talk of the white students and that they define their race implicitly as natural. Their colorblind orientation sustains and reproduces inequalities, but, in contrast to theories that posit colorblind racism as based in self-interest, Perry argues that the orientation arises out of the perceptual blind spots derived from limited experiences with racialized difference and inequality (see also Perry and Shotwell 2009).

In an intersectional analysis of race, class, and morality in the boundaries and self-definitions of working-class men, Michèle Lamont (2000) shows that whiteness, for working-class white men, operates as a form of boundary work through moral configurations. These men described themselves as more moral and with higher character than their black working-class counterparts. In a methodological approach well designed for accessing multidimensionality in categories of belonging and distinction, Lamont employed open-ended interviews – about friends, foes, role models, heroes, and the kinds of people one likes and dislikes – to access the taken-for-granted categories working-class men used when defining their identities and defining themselves against others. The intersections of class and race contributed to different constructions of self-worth and attributions of "our kind of people." Both white and black working men, she argues, believed that morality was demonstrated by hard work, personal integrity, and traditional morality, but they placed greater weight on different dimensions of moral attributes. White workers primarily valued the "disciplined self," while black workers valued protecting and caring for others and the "caring self" (Lamont 2000). These different moral emphases led to strengthening symbolic boundaries between racial groups and to perceptions that others were not "our kind of people," either because they lacked discipline (white perceptions of blacks) or because they lacked caring (black perceptions of whites).

Lamont also demonstrates that the cognitive and symbolic boundaries people form extend beyond material distinctions, and that the self-identifications people develop are often centered on moral self-definition rather than traditional identity characteristics such as race, class, or gender. While these other characteristics played into perceptions of morality, Lamont shows that for working-class men the line demarcating "people like me" (defined morally) both overlapped with and sometimes crossed race and class boundaries. Considering moral self-definition as an attribute of identity further complicates sociological understandings of identity. Individuals' identifications with "people like me" are themselves intersectional and multidimensional, and sometimes transcend more easily visible and measurable demographic categories.

In a quantitative examination of intersectionality and identity, Peter Aspinall and Miri Song (2013) employ an analysis of social surveys in the United Kingdom and the United States to demonstrate that race is losing its place as a master status as family, religion, age/life stage, and study/work take on greater salience. The idea of a master status that overpowers or dominates all other statuses in most situations is a longstanding concept in sociology and one that still shapes many understandings of marked and minority identities. Aspinall and Song test the centrality of race as a salient or dominant identity of self-identification. While they predictably find that ethnic minorities are more likely to see race as their primary status than whites are, they also find that other identities such as family, religion, occupation and life stage are more central even to members of these minority groups. In the UK they note, for instance, that the salience of race appears to have been undermined by the rise of "Muslim" as a central identity, the growing identification of people as mixed race, and the fragmentation of identity as it is increasingly interwoven with a range of attributes. Aspinall and Song (2013: 548) argue that "the 'external' and 'internal' moments in identity construction are clearly mutually entailed" and that while race has continuing structural significance, its influence on identity is mediated by other factors including the changing social salience of other identity strands. As social context changes, groups and individuals undergo shifts in the salience of how they feel and experience various aspects of their own identities.

In her analysis of the uses of identity as an interactional resource by lower to upper middle-class "blue-chip blacks," Karyn Lacy (2007) demonstrates that individuals who negotiate the intersections of a stigmatizing racial identity and a privileging class identity engage in identity performances that do not fit neatly into singular race or class categories. She suggests several kinds of identities that make up the "black middle-class tool kit": public identities, status-based identities, race- and class-based identities, and suburban identities. Middle-class blacks experience different saliences of their racial and class identities in different settings, sometimes experiencing their class identity as more significant, at other times experiencing their racial identity as significantly marked, and often experiencing both identities as significant in how they relate to one another. Randall Schnoor (2006) offers a similar multidimensional analysis of identity as a resource in looking at intersectionality and identity among Jewish gay men in Toronto, highlighting that they manage intersectionality either more or less as Jewish lifestylers (centering

Jewish identity and backgrounding gay identity), gay lifestylers (centering gay identity and backgrounding Jewish identity), gay-Jewish commuters (traveling back and forth between the two different identities and communities), or gay-Jewish integrators (combining the two identities rather than foregrounding one or the other).

Researchers who analyze the multiple collective identity elements within individuals' self-identities access the ways that people balance and combine different attributes of their selves on the basis of contextual concerns. People belong to multiple social categories and groups, and they balance these affiliational claims on their identity in varying ways. Understanding intersectionality requires a non-static view of identity, recognizing that the complexity of managing multiple marked and unmarked attributes of self in relation to others entails constant negotiation and navigation with an ever-shifting social landscape. The multiply influenced self is constituted across time and space. Studying multidimensionality involves recognizing how multiple influences are integrated so that as people present subcultural or sexual identities, for instance, they are also doing social class through race/ethnicity and gender. In addition to understanding the integration of intersecting and competing attributes, analysts can also explore the temporal and spatial segregation of these attributes. Several of the researchers discussed in this section have shown that identity performances are often variable and dependent on audience. This suggests a temporal and spatial mobility to social identity.

Identity mobility

In addition to being multidimensional, modern identities are fluid, mobile, and shifting. Recent scholarship in the sociology of identity shows that individuals may shift their identities from one setting to the next, playing up, trying on, and living out some identities in specific contexts, while performing other identities in other contexts. Goffman's (1959) idea of a dramaturgical self performed on various stages of social life to different audiences informs a longstanding tradition in studying the performative nature of identity and the self (see also Butler 1999). Individuals can accentuate, amplify, mask, or mute different facets of their identity across different social networks and social contexts, and creatively play up and play down different elements of the self to match their setting.

The concept of code-switching, which Elijah Anderson (1999) has applied specifically to the ways lower-class African-American men switch from the cultural code of the street to mainstream codes in order to negotiate both settings, is an instructive concept that can be brought to bear on performances of identities more generally. People code-switch different auxiliary characteristics and identity currencies across different contexts. Prudence Carter (2003), whose ideas we previously examined in understanding identity authenticity, argues that cultural capital is context-dependent and shows that lower-class African-Americans use different linguistic currencies in different settings, cashing in on their "black cultural capital" to gain legitimacy in African-American social spaces while employing mainstream speech patterns in white-dominant work settings. She shows that they deploy these two different cultural capitals as dual currencies, code-switching across cultural contexts to strive for racial authenticity and legitimacy in black social networks and to aspire to mainstream authenticity and legitimacy in white workplaces.

Kerry Rockquemore and David Brunsma (2002) show that for some people racial identity itself is flexible and mobile. In their study of biracial individuals, these authors illustrate a distinction between those who integrate their mixed heritage into a unified biracial identity, those who identify singularly with one side of their mixed heritage, and those who experience a protean, mobile racial identity. These latter individuals develop separate white, black, and biracial cultural competencies and contextually shift their racial identity presentation according to the context and the social networks they are in. Rockquemore and Brunsma explain the protean identity strategy as follows:

Their response was not to integrate their racially fragmented experiences (like the border identifiers) nor to accept one reality and eschew another (like the singular identifiers). Instead, the protean respondents describe themselves as moving in and out of differing social contexts, acting as chameleons who change their identities as quickly and as often as others change their clothes. They are neither compromised nor ashamed of their "shifty" ways and find themselves validated at every turn. (2002: 70–1)

They note that the protean group felt the closest to both blacks and whites of any of the groups they studied, even closer for the two respective racial groups than those who chose a singular black or white identity. This suggests that views of "passing" as necessarily cynical and inauthentic, leading to inevitable role conflict, role strain, or lack of a coherent self, need to be tested rather than simply assumed. Mobility and lack of a consistent singular identity are not inherently a problem for all who switch codes.

Mobility entails adopting different identity personas and cultural codes or performing different cultural competencies or capitals across different contexts. In observing the social construction of authentic cosmopolitan identities through the consumption of urban nightlife, David Grazian (2003; 2008) illustrates the night as a temporal space for performing desired selves. In his study of Chicago blues clubs, Grazian (2003) documents the ways that patrons adopted a "nocturnal self" – a special kind of presentation of self associated with consuming urban nightlife – that allowed them to claim the "nocturnal capital" of maintaining an "authentic" cosmopolitan, subculturally savvy, and urbanely hip persona that matched the surroundings of the most symbolically authentic urban environments, such as the blues clubs perceived as the most legitimate. Grazian (2008) extends his analysis of nocturnal presentations of self and identity in *On the Make: The Hustle of Urban Nightlife*, showing that young denizens of Philadelphia nightlife practice and try out their adult cosmopolitanite identities at night. He demonstrates the centrality of urban nightlife spaces for trying on, amplifying, or temporarily adopting alternative selves and identities. These spaces are organized for leisure, recreational identities, play, masquerade, and drag. While theories of performativity have looked particularly at gender presentations as drag (Butler 1999), other identity performances also resemble drag. Grazian shows that some young heterosexual men in Philadelphia use the play spaces of urban nightlife to collectively perform exaggerated displays of heterosexuality in a ritual "girlhunt," to gain status and social currency among their peers as competent and spirited heterosexual men. Although these men are heterosexual in diurnal everyday spaces, they strategically perform a consciously amplified heterosexuality when in the presence of one another at night. The urban setting and the night are spatial and temporal enclaves that can serve as amplifiers for identity (Brekhus 2003: 25–6).

Whereas Grazian's concept of the nocturnal self illustrates the bracketing of temporary identities in the "leisure time" of night, Karen Stein (2011) looks at the bracketing of "vacation selves" as distinct from one's everyday self. Stein observed international tourists from the United States, Great Britain, and Canada, who volunteered two hours a day for a charitable cause while on vacation in China during the summer of 2008, to identify a variety of characteristics of vacation identities. Like urban nightlife, vacation affords individuals the mobility and freedom to act out different roles within a new context. When individuals go on vacation they use props, behaviors, and interactions with travel companions to bound the experience as distinct from everyday life and to take on a temporary "vacation identity." Stein (2011: 298) shows that vacationers often express their temporary identities as more free and amplify the recreational sides of themselves, including demonstrating more openness to drinking and drugs, partying, and danger and risk. Her informants expressed the idea that vacation affords more "freedom to do and be whatever you want" (Stein 2011: 301) and thus allows for a freer and wider range of deviant or risk-taking behaviors. It can be used as a concealment track (Goffman 1974) to hide behavior inconsistent with one's everyday identity and to enact temporary performances that can be bracketed from counting toward who one is outside of the vacation frame. Traveling companions become an important audience for vacation identities and can often assist in the "teamwork" (Goffman 1959) involved to pull off a convincing performance. They can solicit vacation-appropriate behaviors and reinforce the vacation role. Stein also shows, however, that some traveling companions, such as children, are more likely to force one to integrate one's vacation identity with one's everyday self and to manifest identity as a "vacation integrator" rather than a "vacation commuter." She demonstrates further that vacationers go through role-entrance and role-exit strategies to get into and move out of their vacation identity roles. Modern social media, she argues, break down the neat segmentation of everyday and vacation selves and make it harder to completely "get away from it all," as cell phones, Facebook, and other technological ways to stay always available and ever present, even when physically away, encroach on the time and space of vacations.

Karen Danna Lynch (2011) looks at role and identity mobility and fluidity at the micro-temporal level of rapid everyday role shifts. From in-depth interviews with 60 full-time parents, from a variety of occupations, on the types of roles they play on any given day, she shows the multiplicity and multidimensionality of social roles. She looks at the duration of their role performances, shifts and overlaps in role performances, their role audiences, their social resources, their physical and mental partitioning of roles, and their thoughts and feelings about their roles and role performances. Many social analysts start with the premise that multiple competing roles are inherently a problem that will produce negative consequences such as stress, cognitive dissonance, and lack of authenticity to a core self. Danna Lynch shows, however, that individuals creatively and successfully manage multiple roles in their everyday lives all of the time. Rather than follow a "problems" approach, she documents an everyday life "solutions" approach, demonstrating the multiple ways that people successfully and creatively handle overlapping and competing role commitments. Danna Lynch develops a typology of four "role states" to portray how different configurations of behavior and cognition result in different ways of managing or focusing the self in role(s). The first is single focus (characterized by deliberate cognition and deliberate behavior, where an individual is 100 percent intently focused on a single role. This is the segmented role state that many social analysts seem to assume, even though it may, in fact, be the most statistically rare. The second is behavioral overlap (characterized by deliberate behavior and automatic cognition), where individuals enact the behavioral elements of a role while cognitively wandering to many other roles and possibilities (for instance, behaviorally engaging as a chauffeur to children while also investing cognitively in several other roles as a parent, a commuter, and the like). The third is cognitive overlap (characterized by automatic behavior and deliberate cognition), where individuals are deliberately mentally and cognitively focused on a single role, even while engaged in many behaviors related to other roles. The fourth is complete overlap (characterized by automatic behavior and automatic cognition), where diverse cognitive engagements are performed simultaneously with diverse behavioral enactments. The typology of role performances, and of how people manage simultaneously multiple overlapping roles, that Danna Lynch employs focuses primarily on relational (e.g. parent, spouse) or occupational (e.g. mechanic, doctor) roles, but has analytic parallels to other identity dimensions (e.g. race, class, ethnicity, sexuality, gender).

At the opposite end of the temporal spectrum from Danna Lynch's focus on identity shifts at the very micro-temporal level, identity mobility is also something to negotiate over longer spans of time. In dealing with macro-temporal periods of time, one way that people negotiate their identities and maintain self-consistency in their mobile lives is by constructing narrative identities of the self. Drawing on Mead's ([1934] 1967) idea of the double dialogue between internal conversation and external interaction, narrative theorists of the self (Ezzy 1998; Ricoeur 1984) emphasize that creating a sense of self-continuity involves active work to create a consistent story or plot of whom one is. Narrative theorists of identity emphasize that the self is discovered and articulated through narrative. Paul Ricoeur (1984) uses the idea of emplotment to describe a process of continuing reorientation through which stories become narratively configured to make sense and provide meaning. Human time, he argues, is constructed through stories and events; our autobiographies are similarly created through our narrative plots that give the past sense in the present. Douglas Ezzy (1998) points out that identity is not deep in our personality but rather consists of being recognized by others as being the same person. This brings us to the mobility of the self, and the lack of a deep core self, that Goffman studied; yet we can give the self coherence by selecting parts of our past that maintain our consistency and self-definition.

In her study of high school reunions as autobiographical occasions, Vered Vinitzky-Seroussi (1998) analyzes self-identity and authenticity and identity work in these situations. She demonstrates that the intersection between one's past and one's present generates a tension between a situated identity – enacted, held, and understood in a social setting – and a personal identity that people bring to the situation and leave the situation with; the two types of identity, while analytically separable, overlap in everyday life (Vinitzky-Seroussi 1998: 132). The techniques of self-presentation and identity management that are situationally enacted at a class reunion generally extend beyond the setting and either affect personal identity or require some accounting of the relationship between the situated and the personal identity. Reunions serve as an occasion for a situated identity that is situated temporally and in a social network, tied to a historic past and within social networks that share that past but not necessarily the present, beyond the immediate present of the autobiographical occasion of the reunion. Much as Grazian demonstrates nocturnal identities as situated urban identities in specific spaces at night and Stein demonstrates vacation identities as temporally situated and facilitated by traveling companions in one's situated vacationing social network, Vinitzky-Seroussi highlights the temporal situatedness of a reunion identity, showing that individuals construct autobiographies and personal identities that creatively piece together and integrate a combination of who one is and who one wishes to be. Reunions are also autobiographical occasions that potentially create abrupt discontinuities, sometimes forcing people into more deliberate cognition about their self-identities. Because individuals often try to maintain a consistent self between past and present, and perform for audiences accustomed to a particular past self, they sometimes discover that it takes considerable presentational work to keep the two selves aligned. Vinitzky-Seroussi, in showing people trying to manage these discrepancies, suggests that over a lifetime one's identity and one's primary definition of self may change quite significantly, so that the past self and the present self may share very little in common; such situations may require reparative narrative work to maintain a consistent sense of self.

A class reunion is a rather mundane and small rupture leading to deliberate cognition about identity. More abrupt and more enduringly transformative changes in identity can occur during events metaphorically described as turning points, watershed moments, crossroads, rites of passage, exits (Ebaugh 1988), conversions (Snow and Machalek 1984), revelations, and awakenings. Thomas DeGloma (2010; 2014) analyzes autobiographical awakening narratives and stories people tell about personally discovering truth, demonstrating that such autobiographical tales are characterized by defining two radically distinct selves: a past self that was blind and naive and a new self that is aware and has "seen the light." Using social pattern analysis, DeGloma puts a broad range of "awakeners" into a single analytic social category to highlight the narrative structure of their identity conversions. These awakeners include veterans who oppose wars, born-again Christians, Mormon converts and Mormon apostates, survivors of childhood sex abuse, sexual reconversionists such as ex-gays, and people who have converted from ex-gay (ex ex-gays). In awakening narratives, he shows that individuals express a transition between two mutually exclusive selves and use vocabularies of liminality to depict the cognitive transition from one belief system, worldview, and self to another. They express these transitions in two metaphorical ways. One is an express elevator, where the individual makes a direct and expedited ascent to a new awakening and "higher self." In this version of liminality the individual experiences an abrupt disruption or stunning discovery that leads to an immediately new consciousness. A second metaphorical transition is a staircase, where the individual experiences a step-by-step ascent in which several notable, but not singularly dramatic and transformative, experiences lead to an awakening over a longer time period. These experiences are nested together in a broader awakening episode and contribute to the cumulative shift of the storyteller's consciousness and identity (DeGloma 2010: 531). These descriptions of liminality help storytellers to segment past and present selves.

DeGloma shows that individuals with awakening stories construct distinct temporally situated selves. Awakening narratives articulate radical shifts in identity, worldview, social networks of reference and affiliation, and presentations of self. They split the past and the present into two distinct autobiographical periods, each with a diametrically different standpoint on truth and knowledge. In narrating a shift in the autobiographical self, awakeners articulate the mobility of identities over time. DeGloma (2010: 533) captures this migratory aspect of the self in describing "cognitive migration":

> Awakeners portray their "self as soliloquy" (Athens 1994) in order to personify different socially rooted worldviews. In the process, they articulate a *cognitive migration* out of one autobiographical community and into another, whether religious, clinical, political, sexual, or otherwise. As opposed to the conventional notion of migration, which refers to the physical movement of an individual or group from one geographic location to another, the notion of cognitive migration refers to a change in one's sociomental location or "reference group" (Shibutani 1955).

In addition to cognitive migration we can talk about identity migration. Just as one can commute to different identities on a short time basis, one can migrate to a different identity over the life-course.

Conclusion

This chapter explored identity as a resource and something that is multidimensional. Identity is multidimensional in relation to how authenticity is defined, the complex relationship between marked and unmarked attributes, and the mobility and changes in identity over time and across space. This mobility occurs at both the micro-temporal level of daily shifts and short commutes and at the macro-temporal level of life-course shifts and long migrations. Debates over authenticity focus on both claims to belonging as an authentic member to a collective identity and claims to personal authenticity. The former usually involve a degree of conformity and adherence to auxiliary characteristics and to proving authenticity within one's performance of group identity. The latter typically involve an expression of multidimensionality that transcends complete conformity to group expectations. Authenticity claims also center on the divide between natural and fake performances, and such claims involve employing essentialist metaphors and logics to express the "natural" and unaffected performance of an identity.

Studies of socially marked identities have developed beyond a singular master status approach to explore the interplay between different marked attributes and the relationship and interaction between marked and unmarked attributes, showing that both shape social standpoints and that individuals simultaneously negotiate their statuses of social disadvantage and social privilege. Identity multidimensionality is connected to many different strategies of using identity as a resource. Some individuals combine many attributes of identity, worldviews, and social networks at once to form a complex, multiple-attribute social identity that changes little from setting to setting, while other individuals travel between different roles, selves, and identities, displaying a mobile and ever-shifting social identity. The short-term mobility of identity can occur with "identity commutes" on a weekly or daily basis, or even rapidly switching roles on an hourly or moment-to-moment basis. Micro identity shifts often involve the cultural practice of code-switching between the presentational styles and auxiliary characteristics demanded of a particular social context. The long-term mobility of identity can occur with "identity migrations" over a much longer time period. These shifts in identity are often articulated through narrative and autobiographical accounts that bracket and segment different selves and articulate rites of transition as one shifts from one identity to the next.

5

Memory and Time

Memory and perceptions of timing and time are important dimensions of our cognition. Our collective and collected memories are closely aligned with other key cognitive processes such as attention, frame, relevance, categorization, meaning, and identity. What do we remember and what do we forget? How do we make sense of the past in the present and how do we use the present to culturally construe the past? How do we bridge time, connecting the distant past more directly to the present? How are our memories culturally and socially structured? What events have cultural resonance? How does the sequencing of events in time shape our understandings of those events? How do we experience time? These are questions for a cognitive sociology of memory and time. This chapter explores these questions analyzing collective memory, time sequences (how does the ordering of events shape our moral understandings?), and phenomenological perceptions of time.

In his foundational work on collective memory, Maurice Halbwachs ([1950] 1992) advanced the argument that human memory functions within a social context. Following Durkheim's view of the social existing outside the individual, Halbwachs saw the memory of the collective as a social force that exerts influence on individual memories. Individual memories, he argued, are only understood through a group context such as a family, an organization, a nation, a religion, or a social class. He illustrates cognitive variation between groups, showing, for instance, that the old rich in France have a very different memory of the past than the new rich, and that different groups of religious pilgrims to the Holy Land construct very different versions of the past. Halbwachs also emphasized that collective memories are influenced by the needs of the present. Groups arrange their memories of past events, highlighting, eliminating, and rearranging elements to construct a narrative past that fits within present understandings.

In his influential writings on human time, Paul Ricoeur (1984; 1988) argues that time becomes human when it is organized narratively. Narrative emplotment, he argues, brings elements of the past into a constructed and imagined order, and this narrative configuration of past events gives them meaning and intelligibility. Ricoeur distinguishes between cosmological or linear time and phenomenological time, arguing that we do not only experience time as linear, but are oriented to the movement of time in terms of events and our images of what was, what is, and what will be.

The experience of the movement of time is often event-centered, rather than chronologically centered, and shaped by organizational and cultural expectations and rhythms. Individuals, located in social life, can cognitively experience time as accelerating or slowing down on the basis of the events that happen in time, the social relations tied to the events, and the organizational and subcultural structuring of time and events. Whether in a kitchen, a jail, or the cab of a truck, the movement of time ebbs, flows, and pulses with the movement of social life. The clock, the calendar, and the organizational schedule may discipline time and its users, but users also employ and creatively use time in ways that sometimes contest its orderly and disciplinary structuring. Like identity, discussed in the previous chapter, time can be employed strategically as an interactional and even a moral resource.

The experience of memory, like the experience of time more generally, is also event-centered. We begin our travel in time by looking at collective memory and how we attend to, understand, and use the past.

Collective memory and the construction of the past

Memory is socially shaped and many aspects of the past are ignored as out of frame, while a few aspects are accentuated as salient. In his analysis of the cognitive mechanisms of collective memory, Aaron Beim (2007: 18) develops a culture-and-cognition model of collective memory, arguing that we use culturally available memory schemas to make sense of the past, and that "the social interaction of culturally related individuals with each other among cultural objects and other institutional forms produce these schemata." He focuses on the idea of schemas as an important concept because they both constrain and enable: they constrain because they limit the contexts and frames with which people interpret the world, and they enable because they determine how people store, process, and recall the many cognitive cues in social life. Connecting cognitive sociology to cognitive psychology and anthropology, Beim (2007: 17) notes that research on memory cognition demonstrates that schemas and social structure shape individual memories and that individuals remember better those events that can be encoded by a well-formed schema (see also D'Andrade 1995). Individuals remember by accessing culturally available memory schemas, and schematically linked information is more easily retrieved than information that is non-schematically located and thus likely to fall outside our cognitive attention and focus (see also Cerulo 2002c). Karen Cerulo (2002b: 8) discusses how cognitive scientists look at how schemas work in the individual brain and suggests that they play an equally important role in the construction of collective memory. Our apprehension, retrieval, and remembrance of the past are connected to our schema of the present (Cerulo 2002c: 204).

Jeffrey Olick (1999) makes a distinction between two traditions in understanding memory. Collected memories he defines as referring to the ways that individuals recount significant historical events as part of aggregates (e.g. how members of one generation remember an event compared to members of another generation). Collective memories on the other hand refer to the social and cultural patterns of memory constituted in the social arena, such as symbols, commemorative rituals, museums, discourses, and authoritative public narratives. The distinction between collective elements in individual memories (collected memories) and collective memories is similar to the distinction between collective elements in individual identities and identities as collectives discussed in the previous chapter. I highlight both approaches to collective memory, starting with collected memories.

Howard Schuman and Jacqueline Scott (1989) demonstrate generational cognitive variation in collected memories using a probability sample of 1,410 adult Americans, asking them to identify the most important events and changes over the last 50 years. In doing so, these authors demonstrate how within generations individuals remember things similarly to one another (and differently from other generations) on the basis of their shared generational standpoints and experiences of world events, particularly in adolescence and early adulthood. In Schuman and Scott's analysis the hypotheses that memories of important political events and social change are structured by age, and that adolescence and early adulthood are the primary period for "generational imprinting" of political memories, were strongly supported (1989: 377). The researchers found that individuals who mentioned an event that happened during their adolescence or early adulthood showed a strong tendency to explain it in terms of their personal, individual experience at the time – for example service in a war, or a "flashbulb memory" of where they were when they heard Kennedy was assassinated – while events that did not happen in their youth were typically contrasted implicitly with ones from their own youth or childhood (Schuman and Scott 1989: 378). As an example, Schuman and Scott (1989) discuss how those who experienced World War II focused their memories on the direct personal meaning of the event, while the more narrative and moral meaning of the event as a "good war" and a "victorious war" came from the later Vietnam generation. These authors go on to argue that the importance of adolescence and early adulthood arises out of the congruence of several life-course factors including the low salience of and general disattention to events that occurred prior to their own lifetime, the openness and exposure of adolescents and young adults to events and influences outside their home and neighborhood, and the importance of first political and social events that they encounter for shaping their later worldviews. Subsequent events seldom seemed as significant as those that individuals encountered when they first moved outside the immediacy of their home. In this respect, they relate to Mullaney's (2006) observation that first times and jumps from zero to one are a more significant cognitive leap than subsequent moves.

Schuman and Scott (1989) argue ultimately that generational effects on memory are not simply a mental recording of general historical importance or judgments that reflect primarily the perspective of historians on the past, but are rather the intersection of personal history and collective history that provides the most strongly remembered connections to the times we have lived through and particularly came of age in. These authors also found that blacks' and women's experiences of the civil rights and women's liberation movements were very generationally influenced by who experienced those movements as adolescents or young adults, while the same generational effects did not show in whites or men. Generational effects in collective memory are the results of the intersection of personal and national history. Karl Mannheim ([1928] 1952) argued that generational effects or cohort effects on people who experienced events as 17- to 25-year-olds have effects on worldview that are comparable in importance to social class (see also Schuman and Rieger 1992: 315). Schuman and Scott, in studying cohort effect as a variable potentially comparable to other variables of social standpoint, discover strong support for generations as "thought communities" when it comes to collectively remembering some events and collectively ignoring others. As the women's liberation and civil rights data show, however, generation is itself intersectional with other identity attributes such as race and sex and also region (see also Griffin 2004).

Howard Schuman and Cheryl Rieger (1992) build upon Schuman and Scott's earlier work in studying the historical analogies and analogical reasoning that people used in the buildup to the 1990s Iraq or Persian Gulf War. Two analogies from the past were most commonly used: World War II or the Vietnam War. Generational experience was related to which analogy was chosen. Before the war, for instance, approximately 70 percent of older Americans favored the Hitler analogy over the Vietnam analogy, but for those born in the years 1946–50, who would have been 15 to 19 years old when the Vietnam War began with the US bombing of North Vietnam, and 18 to 22 years old during the Tet Offensive of 1968, this cohort was much more likely to choose the Vietnam War analogy in the pre-Iraq War period (Schuman and Rieger 1992: 320). These authors add that "in each case, the collective memory of the last profound war experience seemed to continue to affect later cohorts until an equally profound new war experience began to construct a new collective memory for youths growing up at that time" (Schuman and Rieger 1992: 324). Although they found a strong influence of generational experience in being attracted to one analogy over the other, they found that these analogy preferences did not necessarily line up with stark contrasts in policy preferences.

Social standpoint and intersectionality within social standpoints, important to identity, also shape memory. Larry Griffin (2004) looks at collective memory of civil rights, demonstrating that region and race shape understandings of the past. He re-examines Schuman and Scott's (1989) study of generations and collective memories, looking specifically at their finding that there was no generational effect on whites' recollections of the civil rights movement. He separates whites into Northern and Southern whites to see if this effect remains the same. Griffin finds that civil rights memory was significantly more salient for Southern whites who experienced the movement as mature teenagers or young adults than for their same-aged peers elsewhere or for Southern whites in different age cohorts. This indicates that the social location of generation interacts with the spatial location of region or place in shaping collective memories. Griffin (2004: 544) concludes that where highly charged events happen, along with when they happen in the stage of one's life-course, shape consciousness and memory, thus suggesting that "Mannheim's idea of the 'social location' of generational identity formation is place-specific as well as age-specific." Griffin gets at the multidimensional and intersectional character of memories by arguing that multiple intersecting social standpoints shape the salience and recollection of past events:

> Region, along with race, gender, age, and other social factors, matters in the construction of collective memories, and the real question is not whether it (or place, more generally) or something else has causal primacy, but how, conjoined, they produce – as race, region and age do in these data – what is remembered and thought to be historically important. (Griffin 2004: 556)

Jens Rydgren (2007) analyzes the ways that collective memory of ethnic conflict is biased toward remembering vivid events such as war and conflict and that these events appear to take up a greater share of the past, because long periods of peace are ignored and thus mentally shrunk, giving the past a more violent coloring than it actually had. He suggests that the memory biases inherent in analogical reasoning, especially as folks are likely to interpret events in relation to significant "marked" events such as past wars and conflicts, lead them to overestimate the likelihood of future conflict and to color the present with the most dramatic elements of the past.

Reuben Buford May (2000) focused on micro "communities of memory" among African-American men in a neighborhood tavern who shared stories of negative racial encounters that then influenced their view on race relations. Similar to Rydgren's findings at the macro level, his observations were that patrons' discussions had a compounding effect in disseminating and narrating stories about marked inter-racial encounters. Their stories became a mass of local collective memory. This race talk helped patrons to maintain a positive racial identity, to find support for negotiating their racial identity in the face of negative inter-racial encounters outside of the bar space, and to reduce the psychological effects of racist and discriminatory acts through the catharsis of venting. But the same talk also led to similar issues to those that Rydgren identifies. Since many African-Americans live in highly segregated communities and socialize within race-segregated enclaves and social networks, race talk within these settings often reified a narrow perspective of race relations (May 2000: 212). The collective stories led to a distrust of other races and to a collective memory that reinforced the racial attitudes that Elijah Anderson (2011) refers to as "ethnos" (ethnocentric views that involve distrust of out-groups and high degrees of in-group identification) rather than "cosmos" (cosmopolitan views that involve social network integration, lack of strong in-group specific identification, and a heterogeneous identification). Anderson argues (2011: 190) that African-Americans who interact in mostly segregated social networks often assume an ethno (or ethnocentric) position as a way to shield themselves and others from potential or actual racial discrimination or injury. The same is true of "ethnos" in other racial groups. May (2000: 212–13) notes that local collective memories in segregated settings focus primarily on negative talk about marked inter-racial interactions:

> Specifically, as individuals in these mnemonic communities recall negative racial encounters, they develop a collective memory that helps to restrict the ways they might view race relations. However, such a limited view of race relations in America is not specific to African-Americans. Members of other racial and ethnic groups also come together in micro "communities of memory" to share their stories of negative racial encounters. They too develop a narrow view of race relations. Again the paradox of local collective memory becomes evident. In one sense the racially and ethnically segregated micro-"communities of memory" help individuals relieve tension and stress related to interracial interactions in everyday life; in another sense they work to reassert the negative perception of race.

Thus the narrative sharing of negative racial discrimination both built community and helped to share stories of mistreatment in a racist society at a collective level, and also marked the salience of race in the local collective memory of patrons.

Rydgren highlighted how collective memory can reinforce the most marked and salient aspects of the past, and Schuman and

Scott and Griffin demonstrated that memory is highly shaped by social location. Barry Schwartz (2009) highlights the other side of the memory coin in discussing collective forgetting or collective amnesia. Part of highlighting the marked, for instance, involves forgetting the unmarked and discarding that which does not fit into existing cognitive schemas. Just as remembering is shaped by social and physical location and unevenly distributed by social location, forgetting is also highly dependent on social location. Schwartz argues that how we remember civil rights heroine Rosa Parks is as much about what we forget and discard as what we remember. Schwartz (2009: 123) explains that:

> Joining the adjective "collective" to forgetting does not imply an emer-
> gent "social mind" or that every member of a society forgets the same
> thing: it means that remembering and forgetting, knowledge and igno-
> rance, are distributed unevenly among different communities, groups,
> and individuals. Events and people of comparable significance are also
> remembered differently *within* these same communities, groups, and
> individuals.

Schwartz further adds that forgetting results not only from efforts to suppress painful, dissonant, immoral, or ignoble experiences and events but also from excluding virtuous actions; our memory cannot maintain everything and we therefore suppress the noble as well as the ignoble. In particular he analyzes the "oneness" of the Rosa Parks story, noting that the construction of Parks as a lone heroine involved collective forgetting of much of the context of her actions as it involved remembering her heroism. He notes, for instance, that we forgot many invisible civil rights heroes and heroines who like Parks defied and resisted bus segregation. The sole figure of a lone black woman who refused to relinquish her seat provided a convenient shorthand with a clear moral message that a commemoration of everyone involved could not provide. Schwartz argues that memory is necessarily selective and that the memory of Parks involved selective forgetting and remembering in a way that made the civil rights movement easier to commemorate and locate in a lone heroine figure. Rosa Parks' story is sche-matic because it packages the Montgomery protests into an easily remembered story about an oppressed people's struggle for justice in the Jim Crow South (Schwartz 2009: 136).

Schwartz (1997; 2000; 2008) also looks at changes in collective memory over time, using the memory of Abraham Lincoln as an example. Schwartz analyzes, for instance, how despite no changes in actual information about Lincoln's racial attitudes, his collective reputation changed from that of a conservative symbol of the status quo during the Jim Crow era into the personification of racial equality and justice during the New Deal and the civil rights movement (Schwartz 1997). Schwartz (2000) demonstrates how the collective national and community memories of Abraham Lincoln were shaped by the present, and that the symbol of the man was used both as a "mirror" to reflect the nation's current concerns and a "lamp" to illuminate its ideals (see also Schwartz and Schuman 2005).

Gary Alan Fine (2001) explores the opposite end of the iconic spectrum in looking at the difficult reputations of historical villains, incompetents, and notorious people, showing how individual reputations emerge and are collectively solidified as cultural fables and morality tales. Like Schwartz, Fine too sees collective memories and reputations of figures as tied to the reflections, character, and goals of a society or community. Historical reputations, including difficult ones, are reflective of the shifting moral boundaries and visions of a society. Fine sees reputations as a form of "social capital" or also, especially in the case of difficult reputations, "social debt." In his analysis of Warren Harding's reputation for incompetence, Fine (2001: 60–94) argues that reputations are not only made but used for purposes that address messages about leadership, the role of an active citizenry, and related issues. Cultural resonance with available schemas is important for reputations to stick.

Jeffrey Olick (2005; 2007) looks at difficult pasts and reputations among nations with troubled histories, such as Germany and South Africa. In his study of collective memory and political culture in post-war Germany, Olick (2005) analyzes the memories and silences around World War II atrocities and the public discourses of guilt that involved remembering and forgetting and the framing of guilt. He notes that memory occurs in dialogue with the past, the present, and the accumulated development of preceding memory. Memories are shaped by our collective memories themselves as well as by the actual events we remember. Jeffrey Olick and Daniel Levy (1997) discuss the relationship between remembered pasts and constructed presents in looking at how the collective memory of the Holocaust is shaped by and shapes Germany's political culture. These authors demonstrate that from different moments in West German history the impact of the Holocaust unfolds in changing meanings, and that collective memory is a continuous negotiation between the past and the present. Collective memory is neither entirely constrained by, nor a contemporary strategic manipulation of, the past but rather a negotiated interplay between the two (Olick and Levy 1997: 934).

Ron Eyerman (2001) analyzes the cultural trauma of African-American collective memories of slavery, showing that two narratives of African-American representation in the post-slavery United States developed. The "progressive narrative" emphasized African-American advances in the post-slavery years while the "tragic narrative" emphasized the oppressive, totalizing force of white society. These different narratives emphasized different narrative plotlines about the relationship of the past to the present and involved different ways of constructing the present and the future (Eyerman 2001).

In their analysis of South African commemorations of apartheid, Chana Teeger and Vered Vinitzky-Seroussi (2007) similarly demonstrate how memories and understandings of the past help to define and construct the present. They show that while apartheid was a difficult past constituted by moral trauma, oppression, violence, tensions, and conflict, South Africa's first museum to commemorate apartheid framed the commemoration through a narrative of consensus rather than conflict. Through its narrative framing the museum divorces a dreadful past from a hopeful present to create historical discontinuity between the two (Teeger and Vinitzky-Seroussi 2007: 64). The museum also frames a oneness around Nelson Mandela that enhances a consensus narrative and aids in legitimating the present. Mandela survived the harsh realities of the difficult past and at the same time responded to this traumatic past by celebrating the new South Africa, thus metaphorically positing a leap in time and a discrete break and historical discontinuity between apartheid and post-apartheid South Africa; this break fits with the reimagined nation concept and with a consensus rather than conflict narrative (Teeger and Vinitzky-Seroussi 2007: 67).These authors argue that by focusing on Mandela and his political party, the African National Congress (ANC), and limiting others' contributions the museum constructs a memory of the struggle where the ANC's vision of resolving the difficult past seems obvious and inevitable, and the museum mnemonically socializes patrons to view the past and the present through a narrative lens of current consensus and historical discontinuity. The museum encourages patrons to forget the divisiveness of the past by presenting a narrative highlighting reconciliation, forgiveness, good will, and acceptance of the past (Teegar and Vinitzky-Seroussi 2007).

Arlene Stein (2009) observes changes in the collective memory of the Holocaust in the United States, showing that in the early post-war years, before the Holocaust was named and widely acknowledged and the diagnosis of post traumatic stress emerged, survivors of Hitler's genocide struggled to tell their stories in a world where people did not wish to hear and often silenced them. Before widespread Holocaust consciousness and before recognition of the role storytelling plays in helping survivors of trauma refashion a sense of self and do narrative work to get through their traumatic experiences, Holocaust survivors in order to avoid stigma had to remain largely silent about their past and create a biographical discontinuity between their past and present selves (Stein 2009: 58). Only after survivors created backstage identity communities that they later brought frontstage collectively did a Holocaust consciousness emerge and a new narrative of redemption replace the stigma of Holocaust narratives, delivering them from collective silence and forgetting into collective memory and remembrance (Stein 2009).

Eviatar Zerubavel (2003) develops a sociomental topography of the past focusing on how people remember it as members of social groups, not simply as individuals. He refers to these communities of memory as "mnemonic communities." Zerubavel analyzes constructions of historical continuity and the ways mnemonic communities collectively shape their pasts. He observes social sites of memory such as history texts, museums, memorials, ritual displays, and monuments where we identify important parts of the past that are to be commemorated and remembered. He emphasizes that some periods of the past are heavily articulated, highlighted, and commemoratively celebrated while others are virtually commemoratively empty. The past is unevenly distributed chronologically with some time periods weighing far more heavily than others (Zerubavel 2003: 29).

Zerubavel also focuses on discursive continuity and the ways that communities use collective memory as a strategic resource to bridge the past and the present. Communities and individuals often symbolically shrink commemoratively empty time periods and expand highly monumental time periods, making the latter appear much closer to the present or part of a plotline or trajectory leading to the present. Daniel Petrin (2014) shows, for instance, that militia members construct a history that bridges the American Revolution and the early United States Republic with the present as a form of "historical capital" that ties them to the heroes of the early American Revolution and omits a vast expanse of United States history. Anastacia Schulhoff (2010) shows similarly how Native American storytellers bridge themselves with tribal pasts, engaging in a "temporal shift" that allows them to claim the past as a part of their present identities and to amplify those aspects of the past that are most valued in the present. Temporal shifting allows individuals to immediately align the past and the present, by making a role switch from the past to the present and integrating the two, while skipping the historical space in between. Both militias and Native American storytellers link the distant past to the present while essentially cutting out the long, "empty" history in between the more distant past and the present. Zerubavel (2003: 52–3) discusses discursive continuity both at the macro level of societal and group histories and at the micro level of individual biographies, noting that people try to bridge historical gaps and connect a past history or a past self to the present reality or the present self. Bridging our present selves to ancestors brings the past and the present closer together (Zerubavel 2003: 55–81; 2012 81–2). Shifts and compressions of time between the past and the present are general temporal strategies observed across the cognitive variation of the particular historical events that communities remember and forget.

The specific uses of the past in the present are highly variable, while strategies of using the past in the present, such as bridging to the pasts that fit current identity concerns or framing oneness to make events more culturally resonant in the present (as we saw in the memories of Rosa Parks and Nelson Mandela), are general across cases. Time matters not only in the past but in the present. Timing and the sequence of events also matter.

Timing frames and time sequencing

Time framing and time sequencing of events shape perceptions, especially moral perceptions of an issue or event. Kathleen Lowney and James Holstein (2003) analyze how television talk shows construct victim and villain archetypes out of moral situations and how they sequence the appearance of victims and villains to channel audience reactions and prime their audiences. Talk shows draw upon familiar archetypes of victim and villain as identity templates for their guests and provide uniquely embodied, yet recognizable and familiar, stock characters that generate emotion and excitement among audiences. Lowney and Holstein (2003) demonstrate that talk shows first use affective framing devices such as titles, opening statements, introductions, and a narrative verbal framing of the issue at hand. These framings prime the audience to view the issue in a certain way, highlighting the moral framework they are to use and what they should attend to (and therefore also what nuances are morally irrelevant or not worth attending to). Talk shows sequence the appearance of victims and villains, starting with the story's "victim" sitting on stage telling their version of events without the presence of the "villain"; by the time the villain is walked out on a runway the audience has already been primed with the story's details, and he or she is paraded for the audience to view as a miscreant, troubled identity spectacle. Lowney and Holstein demonstrate that talk shows sequence the appearance of victims first, followed by villains, as a way of morally framing and constructing clear victims and clear villains for the audience.

Karen Cerulo (1998) analyzes how storytellers' narrative sequencing of stories about violence follow cultural scripts and sequential plotlines according to whether the narrator wants to portray the violence as heinous and deviant or normal and acceptable. She identifies four informational sequences by which storytellers narrate accounts of violence. These include victim sequences (presenting violence from the perspective of the injured party), performer sequences (unfolding the story and presenting violence from the perspective of the person who commits it), contextual sequences (emphasizing the circumstances of the violent act), and doublecasting sequences (highlighting an individual who plays a dual role as both victim and perpetrator). She observes that storytellers emphasize victim sequences for accounts of heinous violence, performer sequences for accounts of justifiable violence, and contextual or doublecasting sequences for accounts of ambiguous violence. Cerulo finds that sequencing has a strong influence on evaluations of violent acts about whose rightness or wrongness there is low moral consensus. The implications of this cognitive finding are interesting to consider in cases such as the 2012 United States one where neighborhood watchman George Zimmerman was acquitted of killing unarmed black teenager Trayvon Martin. In cases such as this, where the shooter is the only surviving witness to the entire incident, witness testimony is constrained to unfold from a performer sequence.

Applying a similar time-sequence understanding to apologies, Karen Cerulo and Janet Ruane (2014) analyze 183 public apologies of the rich and famous spanning from October 2000 to October 2012. They employ a regression analysis, using several offender and victim characteristics and apology discursive and sequential styles as their independent variables and public forgiveness as the dependent variable. They break up apologies into five discursive styles (denial, evasion, reduction, corrective action, and mortification) and five sequential structures (victim-driven, offender-driven, action-ownership, context-driven, and double-casting). These sequential structures follow closely those Cerulo identified in stories of violence. These authors found that public forgiveness for apologies was closely linked to discursive characteristics of the apologies, especially the time-sequenced structuring of the apologies. Effective apologies followed time sequences that appeared to cognitively prime the public, creating associative links to established cultural scripts of atonement, while apologies that failed tended to violate the sequential scripts most easily associated with atonement. In particular, Cerulo and Ruane found that the first thing that the person said in seeking forgiveness primed an audience for particular conclusions. Entry points could focus on the victim, the actor, the act, or the context. Apologies that use the victim as an entry point and end with atonement in the form of remorse, corrective action, or returning to the victim are victim-centered atonement scripts in this analysis, while apologies that use the actor, act, or context as entry points with remorse or corrective action as exit points are victim-free atonement scripts. The authors found that victim-driven entries combined with atonement exits focused on corrective action, remorse, or the victim were the most successful apologies in receiving forgiveness. Atonement exits that were not properly primed with victim-centered entries usually failed to win public forgiveness (Cerulo and Ruane 2014).

Dan Ryan (2006) examines the cognitive, cultural, and moral meanings of time in the context of notification norms – norms about who gets notified in what sequential order after significant events. Notification norms are social rules that govern information transmission on the basis of the role obligations of the participants. The possession of information, Ryan argues, is accompanied by a distinctly normative feeling of obligation to inform (and not inform) the appropriate people in the appropriate manner, at the appropriate time, and in the proper order. A complex array of variables factors into notification norms; with whom and when one shares what kind of information is tied to the nature of the social relationship between parties and the type of news shared. The sequencing of notification also varies depending on the kind of information being shared. For highly monumental or marked information, one medium may be used to simply pre-notify someone – that is, to tell them that the notifier would like to notify them of something (Ryan 2006: 239). Good news and bad news are often pre-notified in different ways. Good news often arrives quickly, even in public via an interruption or someone running down the hall, while bad news may require escorting one to a private area, asking "are you sitting down?" or the appearance of a medium that is itself the message, such as a "pink slip," a "dear John or Jane letter," or the arrival of uniformed officers at one's doorstep (Ryan 2006: 242). Meta-notification is also used to frame and shape social meanings. Ryan notes, for instance, that meta-notifications can be used to bracket the deviance of violating a notification norm or going outside traditional network rules, or to define the circle of insiders and outsiders who are or are not entitled to be "in the loop" about shared information. A sociology of notification timing and sequence illustrates social relationships and social rules and the underlying cultural rules that organize them.

Doing time: the sociocognitive meanings and manipulations of time

Much like money and meaning, discussed in chapter 3, all time is not equal and identical. Cognitively, people experience time as an event-centered experience rather than a strictly chronological or clock-centered one. Organizations and subcultures shape the cultural experience of time at both work and play and in the spaces in between.

Focusing on the sociocultural constructions of work and leisure time, Jeremy Schulz (2010) compares the use of evening time by elite professionals in Paris, Oslo, and San Francisco, demonstrating that how evening time is understood and the meaning given to it vary significantly by national cultures (in Paris and Oslo) and by organizational cultures (in San Francisco). In Paris, the evening hours are territorialized at the macrocultural level as working time for elite professionals, and working late is therefore implicitly mandated as a way of establishing elite status group identities; in Oslo, the evening hours are seen as private or family time, and thus workers are expected to leave the office much earlier; and in San Francisco, temporal boundaries between work and private time are controlled at the level of the organization rather than the macrocultural level (Schulz 2010). These experiences and meanings of evening time indicate that how we use time, even "personal time," is social.

Eviatar Zerubavel (1979) examines the organizational use of time and patterning of schedules in hospitals, demonstrating the distinct "sociotemporal order" that a hospital imposes on organizational life and the different ways that time is cognitively and morally used according to one's organizational and social role. He also notes the importance of the division between "private time" and "public time." Within the temporal constraints that organizations and groups place on our time and privacy, we may create "temporal niches" of autonomy (Fine 1990) or private-time "niches of inaccessibility" (Zerubavel 1979) where we are momentarily unavailable. Some empirical examples of this in sociological analyses of work can be found in Michael Burawoy's (1979) *Manufacturing Consent* and Paul Willis' (1981) *Learning to Labor*.

The experience of time shows cognitive variation by occupation and by subculture. Benjamin Snyder (2012) shows how the occupational culture of truck drivers, for instance, experiences time as highly spatialized and context-dependent, unlike standardized clock time. Truck drivers must professionalize the rhythms of their bodies and adapt them to the unpredictable rhythms of their occupation. Time is money for truckers only in how it relates to space, so more accurately, Snyder argues, space is money and time is used and regulated to serve maximum movement in space. Industry and safety regulations prevent truck drivers from working "on their own time," but the drivers find ways to account for time that allow them to transfer awake time to official "sleep time" when needed, and to transfer time to and from other realms.

Unlike shift workers, truck drivers become "rhythm experts," developing a specialized ability to link the mechanical beat of clock time, which governs their regulations and the appointment times of shippers and receivers, with the complex and irregular patchwork of rhythms that affect the speed of freight. The challenge of linking abstract clock time to the concrete reality of moving freight quickly falls upon the truck driver's body, and the driver develops body rhythms such as sleep cycles, shifts in adrenaline, and digestive cycles to convert clock time into efficient freight time (Snyder 2012).

Gary Fine (1990) analyzes organizational time and temporal demands placed on workers in a restaurant kitchen. Organizational demands affect temporal order and this affects how workers experience their work and the passage of time. Temporal constraints act as a form of social control, but workers can also use time to resist and undercut elements of organizational control and achieve individual autonomy through creating temporal niches (Fine 1990). Among cooks, he found that tempo and rhythm were important and that workers desired balanced temporal conditions that were neither too rushed nor too slow. Days with too much pressure did not give workers enough time to maintain quality and organization, and they experienced being out of control and disorganized. Days that were too slow, however, did not allow them to get into a rhythm or tempo of work and this led to their being distracted, to too many side-involvements, and to a lack of focus. The experience of time in restaurant work, Fine observes, is not structured by the clock but by events such as lunch, dinner, or banquets. The effects of an organization's temporal environment are most dramatically witnessed when the system is loaded to its capacity; for restaurants this is the rush, but other organizations such as emergency rooms, airline counters, toll booths, fire stations, and theater aisles have equivalent kinds of temporal rushes (Fine 1990: 107). The rush is temporal but also physical and emotional for the workers. Fine (1990: 108) draws a passage from McPhee's (1979) *New Yorker* article on chefs to show that the rush, as a distinct feature of restaurant life, has a demanding tempo and associated rhythm that cause the worker to get into a zone and operate on automatic pilot, moving into the realm of automatic rather than deliberate cognition:

> As his usual day accelerates toward dinner time, the chef's working rhythms become increasingly intense, increasingly kinetic, and finally all but automatic. His experience becomes his action. He just cruises, functioning by conditioned response. "You cook unconsciously," he says. "You know what you're going to do and you do it. When problems come along your brain spits out the answer." (McPhee 1979: 78, cited in Fine 1990: 108)

Fine's own informants expressed similar ideas about the physical and cognitive experiences of the rush. Several cooks mentioned that their rush reactions are automatic and that they do not consciously plan or control their behavior or emotions as they get caught up in the tempo, rhythm, and "flow" experience of the work.

Rik Scarce (2002) analyzes the way jail inmates "do time" and control time through a host of cognitive feats. These include ignoring diurnal cycles by rolling entire weeks into single days and using a variety of strategies to make time pass more quickly. Scarce breaks up inmate time into four types: administrative time (the jail's formal, bureaucratic, structural time, for example lockdowns, food service times, and changes in guard assignments), inmate time (the times when inmates congregate and interact, and their communal manipulation of time), individual time (a single inmate's cognitive, behavioral, and personal manipulations of time), and street time (the time in which families, friends, attorneys, and courts operate). Street time happens on the classical clock and calendar time, which has very different rhythms than jail time. One challenge for inmates is to manage the disjunction between jail times and street time. Inmates limit the street time of clocks and calendars for self-survival and recognize jail as an overwhelming current present; neither the past nor the future outside the jail can interfere with the self-sustaining work of the present (Scarce 2002: 316). Jail inmates, he argues, are most successful at doing time when they accept time's reconstruction and adopt a new rhythm, finding ways to mentally transform weeks into hours and months into days. Scarce demonstrates that there are distinctly subcultural ways that inmates do time and that, in fact, inmates who emphasize street time too much are disrespected as cognitive deviants whose failure to live primarily in jail time and keep street time out is a problem to be dealt with.

Judith Halberstam (2005) brings identity and social standpoint into the experience of time, identifying "queer time" as a temporality that develops as an alternative to and in opposition to the institutions of family, reproduction, and heterosexuality. Queer time produces temporal logics that lie outside paradigmatic markers of heteronormative life experience such as marriage and reproduction, and it is unscripted by mainstream conventions of family, child rearing, and inheritance. Noting that conceptions such as reproductive time, family time, and industrial time are not experienced as cultural universals, Halberstam points to experiences of time that fall outside these constructs and where other life events center temporal experience. Some queer subcultures also often live outside the logic of capital accumulation and occupy the hours that others have abandoned; this too represents a queer time that destabilizes and stands outside the normative organization of time and space (Halberstam 2005: 21). Because time is largely experienced socially through the reckoning of events and through the pace and experience of social life, queer time is set apart from heteronormative time, as different events and experiences center one's temporal attentions and inattentions.

Michael Flaherty (2003) conducted semi-structured interviews with 398 subjects, asking them to describe the ways that they create or suppress particular kinds of temporal experience or do "time work." He identifies five common ways that individuals manipulate and exercise control over time. These include manipulating duration, frequency, sequence, timing, and allocation. Efforts to influence duration consist of trying to make an interval longer or shorter than its objective clock or calendar length. For instance, someone may try to slow down pleasurable vacation time by stopping to take it all in and reflecting on the here and now, or speed up unpleasant time by filling it in with distracting activities designed to make the time go faster. Manipulating frequency involves controlling the rate at which something is experienced; for example, someone choosing to only golf occasionally so that the time spent golfing feels marked as special. Manipulating temporal sequence involves customizing the time order in which events occur. Manipulating timing involves seeking the optimal time for an event. And manipulating allocation involves specifically setting up times for events; for example, one may specifically allocate time to ensure that one spends some time for pleasure in addition to spending time managing all the tasks that are required in a day or week.

Although the subjects in Flaherty's study conveyed individual strategies for manipulating time, they invoked these within cultural guidelines and prescriptions about time. They treated time metaphorically, for instance, as a commodity that was to be "saved" rather than "wasted." This metaphor of time as a commodity came from the larger cultural context. Similarly, time work was conditioned by organizational context. Employees and students are encouraged to use time efficiently, but the regimentation and structuring of time create compensatory desires to carve out "free time." Organizational contexts facilitate individual forms of adaptation and cultivate predictable kinds of temporal deviance; carving an academic calendar into structured semesters and deadlines, for instance, creates conditions for creative temporal extension such as incompletes (Flaherty 2003: 31). Organizations, he argues, develop their own temporal cultures, which individuals adapt to and at times creatively manipulate. Finally, time work is also influenced by relationships and social networks. Relations place demands on our time that compete with other temporal arrangements, and they also attempt to place their own controls on the ways that we manipulate time. Flaherty (2003) finds overall that most time work is compensatory. People exercise their temporal agency largely within cultural, organizational, and relational constraints and thus maintain power relations and the status quo while playing with the temporal margins and boundaries.

Conclusion

This chapter has examined memory and time as collective enterprises. Our conceptions of the past are patterned by the present and shaped by analogical reasoning. Analogical reasoning often draws analogies to the eventful, that which stands out, and is monumental and socially marked. This can lead to memories that are distorted by the over-recognition of the dramatic and noteworthy and the underrepresentation of the quotidian and mundane. Memory also develops into coherent narratives, narratives that involve filling in gaps, making stories fit with the present, and editing out and ignoring events that do not fit. Memory can have intended or unintended instrumental uses for groups and communities. With memories we also use and construct time and can metaphorically expand or contract decades and time periods, so that "eventful" periods can expand to fill a large amount of historical space, while "uneventful" ones can contract or be bracketed completely.

Time sequencing in organizational settings and in narrative accounts can shape social perceptions and moral accountability. The location of events and individuals in time and the sequencing of events and social actors can significantly influence how they are perceived. Time often has a distinctly moral dimension. Donald Black's (2011) book *Moral Time* provocatively asserts this in the title. He refers to time as the dynamic dimension of reality and social time as the dynamic dimension of social reality, and employs the idea of social time to refer to whenever social life moves. As Black (2011: 5) explains:

> Social time moves when someone increases or decreases intimacy with someone else, achieves more or less than someone else, or accepts or rejects an idea of someone else. It moves when someone allows a relationship to weaken, disobeys an authority, or converts to another religion. It moves when strangers become acquaintances, when a marriage begins or ends, when a business hires or fires an employee, and when a nation rises or falls. It moves when someone gains or loses wealth, gives birth or dies, commits a crime or punishes

a criminal, creates or criticizes a work of art, or introduces or ignores a new theory. Social time is the ceaseless movement of the social universe.

He argues that where social time moves rapidly, greater moral conflict and crime are more likely to occur than when social time moves slowly and gradually. Sudden losses of intimacy or social status, or other instances where social time moves in large, rapid steps rather than slow, incremental ones, are likely to lead to greater conflict and violence; and violence itself is an abrupt, rapid movement of social time that often leads to more of such violence and movement. Notifications and their timing, which Dan Ryan discusses in his cognitive sociology of notification norms, are about significant movements in social time and are themselves minor movements that can develop into larger movements of time when notification norms are violated and responded to.

How we reckon time is often event-centered rather than chronologically centered. We experience its movement in socially and culturally patterned pulses and flows. It speeds up, slows down, and moves in and out of focus as we apprehend it in organizational and interpersonal contexts. Time exerts social control over our lives, but we also manipulate and find ways to creatively control time.

Conclusion

The diverse range of empirical topics covered in this book illustrates that culture and cognition run the gamut of sociological subfields including deviance, race and ethnicity, sexualities, economic sociology, the sociology of risk, gender, criminology, and environmental sociology. Culture and cognition are everywhere. Given this, how can sociologists fully capitalize on understanding the complex interplay between culture and cognition? What issues in culture and cognition should sociologists attend to? What are the possibilities and challenges for the future sociological study of culture and cognition? What roles will the cultural, the social, and the neuropsychological play in our analyses? Where does social action fit into cognition? Where is power, a central concern of many sociologists, and how does it operate in culture and cognition? To address these questions I first focus on the ongoing and sometimes spirited debates among sociologists about questions such as how culture enters into cognition, how we use culture in action, and how to access culture as researchers. Then I discuss contributions and possibilities for the cultural sociology of cognition for understanding (1) cognition and social action, (2) cognition, power, and social inequalities, and (3) general social patterns.

First of all, there are increasing debates about the nature of culture and cognition and the future direction of its study within sociology. These debates are tied to methodological issues of observing culture and to theoretical questions about how we

171

internalize culture, as scholars in the neuropsychology-focused Bourdieusian interdisciplinary tradition raise challenges to other approaches to studying culture and cognition. These challenges and others' responses to them help to illustrate key issues and ongoing debates in the field.

The embodied/neuropsychology challenge to social and cultural approaches

Within the sociology of culture and cognition, scholars emphasizing practical individual actor theories integrated with neuropsychological dual-process models of cognition have developed an emerging body of criticism challenging collective representations, symbolic interactionist, social mindscapes, and cultural toolkit approaches. At the core of these criticisms are questions about how much shared culture we actually internalize and whether our conscious thoughts and explanations for behavior have much connection to the ways we actually act and draw upon culture to think and to respond to situations. Some variant of these criticisms can be found emanating from several neuropsychology-oriented cognitivist sociologists (see Bergesen 2004a; 2004b; Turner 2007; Vaisey 2008; 2009; Lizardo and Strand 2010; Martin 2010; 2011; Lizardo forthcoming). I highlight and discuss Omar Lizardo and Steven Vaisey's criticisms as two representative exemplars of this body of critique.

Omar Lizardo (forthcoming) argues that the study of culture and cognition is divided between a "classical" approach that conceives of culture as internalized by individuals and a grounded, "embodied" approach to cognition that is tightly linked to practical action and primary experience as individuals interact with material environments. He describes as classical the cultural approaches exemplified in modern exemplars such as Alexander and Zerubavel, and found in much of cultural sociology, as based on the idea of mental or collective representations that people internalize through socialization within a culture to organize their perceptual experience. These approaches, he argues, assume that

172

people share cultural contents such as beliefs and worldviews because they internalize those contents from the larger culture. This, he contends, unnecessarily separates bodily, sensory stimulation and mental, abstract, conceptual structure, and falsely assumes that "sensory stimulation (and practical action in the world of objects) . . . is not sufficient for the formation of durable mental categories that generalize from experience" (Lizardo forthcoming: 7). John Levi Martin (2011) similarly argues for a theory of practical action in the world of objects, asserting that there is no need for third person explanations of causes of action because the causal power in how individuals act is located in the heads of individuals (what they know, what they want, what they choose, and how they act). These cognitive sociologists emphasize the embodied minds of individual actors as the source for accessing culture's fragmented role in thought and human action. Lizardo advocates for embodied cognition theories based on a dual-process model, arguing that "proponents of embodied approaches to the culture-cognition link propose that the meaningful component of mental experience is primarily made up of repeated, embodied *simulations* over previous experiences" consistent with dual-process models of learning and memory (Lizardo forthcoming: 13).

In "Socrates, Skinner, and Aristotle: Three Ways of Thinking About Culture in Action," Stephen Vaisey (2008) offers a related critique of other culture and cognition traditions; he uses Socrates and Skinner as analogies to describe the two dominant ways that sociologists conceive of people using culture in action. The "Socrates model" of social action (which he uses to typify collective representations approaches), he argues, assumes that people acquire values through cultural socialization and that these values shape how they act and behave. The "Skinner model" (which he uses to represent cultural toolkit approaches), he asserts, avoids the socialization explanation and instead focuses on the action-shaping power of external environments, emphasizing that culture's primary role is to justify actions after the fact and to make sense of constraints and pressures that cause people to act differently from their stated values. He argues for the understanding and use of a dual-process model where humans have two basic cognitive systems: one "fast, 'hot,' automatic and unconscious" and one "slow, 'cool', reflexive, and conscious" (Vaisey 2008: 607), with the main action on the fast track.

In his influential article on dual-process cognition, Vaisey (2009) advances this critique further, arguing that culture is not accessed and deployed like a tool, but rather "as deep, largely unconscious networks of neural associations that facilitate perception, interpretation and action" (Vaisey 2009: 1686). He emphasizes empirical findings and ideas in other fields such as cognitive psychology to advance a model of two levels of consciousness: a discursive, surface-level consciousness accessed by talk and deliberation, and a deeper, more visceral and embodied consciousness that strongly shapes action. He advocates a neuropsychology approach that privileges automatic cognition as the central way that we think, employing Jonathan Haidt's (2001; 2005) metaphor of a rider on the back of an elephant to illustrate that the unconscious is really in charge:

> The rider, who represents our conscious processes, is the part of ourselves that we know best – she can talk, reason, and explain things to our heart's content. Yet, for the most part, she is not in charge. The elephant, which stands for our automatic processes, is larger and stronger than the rider and is totally unencumbered by the need, or the ability, to justify itself. Driven by the simple mechanism of attraction and repulsion, the elephant goes where it wants. As the metaphor implies, the rider is no match for the elephant in a direct struggle. While the rider usually only pretends to be in control, she can slowly train the elephant over time or perhaps trick it into going a different way. But in any given moment, the elephant – practical consciousness – is usually in charge. For the most part, this is quite advantageous. Having a durable practical consciousness means that rather than having to weigh pros and cons on a daily basis (e.g., "Should I continue to value hard work today?"), we can leave some things up to our habits of judgment and evaluation. Having to consciously reevaluate our political leanings, religious commitments, hygienic habits, and life goals on a daily basis would be cognitively overwhelming. (Vaisey 2009: 1683)

Vaisey portrays the elephant metaphor as a useful one for understanding how society "gets into" human beings that is consistent with Bourdieu's idea of habitus. In this view, culture takes two different forms: one that is conscious, deliberative, and accessible but is primarily connected to accounts and justifications, not a motivator of social action, and another that is unconscious, automatic, and closely connected to social action. This argument has significant methodological and theoretical implications.

Methodologically, proponents of dual-process cognition are skeptical of interviews, suggesting that what people say are only accounts (often inconsistent) and do not access culture at the unconscious level where most of it resides. Vaisey (2009: 1688–9) advocates for surveys because respondents given fixed choices rely more on cognitive efficiency than deliberation when responding, and this form of response is closer to the automatic, visceral cognition we use in everyday decision-making processes. Martin (2010: 240) argues more provocatively against interviews, asserting that "if we want to learn about culture, the last thing we should do is to conduct in-depth interviews, any more than we would expect to strike gold by asking them for whatever change is in their pockets." In this strong dual-process view, there is little to be gained by talking to the rider when the sociological gold is in understanding the elephant that is really in charge. These theorists argue that their critiques have significant, even radical, implications for the ways that we study culture and sociology. They not only point to a new and interesting way for sociologists to understand culture and cognition that aligns more closely with cognitive neuropsychology studies, but also maintain that this renders much of what sociologists currently do untenable (e.g. Lizardo forthcoming). If as it turns out we do not internalize shared culture, or much shared culture, as most sociological theories assume, and if we do not acquire culture through socialization, shared symbols, or language, then most of sociology is doing it wrong.

These challenges have contributed to interesting and important debates over how culture is internalized, how sociologists should study culture, and where culture is located in the thoughts and actions of people. In response to these criticisms, other scholars of culture and cognition have advanced two forms of critical response.

Critical responses to the embodied/ neuropsychology challenge to cultural and social approaches

Two forms of critical response to the critique by Vaisey and Lizardo and their reliance on a dual-process model of cognition are that (1) they make the central questions about mechanics and individual-level, social-psychological data and that, while interesting, this significantly limits the scope of sociological inquiry and forgoes interesting observations at other levels of cultural observation; and (2) they overstate the separation between discursive and practical consciousness and undertheorize their relationship, ceding nearly all of the ground to "the elephant" of practical consciousness and automatic cognition.

The first counterchallenge relates to the embodied neuroscience view that sociologists of culture and cognition should study thought only close to and inside the individual heads where it actually happens. Although it is true that thinking itself happens in individual brains, this does not automatically suggest that the individual is necessarily the best or only unit of analysis from which to understand culture and cognition. Critics of this methodological challenge emphasize its underlying individualism and argue for other units of analysis such as institutions, situations, or structures. Ann Swidler (2008: 617), in response to Vaisey (2008), argues, for instance, that

> cultural meanings are organized and brought to bear at the collective and social, not the individual level ... The question of how culture shapes action can't be answered by figuring out better models of how it operates in the heads of individuals, however interesting (and however difficult) that might be; instead we need better structures that determine how cultural meanings will be organized, and when and where particular sets of meanings will be brought to bear on experience.

Swidler argues that Vaisey's idea that we have deep moral intuitions that we employ automatically in practical action still requires us to examine how those moral intuitions are grounded in a cultural context shaped by institutions and situations; for example, while dual-process cognition is likely to explain the deeply held and automatic moral intuitions by which most Americans are immediately and viscerally revolted by the idea of eating dogs, the sociologist may want to study how the collective cultural institution of pet ownership shapes these culturally specific meanings that affect cognition. Swidler (2008: 617) maintains, for example, that Vaisey's interesting point about the "neurological fact that people have strong intuitive responses that guide their action (more than does their conscious cognition)" still leaves open how those fast intuitions and automatic responses are shaped, and "what role the things we normally think of as 'culture' play in shaping them." Swidler suggests that while looking deep for the motivations for individual action is one important task, it moves the scope of analysis away from the broadly social contexts in which these actions occur.

Even if most cognition and moral intuitions are deep in the brain, some critics of Vaisey's neuropsychology approach suggest that it is not clear that trying to access the individual brain through quick survey responses is the means of observing these intuitions in action. Ethnographers Colin Jerolmack and Shamus Khan (2014) argue that the best way to observe the activation of cultural schemas and unconscious dispositions is not by trying to access individual brains through gathering data at the individual level of quick-response self-reports, but by going to the actual situations and relationships in which individuals are embedded and where they execute, rather than provide accounts or responses for, their cognitive decisions and actions. Matthew Norton (2014), in the collective representations tradition, argues that much of what is sociologically significant about meaning is determined in relations and interactions between actors and in cultural systems, not in the heads of actors, and that as such *situations*, not individual actors, should be the sociologist's primary unit of analysis. Norton uses social action in the widespread social and institutional change response to the 1858 Great Stink of London sewerage crisis as a case study to argue for situations as the unit of analysis for culture in action. He argues that trans-situational codes and structures of meaning shaped cognition and action and that actors in multiple situations, spread across geography and institutional location, arrived at similar meanings of the Great Stink as a signifying danger because three cultural mechanisms – pollution (the perception of stink as dangerous), guilt, and purification – were linked. He, suggests, therefore, that culture can be studied as "a system of meanings that actors laminate into the situations they face through interactive processes of interpretation and performance" (Norton 2014: 162). These scholars attempt to locate the link between culture and action in relationships and situations, things they suggest cannot be studied when the individual is isolated as an individual outside the context of their cognitive decisions and action.

The second form of critical response to the embodied neuroscience challenge centers on the two-track, dual-process model of cognition itself. Critics of this dual-process model argue that its proponents overstate the divide between the conscious discursive and subconscious automatic tracks of thought. Allison Pugh (2013: 47) argues that the two-track model shows a discomfort with the incoherence and contradictions of culture in practice and resolves this contradiction by moving incoherence to the surface, suggesting that people are only contradictory on the surface where it is visible, but very coherent in their internalized dispositions at the deep level of practical consciousness. She argues, however, that it may not be a problem that people report contradictory motivations (that this may be a multivocal explanation of social life rather than radical incoherence), and that they braid together paradoxes and incorporate change at the conscious level.

In defense of interviews and accessing cognition through talk and language, Pugh highlights four types of information available in in-depth interviews: the honorable, the schematic, the visceral, and meta-feelings, each with its own important analytic uses for understanding how individuals use culture. Honorable information is information where interviewees frame their answers to present themselves in a favorable light. It is the impression management work that interview subjects engage in to present themselves as honorable, noble, moral, or authentic and is the in-depth interview parallel to survey research's "socially desirable response bias" (Pugh 2013: 50). Examples include simple belief statements or folk theories about how the world works or simple answers to factual questions. Schematic information is interview information accessed through language, metaphors, jokes, turns of phrase, and discursive innovations to convey the frameworks through which people view the world. Interviewers can probe this kind of information by asking interviewees to elaborate and provide specific examples of stated claims; these examples provide self-constructed windows into ethnographic details that can then be analyzed and interpreted in relation to honorable information (Pugh 2013: 50). Visceral information includes emotions, facial expressions, sighs, pauses, or when an interview informant's normally clear language becomes halting or convoluted. Pugh notes that informants do not just answer questions about where they went to school, for instance, but also tell researchers what things were uncomfortable or horrifying or joyful, and thus provide access to their emotional frameworks and reactions. Meta-feelings are how interviewees feel about their feelings. Meta-feelings, Pugh suggests, offer an account of how individuals are embedded in culture because they measure the distance between how someone feels and how they feel they ought to feel. All four kinds of interview data reflect on culture and each illustrates different points in the process of how culture shapes action (Pugh 2013).

Pugh argues that, rather than separate out messy and contradictory discursive consciousness as useless "noise" or mere self-serving rationalization from the consistency of practical consciousness, researchers should analytically mine these inconsistencies. The honorable serves as a cultural barometer of what the interviewee believes to be desirable, but the other three levels of data that come forth in in-depth interviews provide contradictory cultural accounts that access the interviewees' emotional landscape and bring a broader social dimension to individual motivation. Pugh (2013: 46) challenges the radical separation implied in the two-track model of cognition, arguing ultimately that sociologists need to mine the connection between the discursive and the practical:

> By relying on an image of two unlinked processes ... cognitive cul-
> turalists strike an almost gleeful note as they chronicle the distance
> between them, portraying with vivid fervor our very alienation from
> ourselves. The image of a rider and elephant is a dyadic model that
> emphasizes their ironic estrangement, that mocks, however gently,
> the rider's misguided sense of self-efficacy, and ultimately does not
> ask where the elephant comes from. Instead of the rider and elephant,
> then, we need other metaphors that propose how consciousness is
> related and produced.

She acknowledges the importance of the distinction between automatic practical cognition and deliberative discursive cognition, but
suggests that the analytic value in the distinction is best found in
mining their interactions.

Showing a similar interest in the relationship between the two
styles of cognition, Luis Vila-Henninger (2014) employs insights
from cognitive neuroscience to argue for an "expanded dual-
process model that addresses how and when conscious mental
systems override and interact with subconscious mental systems
in the use of cultural ends for decision-making." Agreeing with
Vaisey and Lizardo on the importance of bringing more insights
from cognitive neuroscience into sociological models of culture, he
argues, however, that their choice of Haidt's (2001; 2005) intuitionist model places too much emphasis on subconscious systems
of decision-making. There is growing evidence within cognitive
neuroscience that Haidt's model, foundational for the sociological
dual-process model, is not a wholly accurate or complete charac-
terization of moral decision-making (Vila-Henninger 2014: 4).

Vila-Henninger draws upon two models of moral judgment
from cognitive neuroscience that critique and modify Haidt's
model. One is Joshua Greene and colleagues' (2004), which
synthesizes rational dual-process models and Haidt's intuitionist
dual-process model. In this model, based on fMRIs of brain activity
around moral judgment, "the causal role of utilitarian reasoning
and emotional response, and by extension discursive and practical consciousness, is socially mediated" (Vila-Henninger 2014:
12–13). This model is important, Vila-Henninger argues, because
it shows how utilitarian reasoning and cognitive override affect

decision-making. The second cognitive neuroscience model of moral reasoning he draws on is Jorge Moll and colleagues' (2005) single-process model. This model looks at "action/event sequence knowledge" that corresponds with activity in the prefrontal cortex (PFC), the perception of social cues, and the processing of social characteristics to produce social perceptual knowledge located around the temporal lobes, and motivation located in a variety of subcortical neural areas. This model shows that activity in these three parts of the brain interacts and that conscious decision-making plays a bigger role than Haidt's model implies:

> Automatic responses, beliefs, and more general knowledge are all utilized to create meaning, interpret situations, generate motives and determine actions. It is not an issue of whether habits or practical schemes have superiority. Instead, activity in different areas of the brain interact and use resources available to them [*sic*] to interpret and define a situation. This process, which draws upon conscious and unconscious resources, is itself a conscious process in which the agent actively interprets and assesses a situation, makes judgments about potential outcomes of the situation, and then decides on the most appropriate action to pursue given his/her assessment of the situation. Thus, while habits and dispositions are important, they are not the sole or even the driving neural function in moral decision-making. Instead, they are one set of resources among many that is used to define a situation and help agents make decisions about how to behave and pursue their goals. (Vila-Henninger 2014: 15)

This model, Vila-Henninger argues, "not only shifts the emphasis of the causal role of cultural ends in moral decision-making to an interaction between conscious and subconscious processes, but specifies a concrete, empirically-supported set of mechanisms for this process." This challenges the radical split between discursive and practical consciousness advanced by Haidt and posited by sociological dual-process models of culture in action. On the basis of these two more recent cognitive neuroscience models, Vila-Henninger proposes a change in metaphor:

> Given this expansion, it seems that the apt metaphor is not a rider on top of an elephant, but a driver in a car. The car, or subconscious

processes, are [*sic*] socially influenced and allow the driver, or conscious processes, the possibility of switching to "cruise control." However, cruise control is never enough on its own, as the driver is responsible to [*sic*] deciding when and at what speed to activate or deactivate cruise control. The car is also able to indicate issues that the driver was not aware of, such as low gas or engine problems. The driver can follow these indicators, or impulses, or ignore them at his/her risk, which is often mediated by the social situation. The driver is required to make important decisions, such as where the car is going, when to go, and how fast. These decisions are based on the driver's interpretation of the context and the signals given to him/her by the car. The car determines to a large extent what the driver can do, and is responsible for a variety of crucial actions that are beyond the driver's control. However the car is also responsible to the driver, who can inhibit or manipulate these actions, and allows him/her to accomplish goals that are feasible given the limits and capacities of the car and driver. (Vila-Henninger 2014: 17–18)

This modification maintains that practical consciousness and automatic cognition are still important, but it elevates deliberate cognition and discursive consciousness to a more significant role. Vila-Henninger (2014: 19–20) also addresses methodological debates in the sociology of culture and cognition, noting that both interviews and fixed-response survey methods access discursive consciousness by measuring the retrieval of declarative memory through two different forms; interviews capture declarative memories through free recall, while surveys do so through recognition. He suggests that conscious declarative memory and procedural unconscious memories both play a role and that they compete and interact in habit acquisition. With this modification, he builds on work in the neuropsychology tradition of cognitive sociology and advances the dialogue about decision-making and social action. As cognitive sociologists become increasingly engaged in cross-disciplinary connections with neuropsychology, the opportunities to consider how social conditions and situational circumstances shape what forms of cognition and recall we use become important and interesting questions.

If we accept Vila-Henninger's driver of a car as a more accurate metaphor for current neuroscience understandings of cognition than a rider on an elephant, this reinforces the case for pluralism in sociological approaches to culture and cognition. We need to understand the car that drives action, the driver that handles the car, and the traffic that the car and the driver operate in and help to constitute. At the neurological and intuitive level, it is important to understand the signals, movement, capacities, and mechanics of "the car," the influences on the car, and the limitations and choices that these place upon the driver. At the social level, it is important to understand the external influences on "the driver" and how the driver adapts to and operates in situational and interactional contexts. When does the driver exercise control and when do they put the car in cruise control? At the cultural and structural level, it is important to understand "the traffic," its patterns and flows, the shared symbols and codes that guide its flows, as well as the unwritten, interactional, informal, unstated "rules of the road" that we internalize and make use of in varying degrees and situations. All of these levels of understanding are interesting and important and worth continued sociological exploration.

Culture and cognition in sociology: prospects for studying social action, social power, and general patterns

In assessing the future of sociological research in culture and cognition, I briefly discuss them with respect to understanding (1) cognition and social action, (2) cognition, power, and social inequalities, and (3) general patterns. Here I revisit research on the different cognitive processes thematically and suggest ways that sociologists can consider culture and cognition within their own research interests. These are three issues of broad interest to sociologists whether or not they study cognition; thus their applicability through a culture and cognition lens can be of value to a wide variety of sociologists.

Conclusion

Cognition and social action

Many sociologists are interested in social action. What does a sociology of culture and cognition offer to the understanding of action? What are the relationships among culture, thought, and action? What role does action play in the sociology of culture and cognition? How do cognitive processes such as perception, boundary creation, metaphor, identity, and memory shape social action? How do sociologists of cognition relate thought to action? Should they do so at the level of the individual actor or try to assess this at some other level of culture? All these questions can be explored through studying culture and cognition.

Sociologists working at the intersections with cognitive neuroscience have developed promising contributions toward considering how even unconscious cognition motivates action. In their finding that people's moral-cultural worldviews unconsciously shaped action by determining who they associated and disassociated with over time, Vaisey and Lizardo (2010) showed that how we think eventually shapes who we think with. Gabriel Ignatow (2009) showed that members of a religious self-help group for overeaters that frequently used cleanliness metaphors maintained a more enduring bond, suggesting that the embodied metaphors the group harnessed predicted action in continuing membership and active participation in a group centered on self-improvement. Studying cognition offers the potential to see the subtle social change of network composition and social tie formation over time at the individual level where social actors make their affiliational decisions. Future research inquiries in the area of social network change might include analyzing other types of worldviews than moral ones to see what kinds of similarities are most important in causing people to affiliate. Are cultural worldviews associated with sport, musical tastes, or hobbies also likely to lead to shifts in social network composition, or does the moral aspect of moral-cultural worldviews make it a more significant part of cognitive intuitions? In addition to studying how the brain subtly shapes network connections over time, cognitive sociologists can also study how our cultural affiliations, social action, and thought styles themselves reshape the brain. Neuroplasticity, the idea that the brain is malleable by social thought and activity, provides rich avenues for continuing to explore the intersections between cognitive sociology and neuroscience. Recent research by political neuroscientists, for instance, has suggested that not only do people with different brain structures self-select into different political parties, but acting and thinking as a political partisan in a partisan environment also changes our brains (e.g. Schreiber et al. 2013).

In his analysis of why countries go to war, Philip Smith links narrative to social action, suggesting that people make sense of the world through stories, and those stories shape and motivate action. Narratives, Smith (2005: 18) argues, define actors and their motivations, indicate the trajectory of the past, suggest the consequences of future choices, align events with cultural codes, and indicate courses of action. Social action, in this view, is deeply embedded in and informed by narrative and speech acts, and wars have their roots in the ways we tell, interpret, and understand stories about events. Donileen Loseke (2009) similarly shows that a vast and heterogeneous audience can be motivated to collective action such as supporting a war when a wide array of emotion codes that structure how one should think and feel are organized to have broad cultural resonance. Structuring of discourse that deploys widely held symbolic codes and their accompanying emotion codes, and that portrays a melodrama with easily polarized cognitive evaluations and moral meanings, can, for instance, discourage disagreements and mobilize moral action.

The connection between culture, cognition, and social action can be explored at the institutional level of domestic social policy as well as foreign policy. The social meanings of the "undeserving poor" as a cultural category, as we saw in chapter 3, constrain welfare policy in the United States by taking policies that appear to benefit the "lazy" unworking poor off the table (Steensland 2006). Researchers concerned with policy issues can explore the relationship between cultural meanings and policy decisions in discourse, not only with respect to the strategic action of policymakers to try to shape relative cognitive consensus but also to understand how existing culture meanings make the implementation of some policies more tenable than that of others.

Studying the connection between culture, cognition, and action involves studying how culture shapes both social action and social inaction. Scholars of social movements have demonstrated how framing can motivate social action around a cause, but cognitive sociology may also provide insights into why many people do not join social movements or leave social problems "seen but unnoticed." Observations from a cognitive sociology of danger and safety suggest that when hazards become routine we often ignore them as they become relationally anchored in the mundane, habitual aspects of our everyday life that we take for granted. Studying inaction on changing environmental habits, voting behavior, talking about inequality, and other issues are all areas for further cognitive sociological inquiry. How do organizations and groups develop organization- and group-specific visions and blinders that channel action in certain directions and away from others?

Cognition, power, and social inequalities

Power and social inequalities are issues of central concern within much of sociology. What does a cultural sociology of cognition offer to scholars whose major interests relate to power and social inequalities?

Research on culture and cognition can be especially instructive on issues of power because it gets at subtle, often unconscious and hidden dimensions of power that are nonetheless important for thought and action. The metaphors we use without much thought, for instance, can subtly define and influence how we see the world or think about a particular problem. Otto Santa Ana (2002) illustrated the significance of metaphor in showing how the tide, flood, or "dangerous waters" metaphor for Latino immigration to the United States structures how people in the United States respond to the issue of immigration. Likewise, the many different contexts in which people "out of place" are metaphorically compared to "weeds" that disrupt the "orderly garden" of a society or community have important implications for the sociology of power, inequalities, and social control. Further documenting the range of frames such as governance, sport, and introspection (see Lizardo 2012) that employ dirt or weeds as metaphor, and considering the ways that these metaphors organize power dynamics across different contexts, provide an interesting avenue for exploring the relationship between cultural cognition and power and inequalities.

A culture and cognition approach is also particularly useful for studying the more subtle aspects of racial inequalities. Social inequality on the axis of race is reproduced in cultural cognition in a variety of ways. Hypodescent rules of racial classification (discussed in chapter 2) reinforce the added social weight and negative power of racial markedness at the cultural level. Aliya Saperstein and Andrew Penner (2012) connected the cultural to the individual level by showing that social science interviewers changed how they coded the race of their respondents on the basis of life events. The interviewers more generously assigned respondents with positive life events to the unmarked racial category and those with negative life events to the marked racial categories. In subconsciously allowing negative life events to tip their classification of a respondent toward a minority classification, interviewers unconsciously used an internal classification strategy that resembles elements of the culture's hypodescent rule in assigning greater social weight and negative power to the marked. Researchers in culture and cognition can further explore these kinds of links between structural inequalities and cognitive biases and influences.

Sociologists of race have become increasingly interested in the more implicit forms of racism referred to as "colorblind racism." Thinking about the often unnoticed privilege of the unmarked can help to advance a cognitive sociological understanding of race. Nancy DiTomaso (2013) observed how the routine practice of whites trusting and hiring qualified people in their own social networks often reproduces the social problem of black unemployment. Even though many whites expressed an interest in diversity and fairness, they were embedded in mostly similar social networks and engaged in everyday, practical, seemingly moral action to hire qualified people that were in the networks they knew and

Conclusion

trusted, without seeing that their behavior was racially biased in its outcomes. Scholars interested in power and inequality can employ a culture and cognition analysis to examine the unconscious ways that the privileged reinforce inequalities through embodying taken-for-granted realities where they do not perceive privilege and power.

Power is also present in definitions of identity authenticity. The ability to be influential in defining and policing what counts as authenticity within an identity category is often tied to power. The most influential insiders within an identity group police definitions and presentations of authenticity and exert the classification power of deciding who and what actions count as authentic and inauthentic. Definitions of authenticity can also reproduce inequalities by limiting the range of acceptable expressions, particularly for members of marked social categories. Julie Bettie's (2003) example of middle-class Mexican-American girls feeling the need to perform working-class identities to maintain Mexican-American group identity, and Prudence Carter's (2003) observation that blacks deployed "black cultural capital" to maintain racial authenticity in ways that limited social mobility, unless they were able to deftly negotiate the dual cultural currencies of "black cultural capital" and "mainstream cultural capital" across settings, both illustrated issues of power and social inequality. Sociologists interested in power in social identities can analyze the various contexts where people negotiate identities and employ different identity currencies across different contextual environments.

Power is manifest in collective memory, especially in who has the power to focus and channel our attention. The collective amnesia that Barry Schwartz (2009) highlighted in the social construction of Rosa Parks as a lone heroine who refused to give up her seat on a bus not only demonstrated the difficulty of packaging a more complex story into an existing cultural schema, but also showed how such schemas can underplay the importance of social movements. Chapter 5 explored a number of ways that our collective mental orderings of the past relate to the present. Sociologists can explore how what pasts get remembered and forgotten affect power relations in the present, and what role institutional and

188

influential actors as well as social movements play in constructing particular pasts.

Power and social inequalities are not only an area of empirical and normative interest in sociology, but one of growing interest in cognitive neuroscience. Martha Farah and colleagues' research on the cognitive neuroscience of childhood poverty, for instance, takes an approach oriented to context and social problems to understanding cognition within the field of neuroscience (e.g. Farah et al. 2006; Farah 2010). As cognitive neuroscience develops context and social problems approaches, the prospects for connecting neuroscience understandings of inequality with sociological research offer continued potential for interdisciplinary intersections and understandings of cognition that relate directly to enduring inequalities. The study of culture and cognition can be enriched by continued and growing attention to issues of inequality, and the sociology of inequality can similarly find that important dimensions of social inequality are informed by studying how the cultural and social shapes our thinking and perception.

General social patterns

Sociologists are interested in generalizable observations of social life beyond a specific case. I have emphasized and highlighted cognitive variation to demonstrate how our cognition is culturally influenced. While this cognitive variation is interesting in its own right, it becomes analytically interesting when the analyst can locate patterns across variation. What similarities do sociologists see in substantively different identities, varying contexts where metaphor is used, or different events and communities that evoke collective memories? What kinds of analytic observations and social patterns can be drawn from the immensely broad range of topics, cultures, and groups that sociologists of culture and cognition study?

Comparative studies between substantively different communities that look not only at variation but at similarity across sites provide potentially interesting analytic insights. For instance, Amy

Conclusion

Wilkins' (2008) comparative ethnographic observation that two quite different subcultures – goths and Christians – shared patterned similarities in strategically deploying whiteness to access privilege when needed, but also sought the exotica of difference by carving out non-mainstream subcultural identities, provides a general theoretical insight about the use of privilege in negotiating identity attributes, which can be applied to other settings. Scholars can ask "When do the privileged seek marginality as a subcultural strategy?" Meta-study comparisons of research across different sites and topics can realize similar analytic possibilities. As we saw in chapter 1, the sensitizing analytic concept of "moral attention styles" can be used to explore differences and similarities across the moral order of a suburb (Baumgartner 1988), the code of the street (Anderson 1999), and public interactions on Greyhound buses (Kim 2012) and Chicago train lines (Raudenbush 2012) to illustrate how neighborhood, social network, and situational contexts have cultural effects on our moral impulses. Sociologists can analyze cognitive variation between populations, while being attuned to analytic patterns that this study across different populations reveals.

Emphasizing patterns across studies of identity presentation in debates over identity authenticity, performances of identity mobility, and expressions of identity multidimensionality revealed general principles of identity. Scholars interested in identity in their own research can pay attention to conflicts over auxiliary characteristics and authenticity claims and explore how individuals shift their identity presentations across time and space. Cross-domain comparisons of perceptual attention to marked identities and inattention to unmarked identities can highlight ways that perception, boundary classification, and identity processes have similarities (as well as differences) across race, age, religion, class, gender/ sex, occupation, and sexuality. Active research on code-switching identities and negotiating competing cultural capitals from setting to setting can explore the relationships between markedness and unmarkedness, deliberate and automatic cognition, and auxiliary characteristics. Iddo Tavory (2010) showed how Orthodox Jews anticipated interactions based on wearing the minimal mark of a religious Jew. Using this as a case study for sites of embodied expectation, he suggested further study of similar kinds of cases. How do individuals incorporate boundary work and identity into their daily habit? When are their strategies for dealing with things deliberative and when do they become automatic, no longer thought about as strategies, and simply performed as a part of everyday habit? Further research across different types of identities could contribute to greater understanding of the complexities of identity and the interactional and cognitive negotiations of social boundaries and multifaceted selves.

Cross-scale comparisons can provide general insights. Reuben Buford May (2000) demonstrated how race talk about marked inter-racial interactions in a local tavern created a local community of memory that reinforced in-group bonds and distrust of out-groups. Jens Rydgren (2007) showed at the macro level of ethnic conflicts how analogical reasoning emphasizing marked aspects of past ethnic conflicts contributed to in-group identification and out-group distrust, and contributed to social action in the form of continued ethnic violence. Future inquiries in this area could attempt to directly link the relationship between collective group-level narratives and their effect on in-group/out-group relations by analyzing changes in network composition over time. Cross-scale comparisons of general patterns of danger and risk assessment ranging from broad, societal-level fears to specific risk assessments of subcultures, can further outline the analytic contours of cognitive frames of safety and danger. What similarities do we see in risk assessment across different levels of scale of social life? Likewise, what similarities do metaphors used in discourse at the macro level of broad social policy and at the micro level of interpersonal interaction in a work setting share? Studying formal similarities in cognition across different units of scale offers continued promise for a sociology of culture and cognition.

Cross-domain comparisons help to illuminate how general concepts operate in real-world conditions. The growing interest within cognitive sociology in understanding how deliberate and automatic cognition operate, and the application of process models for understanding the relationship between these different types of cognition, provide interesting possibilities for continued cross-domain research focusing on conditions under which one type of cognition or the other prevails. When are utilitarian reasoning and cognitive override most pronounced in social settings and in social fields? Sameer Srivastava and Mahzarin Banaji (2011: 228) suggest studying whether values adopted because of social conformity pressures and social desirability have a greater effect on identities in one form of cognition than the other. Cross-domain and cross-scale comparison of punks (Force 2009), French culinary chefs (Rao et al. 2005), and wine manufacturers (Beverland 2005) shows a common general pattern in which authenticity within a subcultural group, a profession, and a corporate brand market are all maintained not only by following cultural codes, but by violating the rules just enough to appear original and not blindly imitative of the code. Researchers interested in the contours of authenticity can observe what kinds of professions, organizations, subcultures, and identities require this kind of deft partial adherence to a code to claim authenticity. Are there classed characteristics to this form of authenticity strategy, or is it general across most types of authenticity claims? Are there settings or subcultures where strict adherence to a cultural code is more valued? If so, how do these environments and groups differ in other ways that might explain the different authenticity codes and strategies? Cross-context observations of how event notifications (Ryan 2006), appearances of talk show villains and victims (Lowney and Holstein 2003), narratives about acts of violence (Cerulo 1998), and public apologies by the rich and famous (Cerulo and Ruane 2014) are sequenced, illustrate that time location within a sequence can affect how morality is interpreted across a seemingly disparate range of issues from wedding announcements to violent acts. Mining a wide variety of domains, sites, and scales for socially patterned similarities allows sociologists of culture and cognition to develop analytic comparisons that transcend subdisciplinary boundaries and traditional macro and micro distinctions.

Conclusion

The diversity in what sociologists of culture and cognition study, how they study it, and how they locate and define the role of culture may appear to pose challenges for coherence, but this challenge is also an opportunity. Just as the cognitive diversity of cultures, subcultures, organizations, and identity affiliations provides for broad and interesting understandings of cognition across a range of contexts and levels of scale, the same diversity in research thought styles, levels of analysis, and methods among cognitive sociologists can give us a full breadth of innovative ideas and substantive empirical sites that allows for vibrant cross-context comparisons and contrasts. Studying culture and cognition has much to offer sociologists who do not define their interests explicitly as cognitive. Attention and inattention, classification and boundaries, meaning, identity, and memory are issues of importance to broad sociological concerns with social action, power, social inequalities, and generalizable patterns of social life. Professional sociologists and students of sociology alike will find that exploring cognitive processes within their own substantive topics of interest and passion is a rich and rewarding experience.

References

Alexander, Jeffrey C. 2003a. *The Meanings of Social Life: A Cultural Sociology.* Oxford; New York: Oxford University Press.

Alexander, Jeffrey C. 2003b. "On the Social Construction of Moral Universals: The 'Holocaust' from War Crime to Trauma Drama." In *The Meanings of Social Life: A Cultural Sociology*, by Jeffrey C. Alexander. Oxford; New York: Oxford University Press.

Alexander, Jeffrey C., and Philip Smith. 2003. "The Strong Program in Cultural Sociology: Elements of a Structural Hermeneutics." In *The Meanings of Social Life: A Cultural Sociology*, by Jeffrey C. Alexander. Oxford; New York: Oxford University Press.

Altheide, David L. 1997. "The News Media, the Problem Frame, and the Production of Fear." *Sociological Quarterly* 38 (4): 647–68.

Altheide, David L. 2002. "Tracking Discourse." In *Culture in Mind: Toward a Sociology of Culture and Cognition*, ed. Karen A. Cerulo. New York: Routledge.

Anderson, Elijah. 1999. *Code of the Street: Decency, Violence, and the Moral Life of the Inner City.* New York: W.W. Norton.

Anderson, Elijah. 2011. *The Cosmopolitan Canopy: Race and Civility in Everyday Life.* New York: W.W. Norton.

Aspinall, Peter J., and Miri Song. 2013. "Is Race a 'Salient' or 'Dominant Identity' in the Early 21st Century: The Evidence of UK Survey Data on Respondents' Sense of Who They Are." *Social Science Research* 42 (2): 547–61.

Athens, Lonnie. 1994. "The Self as a Soliloquy." *Sociological Quarterly* 35 (3): 521–32.

Auyero, Javier, and Debora Swistun. 2008. "The Social Production of Toxic Uncertainty." *American Sociological Review* 73 (3): 357–79.

Auyero, Javier, and Debora Swistun. 2009. *Flammable: Environmental Suffering in an Argentine Shantytown.* Oxford; New York: Oxford University Press.

Bargh, John A., Mark Chen, and Lara Burrows. 1996. "Automaticity of Social

References

Behavior: Direct Effects of Trait Construct and Stereotype Activation on Action." *Journal of Personality and Social Psychology* 71 (2): 230–44.

Bateson, Gregory. 1972. *Steps to an Ecology of Mind: Collected Essays in Anthropology, Psychiatry, Evolution, and Epistemology*. San Francisco: Chandler.

Baum, Dan. 2010. "Happiness Is a Worn Gun: My Concealed Weapon and Me." *Harper's Magazine* 321 (1923): 29–38.

Bauman, Zygmunt. 1989. *Modernity and the Holocaust*. Ithaca: Cornell University Press.

Bauman, Zygmunt. 1991. *Modernity and Ambivalence*. Ithaca: Cornell University Press.

Baumgartner, Mary Pat. 1988. *The Moral Order of a Suburb*. New York; Oxford: Oxford University Press.

Beim, Aaron. 2007. "The Cognitive Aspects of Collective Memory." *Symbolic Interaction* 30 (1): 7–26.

Benford, Robert D., and David A. Snow. 2000. "Framing Processes and Social Movements: An Overview and Assessment." *Annual Review of Sociology* 26 (1): 611–39.

Berger, Peter L., and Thomas Luckmann. 1966. *The Social Construction of Reality: A Treatise in the Sociology of Knowledge*. Garden City: Doubleday.

Bergesen, Albert J. 2004a. "Durkheim's Theory of Mental Categories: A Review of the Evidence." *Annual Review of Sociology* 30 (1): 395–408.

Bergesen, Albert J. 2004b. "Chomsky Versus Mead." *Sociological Theory* 22 (3): 357–70.

Best, Joel. 1987. "Rhetoric in Claims-Making: Constructing the Missing Children Problem." *Social Problems* 34 (2): 101–21.

Best, Joel, and Gerald T. Horiuchi. 1985. "The Razor Blade in the Apple: The Social Construction of Urban Legends." *Social Problems* 32 (5): 488–99.

Bettie, Julie. 2000. "Women without Class: Chicas, Cholas, Trash, and the Presence/Absence of Class Identity." *Signs* 26 (1): 1–35.

Bettie, Julie. 2003. *Women without Class: Girls, Race, and Identity*. Berkeley: University of California Press.

Beverland, Michael B. 2005. "Crafting Brand Authenticity: The Case of Luxury Wines." *Journal of Management Studies* 42 (5): 1003–29.

Black, Donald. 1983. "Crime as Social Control." *American Sociological Review* 48 (1): 34–45.

Black, Donald. 2011. *Moral Time*. New York: Oxford University Press.

Bloch, Maurice. 1998. *How We Think They Think: Anthropological Approaches to Cognition, Memory, and Literacy*. Boulder: Westview Press.

Bonilla-Silva, Eduardo, and David G. Embrick. 2007. "'Every Place Has a Ghetto . . . ': The Significance of Whites' Social and Residential Segregation." *Symbolic Interaction* 30 (3): 323–45.

References

Bornstein, Kate. 1994. *Gender Outlaw: On Men, Women, and the Rest of Us.* New York: Routledge.

Bourdieu, Pierre. 1969. "Intellectual Field and Creative Project." *Social Science Information* 8 (2): 89–119.

Bourdieu, Pierre. 1977. *Outline of a Theory of Practice.* Cambridge; New York: Cambridge University Press.

Bourdieu, Pierre. 1984. *Distinction: A Social Critique of the Judgment of Taste.* Cambridge, MA: Harvard University Press.

Bourdieu, Pierre. 1990. *The Logic of Practice.* Stanford: Stanford University Press.

Bourdieu, Pierre. 1998. *Practical Reason: On the Theory of Action.* Stanford: Stanford University Press.

Bourdieu, Pierre. 2000. *Pascalian Meditations.* Stanford: Stanford University Press.

Bowers, Chet A. 2009. "How the Linguistic Colonization of the Present by the Past Influences the Linguistic Colonization of Other Cultures Adopting English as Second Language." *Language Value* 1 (1): 39–50.

Brekhus, Wayne H. 1996. "Social Marking and the Mental Coloring of Identity: Sexual Identity Construction and Maintenance in the United States." *Sociological Forum* 11 (3): 497–522.

Brekhus, Wayne H. 1998. "A Sociology of the Unmarked: Redirecting Our Focus." *Sociological Theory* 16 (1): 34–51.

Brekhus, Wayne H. 2003. *Peacocks, Chameleons, Centaurs: Gay Suburbia and the Grammar of Social Identity.* Chicago: University of Chicago Press.

Brekhus, Wayne H. 2007. "The Rutgers School: A Zerubavelian Culturalist Cognitive Sociology." *European Journal of Social Theory* 10 (3): 448–64.

Brekhus, Wayne H. 2008. "Trends in the Qualitative Study of Social Identities." *Sociology Compass* 2 (3): 1059–78.

Brekhus, Wayne H. 2012. "Gay Pendoiari, Gay Integranti: Strategie Identitarie dei Gay di Periferia nell'Era Post-Closet." In *Alterazioni: introduzione alle sociologie delle omosessualità,* ed. Cirus Rinaldi. Milan: Mimesis.

Brekhus, Wayne H., David L. Brunsma, Todd Platts, and Priya Dua. 2010. "On the Contributions of Cognitive Sociology to the Sociological Study of Race." *Sociology Compass* 4 (1): 61–76.

Brooks, Abigail. 2004. "'Under the Knife and Proud of It:' An Analysis of the Normalization of Cosmetic Surgery." *Critical Sociology* 30 (2): 207–39.

Brubaker, Rogers, Mara Loveman, and Peter Stamatov. 2004. "Ethnicity as Cognition." *Theory and Society* 33 (1): 31–64.

Bryson, Bethany. 1996. "'Anything But Heavy Metal': Symbolic Exclusion and Musical Dislikes." *American Sociological Review* 61 (5): 884–99.

Burawoy, Michael. 1979. *Manufacturing Consent: Changes in the Labor Process under Monopoly Capitalism.* Chicago: University of Chicago Press.

References

Butler, Judith. 1999. *Gender Trouble: Feminism and the Subversion of Identity.* New York: Routledge.

Callahan, Sara B. Dykins. 2008. "Academic Outings." *Symbolic Interaction* 31 (4): 351–75.

Carter, Prudence L. 2003. "'Black' Cultural Capital, Status Positioning, and Schooling Conflicts for Low-Income African American Youth." *Social Problems* 50 (1): 136–55.

Cerulo, Karen A. 1998. *Deciphering Violence: The Cognitive Structure of Right and Wrong.* New York: Routledge.

Cerulo, Karen A. 2002a. *Culture in Mind: Toward a Sociology of Culture and Cognition.* New York: Routledge.

Cerulo, Karen A. 2002b. "Establishing a Sociology of Culture and Cognition." In *Culture in Mind: Toward a Sociology of Culture and Cognition*, ed. Karen A. Cerulo. New York: Routledge.

Cerulo, Karen A. 2002c. "Storage and Retrieval." In *Culture in Mind: Toward a Sociology of Culture and Cognition*, ed. Karen A. Cerulo. New York: Routledge.

Cerulo, Karen A. 2006. *Never Saw It Coming: Cultural Challenges to Envisioning the Worst.* Chicago: University of Chicago Press.

Cerulo, Karen A. 2010. "Mining the Intersections of Cognitive Sociology and Neuroscience." *Poetics* 38 (2): 115–32.

Cerulo, Karen A., and Janet M. Ruane. 2014. "Apologies of the Rich and Famous: Cultural, Cognitive, and Social Explanations of Why We Care and Why We Forgive." *Social Psychology Quarterly* 77 (2): 123–49.

Chatterton, Paul, and Robert Hollands. 2002. "Theorising Urban Playscapes: Producing, Regulating and Consuming Youthful Nightlife City Spaces." *Urban Studies* 39 (1): 95–116.

Clarke, Lee. 2006. *Worst Cases: Terror and Catastrophe in the Popular Imagination.* Chicago: University of Chicago Press.

Cook, Nicole, Susan J. Smith, and Beverley A. Searle. 2009. "Mortgage Markets and Cultures of Consumption." *Consumption Markets & Culture* 12 (2): 133–54.

Cousineau, Matthew. 2014. "Discursive Resources in the Everyday Construction of Engineering Knowledge." Dissertation, Columbia: University of Missouri.

Crawley, Sara L. 2008. "The Clothes Make the Trans: Region and Geography in Experiences of the Body." *Journal of Lesbian Studies* 12 (4): 365–79.

Daipha, Phaedra. 2010. "Visual Perception at Work: Lessons from the World of Meteorology." *Poetics* 38 (2): 151–65.

D'Andrade, Roy G. 1995. *The Development of Cognitive Anthropology.* Cambridge: Cambridge University Press.

Danna Lynch, Karen. 2009. "Objects, Meanings, and Role Identities: The Practices That Establish Association in the Case of Home-Based Employment." *Sociological Forum* 24 (1): 76–103.

Danna Lynch, Karen. 2011. *The Chameleon Factor: The Mental Management of*

References

Multiple Roles (and What It Reveals about the Organization of Culture). S.l.: ProQuest, UMI Dissertation Publishing.

Davis, F. James. 1991. *Who Is Black? One Nation's Definition.* University Park: Pennsylvania State University Press.

Davis, F. James. 2006. "Defining Race: Comparative Perspectives." In *Mixed Messages: Multiracial Identities in the "Color-Blind" Era,* ed. David L. Brunsma. Boulder: Lynne Rienner.

Davis, Mike. 1992. *Beyond Blade Runner: Urban Control, the Ecology of Fear.* Westfield: Open Media.

Davis, Murray S. 1983. *Smut: Erotic Reality/Obscene Ideology.* Chicago: University of Chicago Press.

DeGloma, Thomas. 2010. "Awakenings: Autobiography, Memory, and the Social Logic of Personal Discovery." *Sociological Forum* 25 (3): 519–40.

DeGloma, Thomas. 2014. *Seeing the Light: The Social Logic of Personal Discovery.* Chicago: University of Chicago Press.

DiMaggio, Paul. 1997. "Culture and Cognition." *Annual Review of Sociology* 23 (1): 263–87.

DiTomaso, Nancy. 2013. *The American Non-Dilemma: Racial Inequality without Racism.* New York: Russell Sage Foundation.

Douglas, Mary. 1966. *Purity and Danger: An Analysis of Concepts of Pollution and Taboo.* New York: Praeger.

Duneier, Mitchell. 1999. *Sidewalk.* New York: Farrar, Straus and Giroux.

Durkheim, Émile. [1912] 1965. *The Elementary Forms of the Religious Life.* New York: Free Press.

Durkheim, Émile. [1913–14] 1983. *Pragmatism and Sociology.* Cambridge; New York: Cambridge University Press.

Durkheim, Émile, and Marcel Mauss. 1963. *Primitive Classification.* Chicago: University of Chicago Press.

Ebaugh, Helen Rose Fuchs. 1988. *Becoming an Ex: The Process of Role Exit.* Chicago: University of Chicago Press.

Eliasoph, Nina. 1999. "'Everyday Racism' in a Culture of Political Avoidance: Civil Society, Speech, and Taboo." *Social Problems* 46 (4): 479–502.

Eliasoph, Nina, and Paul Lichterman. 2003. "Culture in Interaction." *American Journal of Sociology* 108 (4): 735–94.

Erikson, Kai T. 1976. *Everything in Its Path: Destruction of Community in the Buffalo Creek Flood.* New York: Simon & Schuster.

Eyerman, Ron. 2001. *Cultural Trauma: Slavery and the Formation of African American Identity.* Cambridge; New York: Cambridge University Press.

Ezzy, Douglas. 1998. "Theorizing Narrative Identity: Symbolic Interactionism and Hermeneutics." *Sociological Quarterly* 39 (2): 239–52.

Farah, Martha. 2010. "Mind, Brain and Education in Socioeconomic Context." In *The Developmental Relations among Mind, Brain and Education: Essays*

References

in Honor of Robbie Case, ed. Michel Ferrari and Ljiljana Vuletić. Dordrecht; New York: Springer.

Farah, Martha J., David M. Shera, Jessica H. Savage, Laura Betancourt, Joan M. Giannetta, Nancy L. Brodsky, Elsa K. Malmud, and Hallam Hurt. 2006. "Childhood Poverty: Specific Associations with Neurocognitive Development." *Brain Research* 1110 (1): 166–74.

Farrell, Michael P. 2001. *Collaborative Circles: Friendship Dynamics and Creative Work*. Chicago: University of Chicago Press.

Fine, Gary Alan. 1979. "Small Groups and Culture Creation: The Idioculture of Little League Baseball Teams." *American Sociological Review* 44 (5): 733–45.

Fine, Gary Alan. 1990. "Organizational Time: Temporal Demands and the Experience of Work in Restaurant Kitchens." *Social Forces* 69 (1): 95–114.

Fine, Gary Alan. 1998. *Morel Tales: The Culture of Mushrooming*. Cambridge, MA: Harvard University Press.

Fine, Gary Alan. 2001. *Difficult Reputations: Collective Memories of the Evil, Inept, and Controversial*. Chicago: University of Chicago Press.

Fiske, Susan T., and Shelley E. Taylor. 2013. *Social Cognition: From Brains to Culture*. 2nd edn. Los Angeles: Sage.

Flaherty, Michael G. 2003. "Time Work: Customizing Temporal Experience." *Social Psychology Quarterly* 66: 17–33.

Fleck, Ludwik. [1935] 1979. *Genesis and Development of a Scientific Fact*. Chicago: University of Chicago Press.

Force, William Ryan. 2009. "Consumption Styles and the Fluid Complexity of Punk Authenticity." *Symbolic Interaction* 32 (4): 289–309.

Force, William Ryan. 2010. "The Code of Harry: Performing Normativity in Dexter." *Crime, Media, Culture* 6 (3): 329–45.

Friedman, Asia. 2013. *Blind to Sameness: Sexpectations and the Social Construction of Male and Female Bodies*. Chicago; London: University of Chicago Press.

Fuller, Sylvia. 2003. "Creating and Contesting Boundaries: Exploring the Dynamics of Conflict and Classification." *Sociological Forum* 18 (1): 3–30.

Fussell, Elizabeth. 2006. "Leaving New Orleans: Social Stratification, Networks, and Hurricane Evacuation." In *Understanding Katrina: Perspectives from the Social Sciences*, ed. SSRC. New York: Social Science Research Council. http://understandingkatrina.ssrc.org/Fussell.

Garfinkel, Harold. 1967. *Studies in Ethnomethodology*. Englewood Cliffs: Prentice Hall.

Garroutte, Eva Marie. 2003. *Real Indians: Identity and the Survival of Native America*. Berkeley: University of California Press.

Gaytan, Marie Sarita. 2008. "From Sombreros to Sincronizadas: Authenticity, Ethnicity, and the Mexican Restaurant Industry." *Journal of Contemporary Ethnography* 37 (3): 314–41.

References

Geertz, Clifford. [1973] 2000. *The Interpretation of Cultures: Selected Essays.* New York: Basic Books.

Gergen, Kenneth J. 1991. *The Saturated Self: Dilemmas of Identity in Contemporary Life.* New York: Basic Books.

Glassner, Barry. 1999. *The Culture of Fear: Why Americans Are Afraid of the Wrong Things.* New York: Basic Books.

Goff, Phillip Atiba, Matthew Christian Jackson, Andrew H. Nichols, and Brooke Allison Lewis Di Leone. 2013. "Anything but Race: Avoiding Racial Discourse to Avoid Hurting You or Me." *Psychology* 4 (3A): 335–9.

Goffman, Erving. 1955. "On Face-Work: An Analysis of Ritual Elements in Social Interaction." *Psychiatry: Journal for the Study of Interpersonal Processes* 18: 213–31.

Goffman, Erving. 1959. *The Presentation of Self in Everyday Life.* New York: Anchor.

Goffman, Erving. 1961. *Asylums: Essays on the Social Situation of Mental Patients and Other Inmates.* Garden City: Anchor Books/Doubleday.

Goffman, Erving. 1963. *Behavior in Public Places: Notes on the Social Organization of Gatherings.* New York: Free Press of Glencoe.

Goffman, Erving. 1974. *Frame Analysis: An Essay on the Organization of Experience.* New York: Harper & Row.

Goffman, Erving. [1963] 1986. *Stigma: Notes on the Management of Spoiled Identity.* Reissue edn. New York: Touchstone.

Goodwin, Charles. 1994. "Professional Vision." *American Anthropologist* 96 (3): 606–33.

Grazian, David. 2003. *Blue Chicago: The Search for Authenticity in Urban Blues Clubs.* Chicago: University of Chicago Press.

Grazian, David. 2008. *On the Make: The Hustle of Urban Nightlife.* Chicago: University of Chicago Press.

Greenberg, Joseph H. 1966. *Language Universals, with Special Reference to Feature Hierarchies.* The Hague: Mouton.

Greene, Joshua D., Leigh E. Nystrom, Andrew D. Engell, John M. Darley, and Jonathan D. Cohen. 2004. "The Neural Bases of Cognitive Conflict and Control in Moral Judgment." *Neuron* 44 (2): 389–400.

Griffin, Larry. J. 2004. "'Generations and Collective Memory' Revisited: Race, Region, and Memory of Civil Rights." *American Sociological Review* 69 (4): 544–57.

Gubrium, Jaber F., and James A. Holstein. 2000. "The Self in a World of Going Concerns." *Symbolic Interaction* 23 (2): 95–115.

Haidt, Jonathan. 2001. "The Emotional Dog and Its Rational Tail: A Social Intuitionist Approach to Moral Judgment." *Psychological Review* 108 (4): 814–34.

Haidt, Jonathan. 2005. *The Happiness Hypothesis: Finding Modern Truth in Ancient Wisdom.* New York: Basic Books.

References

Halberstam, Judith. 2005. *In a Queer Time and Place: Transgender Bodies, Subcultural Lives*. New York: New York University Press.

Halbwachs, Maurice. [1950] 1992. *On Collective Memory*. Chicago: University of Chicago Press.

Hartsock, Nancy C. M. 1983. *Money, Sex, and Power: Toward a Feminist Historical Materialism*. New York: Longman.

Harvey, Daina Cheyenne. 2012. "A New Geography of Trouble." In *Black Beaches and Bayous: The BP Deepwater Horizon Oil Spill Disaster*, ed. Lisa A. Eargle and Ashraf Esmail. Lanham: University Press of America.

Heath, Melanie. 2013. "Sexual Misgivings: Producing Un/Marked Knowledge in Neoliberal Marriage Promotion Policies." *Sociological Quarterly* 54 (4): 561–83.

Henrich, Joseph, Steven J. Heine, and Ara Norenzayan. 2010. "The Weirdest People in the World?" *Behavioral and Brain Sciences* 33 (2–3): 61–83.

Hollands, Robert, and Paul Chatterton. 2003. "Producing Nightlife in the New Urban Entertainment Economy: Corporatization, Branding and Market Segmentation." *International Journal of Urban and Regional Research* 27 (2): 361–85.

Howard, Jenna. 2006. "Expecting and Accepting: The Temporal Ambiguity of Recovery Identities." *Social Psychology Quarterly* 69 (4): 307–24.

Hsu, Greta, Michael T. Hannan, and Özgecan Koçak. 2009. "Multiple Category Memberships in Markets: An Integrated Theory and Two Empirical Tests." *American Sociological Review* 74 (1): 150–69.

Hughes, Everett Cherrington. 1945. "Dilemmas and Contradictions of Status." *American Journal of Sociology* 50 (5): 353–9.

Ignatow, Gabriel. 2003. "'Idea Hamsters' on the 'Bleeding Edge:' Profane Metaphors in High Technology Jargon." *Poetics* 31 (1): 1–22.

Ignatow, Gabriel. 2007. "Theories of Embodied Knowledge: New Directions for Cultural and Cognitive Sociology?" *Journal for the Theory of Social Behaviour* 37 (2): 115–35.

Ignatow, Gabriel. 2009. "Culture and Embodied Cognition: Moral Discourses in Internet Support Groups for Overeaters." *Social Forces* 88 (2): 643–69.

Jackson, John L. 2001. *Harlem World: Doing Race and Class in Contemporary Black America*. Chicago: University of Chicago Press.

Jackson, John L. 2005. *Real Black: Adventures in Racial Sincerity*. Chicago: University of Chicago Press.

Jakobson, Roman (ed.). 1975. *N. S. Trubetzkoy's Letters and Notes*. The Hague; Paris: Mouton.

Jerolmack, Colin. 2008. "How Pigeons Became Rats: The Cultural-Spatial Logic of Problem Animals." *Social Problems* 55 (1): 72–94.

Jerolmack, Colin. 2013. *The Global Pigeon*. Chicago: University of Chicago Press.

References

Jerolmack, Colin, and Shamus Khan. 2014. "Talk Is Cheap: Ethnography and the Attitudinal Fallacy." *Sociological Methods & Research* 43 (2): 178–209.

Johnson, Kirk A., Mark K. Dolan, and John Sonnett. 2011. "Speaking of Looting: An Analysis of Racial Propaganda in National Television Coverage of Hurricane Katrina." *Howard Journal of Communications* 22 (3): 302–18.

Johnston, Erin F. 2013. "'I Was Always This Way . . . ': Rhetorics of Continuity in Narratives of Conversion." *Sociological Forum* 28 (3): 549–73.

Johnston, Josée, and Shyon Baumann. 2007. "Democracy versus Distinction: A Study of Omnivorousness in Gourmet Food Writing." *American Journal of Sociology* 113 (1): 165–204.

Kane, Anne E. 1997. "Theorizing Meaning Construction in Social Movements: Symbolic Structures and Interpretation during the Irish Land War, 1879–1882." *Sociological Theory* 15 (3): 249–76.

Kato, Yuki. 2011. "Coming of Age in the Bubble: Suburban Adolescents' Use of a Spatial Metaphor as a Symbolic Boundary." *Symbolic Interaction* 34 (2): 244–64.

Kefalas, Maria J. 2003. *Working-Class Heroes: Protecting Home, Community, and Nation in a Chicago Neighborhood.* Berkeley: University of California Press.

Kelling, George L., and James Q. Wilson. 1982. "Broken Windows." *Atlantic*, March. http://www.theatlantic.com/magazine/archive/1982/03/broken-wind ows/304465.

Kendall, Diana Elizabeth. 2005. *Framing Class: Media Representations of Wealth and Poverty in America.* Lanham: Rowman & Littlefield.

Kidder, Jeffrey L., and Isaac William Martin. 2012. "What We Talk About When We Talk About Taxes." *Symbolic Interaction* 35 (2): 123–45.

Kim, Esther C. 2012. "Nonsocial Transient Behavior: Social Disengagement on the Greyhound Bus." *Symbolic Interaction* 35 (3): 267–83.

King, Deborah K. 1988. "Multiple Jeopardy, Multiple Consciousness: The Context of a Black Feminist Ideology." *Signs: Journal of Women in Culture and Society* 14 (1): 42–72.

Knorr-Cetina, Karin. 1999. *Epistemic Cultures: How the Sciences Make Knowledge.* Cambridge, MA: Harvard University Press.

Lacy, Karyn R. 2007. *Blue-Chip Black: Race, Class, and Status in the New Black Middle Class.* Berkeley: University of California Press.

Lakoff, George. 1996. *Moral Politics: What Conservatives Know That Liberals Don't.* Chicago: University of Chicago Press.

Lakoff, George. 2002. *Moral Politics: How Liberals and Conservatives Think.* Chicago: University of Chicago Press.

Lakoff, George, and Mark Johnson. 1980. *Metaphors We Live by.* Chicago: University of Chicago Press.

Lamont, Michèle. 2000. *The Dignity of Working Men: Morality and the*

References

Boundaries of Race, Class, and Immigration. New York: Russell Sage Foundation; Cambridge, MA: Harvard University Press.

Lamont, Michèle. 2009. *How Professors Think: Inside the Curious World of Academic Judgment*. Cambridge, MA: Harvard University Press.

Lamont, Michèle, and Virág Molnár. 2002. "The Study of Boundaries in the Social Sciences." *Annual Review of Sociology* 28 (1): 167–95.

Lang, Robert E., and Karen A. Danielsen. 1997. "Gated Communities in America: Walling out the World?" *Housing Policy Debate* 8 (4): 867–99.

Leschziner, Vanina. 2007. "Kitchen Stories: Patterns of Recognition in Contemporary High Cuisine." *Sociological Forum* 22 (1): 78–102.

Leschziner, Vanina, and Adam Isaiah Green. 2013. "Thinking about Food and Sex: Deliberate Cognition in the Routine Practices of a Field." *Sociological Theory* 31 (2): 116–44.

Levine, Martin P. 1998. *Gay Macho: The Life and Death of the Homosexual Clone*. New York: New York University Press.

Lévi-Strauss, Claude. 1963. *Structural Anthropology*. New York: Basic Books.

Lizardo, Omar. 2004. "The Cognitive Origins of Bourdieu's Habitus." *Journal for the Theory of Social Behaviour* 34 (4): 375–401.

Lizardo, Omar. 2007. "'Mirror Neurons,' Collective Objects and the Problem of Transmission: Reconsidering Stephen Turner's Critique of Practice Theory." *Journal for the Theory of Social Behaviour* 37 (3): 319–50.

Lizardo, Omar. 2012. "The Conceptual Bases of Metaphors of Dirt and Cleanliness in Moral and Non-Moral Reasoning." *Cognitive Linguistics* 23 (2): 367–93.

Lizardo, Omar. forthcoming. "Culture and Cognition." In *International Encyclopedia of the Social and Behavioral Sciences*. http://www3.nd.edu/~olizardo/papers/culture-cognition-entry-short.pdf.

Lizardo, Omar, and Michael Strand. 2010. "Skills, Toolkits, Contexts and Institutions: Clarifying the Relationship between Different Approaches to Cognition in Cultural Sociology." *Poetics* 38 (2): 205–28.

Loseke, Donileen R. 2009. "Examining Emotion as Discourse: Emotion Codes and Presidential Speeches Justifying War." *Sociological Quarterly* 50 (3): 497–524.

Lowney, Kathleen, and James A. Holstein. 2003. "Victims, Villains, and Talk Show Selves." In *Inner Lives and Social Worlds: Readings in Social Psychology*, ed. James A. Holstein and Jaber F. Gubrium. New York: Oxford University Press.

Mannheim, Karl. [1936] 1985. *Ideology and Utopia: An Introduction to the Sociology of Knowledge*. San Diego: Harcourt Brace Jovanovich.

Mannheim, Karl. [1928] 1952. "The Problem of Generations." In *Essays on the Sociology of Knowledge*, by Karl Mannheim. London: Routledge & Kegan Paul.

Martin, John Levi. 2010. "Life's a Beach but You're an Ant, and Other Unwelcome News for the Sociology of Culture." *Poetics* 38 (2): 229–44.

References

Martin, John Levi. 2011. *The Explanation of Social Action*. Oxford; New York: Oxford University Press.

Martin, John Levi, and Matthew Desmond. 2010. "Political Position and Social Knowledge." *Sociological Forum* 25 (1): 1–26.

Massengill, Rebekah Peeples. 2008. "Prayers of the People: Moral Metaphors in the Right-to-Life and Faith-Based Labor Movements." *Poetics* 36 (5): 338–57.

Massengill, Rebekah Peeples. 2013. *Wal-Mart Wars: Moral Populism in the Twenty-First Century*. New York: New York University Press.

May, Reuben A. Buford. 2000. "Race Talk and Local Collective Memory among African American Men in a Neighborhood Tavern." *Qualitative Sociology* 23 (2): 201–14.

McLeod, Kembrew. 1999. "Authenticity within Hip-Hop and Other Cultures Threatened with Assimilation." *Journal of Communication* 49 (4): 134–50.

McPhee, John. 1979. "Profiles: Brigade de Cuisine." *New Yorker*, February 19.

Mead, George Herbert. [1934] 1967. *Mind, Self, and Society: From the Standpoint of a Social Behaviorist*. Chicago: University of Chicago Press.

Melbin, Murray. 1978. "Night As Frontier." *American Sociological Review* 43 (1): 3–22.

Melbin, Murray. 1987. *Night as Frontier: Colonizing the World after Dark*. New York: Free Press; London: Collier Macmillan.

Moll, Jorge, Roland Zahn, Ricardo de Oliveira-Souza, Frank Krueger, and Jordan Grafman. 2005. "The Neural Basis of Human Moral Cognition." *Nature Reviews Neuroscience* 6 (10): 799–809.

Mullaney, Jamie L. 1999. "Making It 'Count': Mental Weighing and Identity Attribution." *Symbolic Interaction* 22 (3): 269–83.

Mullaney, Jamie L. 2006. *Everyone Is NOT Doing It: Abstinence and Personal Identity*. Chicago: University of Chicago Press.

Nagel, Joane. 1994. "Constructing Ethnicity: Creating and Recreating Ethnic Identity and Culture." *Social Problems* 41 (1): 152–76.

New York Times. 1966. "Hoving Calls a Meeting to Plan for Restoration of Bryant Park: Cleanup Is Urged for Bryant Park." *New York Times*, June 22.

Nippert-Eng, Christena E. 1996. *Home and Work: Negotiating Boundaries through Everyday Life*. Chicago: University of Chicago Press.

Norton, Matthew 2014. "Mechanisms and Meaning Structures." *Sociological Theory* 32 (2): 162–87.

Obasogie, Osagie K. 2013. *Blinded by Sight: Seeing Race through the Eyes of the Blind*. Stanford: Stanford University Press.

Ocasio, William. 1997. "Towards an Attention-Based View of the Firm." *Strategic Management Journal* 18: 187–206.

Olick, Jeffrey K. 1999. "Collective Memory: The Two Cultures." *Sociological Theory* 17 (3): 333–48.

References

Olick, Jeffrey K. 2005. *In the House of the Hangman: The Agonies of German Defeat, 1943–1949.* Chicago: University of Chicago Press.

Olick, Jeffrey K. 2007. *The Politics of Regret: On Collective Memory and Historical Responsibility.* New York: Routledge.

Olick, Jeffrey K., and Daniel Levy. 1997. "Collective Memory and Cultural Constraint: Holocaust Myth and Rationality in German Politics." *American Sociological Review* 62 (6): 921–36.

Papachristos, Andrew V. 2009. "Murder by Structure: Dominance Relations and the Social Structure of Gang Homicide." *American Journal of Sociology* 115 (1): 74–128.

Perry, Pamela. 2001. "White Means Never Having to Say You're Ethnic." *Journal of Contemporary Ethnography* 30 (1): 56–91.

Perry, Pamela. 2002. *Shades of White: White Kids and Racial Identities in High School.* Durham, NC: Duke University Press.

Perry, Pamela, and Alexis Shotwell. 2009. "Relational Understanding and White Antiracist Praxis." *Sociological Theory* 27 (1): 33–50.

Peterson, Richard A. 1997. *Creating Country Music: Fabricating Authenticity.* Chicago: University of Chicago Press.

Petrin, Daniel. 2014. "RetroRevolutionaries: The Use of History in Internet-Based Identity Presentation in Contemporary American Militias." Presented at the Annual Stony Brook Graduate Student Ethnography Conference: New York.

Phillips, Frances. 2007. "Collaborative Circles: A Review." *Grantmakers in the Arts Reader* 18 (1). http://www.giarts.org/article/collaborative-circles.

Pollock, Mica. 2004. *Colormute: Race Talk Dilemmas in an American School.* Princeton: Princeton University Press.

Pugh, Allison J. 2009. *Longing and Belonging: Parents, Children, and Consumer Culture.* Berkeley: University of California Press.

Pugh, Allison J. 2013. "What Good Are Interviews for Thinking about Culture? Demystifying Interpretive Analysis." *American Journal of Cultural Sociology* 1 (1): 42–68.

Rao, Hayagreeva, Philippe Monin, and Rodolphe Durand. 2005. "Border Crossing: Bricolage and the Erosion of Categorical Boundaries in French Gastronomy." *American Sociological Review* 70 (6): 968–91.

Raudenbush, Danielle T. 2012. "Race and Interactions on Public Transportation: Social Cohesion and the Production of Common Norms and a Collective Black Identity." *Symbolic Interaction* 35 (4): 456–73.

Rawls, Anne Warfield. 1996. "Durkheim's Epistemology: The Neglected Argument." *American Journal of Sociology* 102 (2): 430–82.

Rawls, Anne Warfield. 1997. "Durkheim and Pragmatism: An Old Twist on a Contemporary Debate." *Sociological Theory* 15 (1): 5–29.

Richeson, Jennifer A., and Sophie Trawalter. 2005. "On the Categorization of Admired and Disliked Exemplars of Admired and Disliked Racial Groups." *Journal of Personality and Social Psychology* 89 (4): 517–30.

References

Ricoeur, Paul. 1984. *Time and Narrative. Vol. 1.* Chicago: University of Chicago Press.

Ricoeur, Paul. 1988. *Time and Narrative. Vol. 3.* Chicago: University of Chicago Press.

Rockquemore, Kerry, and David L. Brunsma. 2002. *Beyond Black: Biracial Identity in America.* Thousand Oaks: Sage.

Rodgers, Diane M. 2008. *Debugging the Link between Social Theory and Social Insects.* Baton Rouge: Louisiana State University Press.

Roffman, Andrew E. 2008. "Men Are Grass: Bateson, Erickson, Utilization and Metaphor." *American Journal of Clinical Hypnosis* 50 (3): 247–57.

Ryan, Dan. 2006. "Getting the Word Out: Notes on the Social Organization of Notification." *Sociological Theory* 24 (3): 228–54.

Rydgren, Jens. 2007. "The Power of the Past: A Contribution to a Cognitive Sociology of Ethnic Conflict." *Sociological Theory* 25 (3): 225–44.

Santa Ana, Otto. 2002. *Brown Tide Rising: Metaphors of Latinos in Contemporary American Public Discourse.* Austin: University of Texas Press.

Saperstein, Aliya, and Andrew M. Penner. 2012. "Racial Fluidity and Inequality in the United States." *American Journal of Sociology* 118 (3): 676–727.

Scarce, Rik. 2000. *Fishy Business: Salmon, Biology, and the Social Construction of Nature.* Philadelphia: Temple University Press.

Scarce, Rik. 2002. "Doing Time as an Act of Survival." *Symbolic Interaction* 25 (3): 303–21.

Schnoor, Randal F. 2006. "Being Gay and Jewish: Negotiating Intersecting Identities." *Sociology of Religion* 67 (1): 43–60.

Schreiber, Darren, Greg Fonzo, Alan N. Simmons, Christopher T. Dawes, Taru Flagan, James H. Fowler, and Martin P. Paulus. 2013. "Red Brain, Blue Brain: Evaluative Processes Differ in Democrats and Republicans." *PLOS ONE* 8 (2): e52970.

Schulhoff, Anastacia. 2010. "More Than Bows and Arrows: Subversion and Double-Consciousness in Native American Storytelling." *Graduate Theses and Dissertations*, October. http://scholarcommons.usf.edu/etd/3545.

Schulz, Jeremy Markham. 2010. "Work and Life in the Balance: Ways of Working and Living Among Elite French, Norwegian, and American Professionals." Dissertation Berkeley: University of California.

Schuman, Howard, and Cheryl Rieger. 1992. "Historical Analogies, Generational Effects, and Attitudes Toward War." *American Sociological Review* 57 (3): 315–26.

Schuman, Howard, and Jacqueline Scott. 1989. "Generations and Collective Memories." *American Sociological Review* 54 (3): 359–81.

Schwartz, Barry. 1981. *Vertical Classification: A Study in Structuralism and the Sociology of Knowledge.* Chicago: University of Chicago Press.

Schwartz, Barry. 1997. "Collective Memory and History: How Abraham Lincoln Became a Symbol of Racial Equality." *Sociological Quarterly* 38 (3): 469–96.

References

Schwartz, Barry. 2000. *Abraham Lincoln and the Forge of National Memory.* Chicago: University of Chicago Press.

Schwartz, Barry. 2008. *Abraham Lincoln in the Post-Heroic Era: History and Memory in Late Twentieth-Century America.* Chicago: University of Chicago Press.

Schwartz, Barry. 2009. "Collective Forgetting and the Symbolic Power of Oneness: The Strange Apotheosis of Rosa Parks." *Social Psychology Quarterly* 72 (2): 123–42.

Schwartz, Barry, and Howard Schuman. 2005. "History, Commemoration, and Belief: Abraham Lincoln in American Memory, 1945–2001." *American Sociological Review* 70 (2): 183–203.

Shepherd, Hana. 2011. "The Cultural Context of Cognition: What the Implicit Association Test Tells Us About How Culture Works." *Sociological Forum* 26 (1): 121–43.

Shibutani, Tamotsu. 1955. "Reference Groups as Perspectives." *American Journal of Sociology* 60 (6): 562–9.

Simmel, Georg. [1955] 1964. *Conflict/The Web of Group-Affiliations*, trans. Reinhard Bendix. New York: Free Press.

Simpson, Ruth. 1996. "Neither Clear nor Present: The Social Construction of Safety and Danger." *Sociological Forum* 11 (3): 549–62.

Smith, Philip. 2005. *Why War? The Cultural Logic of Iraq, the Gulf War, and Suez.* Chicago: University of Chicago Press.

Snow, David A., and Robert D. Benford. 1988. "Ideology, Frame Resonance and Particpant Mobilization." In *From Structure to Action*, ed. Bert Klandermans, Hanspeter Kriesi, and Sidney G. Tarrow. Greenwich: JAI Press.

Snow, David A., and Richard Machalek. 1984. "The Sociology of Conversion." *Annual Review of Sociology* 10 (1): 167–90.

Snow, David A., E. Burke Rochford Jr., Steven K. Worden, and Robert D. Benford. 1986. "Frame Alignment Processes, Micromobilization, and Movement Participation." *American Sociological Review* 51 (4): 464–81.

Snow, David A., Daniel M. Cress, Liam Downey, and Andrew W. Jones. 1998. "Disrupting the 'Quotidian': Reconceptualizing the Relationship between Breakdown and the Emergence of Collective Action." *Mobilization: An International Quarterly* 3 (1): 1–22.

Snyder, Benjamin. 2012. "Dignity and the Professionalized Body: Truck Driving in the Age of Instant Gratification." *Hedgehog Review* 14 (3): 8–20.

Snyder, Benjamin. 2013. "Unsettled Rhythms: The Temporal Dynamics of Culture in Times of Crisis and Uncertainty." Presented at the Annual Meetings of the American Sociological Association: New York.

Spillman, Lyn. 1995. "Culture, Social Structures, and Discursive Fields." *Current Perspectives in Social Theory* 15: 129–54.

Srivastava, Sameer B., and Mahzarin R. Banaji. 2011. "Culture, Cognition, and

References

Collaborative Networks in Organizations." *American Sociological Review* 76 (2): 207–33.

Steensland, Brian. 2006. "Cultural Categories and the American Welfare State: The Case of Guaranteed Income Policy." *American Journal of Sociology* 111 (5): 1273–326.

Stein, Arlene. 1997. *Sex and Sensibility: Stories of a Lesbian Generation.* Berkeley: University of California Press.

Stein, Arlene. 2009. "'As Far as They Knew I Came from France': Stigma, Passing, and Not Speaking about the Holocaust." *Symbolic Interaction* 32 (1): 44–60.

Stein, Karen. 2011. "Getting Away from It All: The Construction and Management of Temporary Identities on Vacation." *Symbolic Interaction* 34 (2): 290–308.

Strydom, Piet. 2007. "Introduction: A Cartography of Contemporary Cognitive Social Theory." *European Journal of Social Theory* 10 (3): 339–56.

Swidler, Ann. 1986. "Culture in Action: Symbols and Strategies." *American Sociological Review* 51 (2): 273–86.

Swidler, Ann. 1995. "Cultural Power and Social Movements." In *Social Movements and Culture*, ed. Hank Johnston and Bert Klandermans. Minneapolis: University of Minnesota Press.

Swidler, Ann. 2001. *Talk of Love: How Culture Matters.* Chicago: University of Chicago Press.

Swidler, Ann. 2008. "Comment on Stephen Vaisey's 'Socrates, Skinner, and Aristotle: Three Ways of Thinking About Culture in Action.'" *Sociological Forum* 23 (3): 614–18.

Tavory, Iddo. 2010. "Of Yarmulkes and Categories: Delegating Boundaries and the Phenomenology of Interactional Expectation." *Theory and Society* 39 (1): 49–68.

Teeger, Chana, and Vered Vinitzky-Seroussi. 2007. "Controlling for Consensus: Commemorating Apartheid in South Africa." *Symbolic Interaction* 30 (1): 57–78.

Thorne, Barrie. 1993. *Gender Play: Girls and Boys in School.* New Brunswick: Rutgers University Press.

Turner, Stephen. 2007. "Social Theory as a Cognitive Neuroscience." *European Journal of Social Theory* 10 (3): 357–74.

Turner, Victor W. 1967. *The Forest of Symbols: Aspects of Ndembu Ritual.* Ithaca: Cornell University Press.

Vaisey, Stephen. 2008. "Socrates, Skinner, and Aristotle: Three Ways of Thinking About Culture in Action." *Sociological Forum* 23 (3): 603–13.

Vaisey, Stephen. 2009. "Motivation and Justification: A Dual-Process Model of Culture in Action." *American Journal of Sociology* 114 (6): 1675–715.

Vaisey, Stephen, and Omar Lizardo. 2010. "Can Cultural Worldviews Influence Network Composition?" *Social Forces* 88 (4): 1595–618.

References

Van Gennep, Arnold. 1960. *The Rites of Passage*. Chicago: University of Chicago Press.

Vaughan, Diane. 1996. *The Challenger Launch Decision: Risky Technology, Culture, and Deviance at NASA*. Chicago: University of Chicago Press.

Vaughan, Diane. 2002. "Signals and Interpretive Work: The Role of Culture in a Theory of Practical Action." In *Culture in Mind: Toward a Sociology of Culture and Cognition*, ed. Karen A. Cerulo. New York: Routledge.

Vila-Henninger, Luis Antonio. 2014. "Towards Defining the Causal Role of Consciousness: Using Models of Memory and Moral Judgement from Cognitive Neuroscience to Expand the Sociological Dual-Process Model." *Journal for the Theory of Social Behaviour* (online).

Vinitzky-Seroussi, Vered. 1998. *After Pomp and Circumstance: High School Reunion as an Autobiographical Occasion*. Chicago: University of Chicago Press.

Wagner-Pacifici, Robin Erica. 1994. *Discourse and Destruction: The City of Philadelphia versus MOVE*. Chicago: University of Chicago Press.

Warikoo, Natasha Kumar. 2007. "Racial Authenticity among Second Generation Youth in Multiethnic New York and London." *Poetics* 35 (6): 388–408.

Warner, W. Lloyd, Marchia Meeker, and Kenneth Eells. 1949. *Social Class in America: A Manual of Procedure for the Measurement of Social Status*. Chicago: Science Research Associates.

Watters, Ethan. 2013. "We Aren't the World." *Pacific Standard*, February 25. http://www.psmag.com/magazines/pacific-standard-cover-story/joe-henrich-weird-ultimatum-game-shaking-up-psychology-economics-53135.

Waugh, Linda R. 1982. "Marked and Unmarked: A Choice between Unequals in Semiotic Discourse." *Semiotica* 38: 299–318.

Weber, Max. [1925] 1978. *Economy and Society: An Outline of Interpretive Sociology*. New edn. Berkeley: University of California Press.

Wherry, Frederick F. 2008. "The Social Characterizations of Price: The Fool, the Faithful, the Frivolous, and the Frugal." *Sociological Theory* 26 (4): 363–79.

Wherry, Frederick F. 2012. *The Culture of Markets*. Cambridge; Malden: Polity.

Widdicombe, Sue, and Rob Wooffitt. 1990. "'Being' Versus 'Doing' Punk: On Achieving Authenticity as a Member." *Journal of Language and Social Psychology* 9 (4): 257–77.

Wilkins, Amy C. 2008. *Wannabes, Goths, and Christians: The Boundaries of Sex, Style, and Status*. Chicago: University of Chicago Press.

Williams, J. Patrick. 2006. "Authentic Identities: Straightedge Subculture, Music, and the Internet." *Journal of Contemporary Ethnography* 35 (2): 173–200.

Williams, Richard E. 1990. *Hierarchical Structures and Social Value: The Creation of Black and Irish Identities in the United States*. Cambridge; New York: Cambridge University Press.

Willis, Paul E. 1981. *Learning to Labor: How Working Class Kids Get Working Class Jobs*. New York: Columbia University Press.

References

Wilson, Mandy. 2002. "'I Am the Prince of Pain, for I Am a Princess in the Brain': Liminal Transgender Identities, Narratives and the Elimination of Ambiguities." *Sexualities* 5 (4): 425–48.

Wiltse, Jeff. 2007. *Contested Waters: A Social History of Swimming Pools in America*. Chapel Hill: University of North Carolina Press.

Winchester, Daniel. 2008. "Embodying the Faith: Religious Practice and the Making of a Muslim Moral Habitus." *Social Forces* 86 (4): 1753–80.

Wuthnow, Robert. 2010. *Be Very Afraid: The Cultural Response to Terror, Pandemics, Environmental Devastation, Nuclear Annihilation, and Other Threats*. Oxford; New York: Oxford University Press.

Zavisca, Jane. 2010. *To Owe Is Not to Own: Why Russians Reject Mortgages (and Why Americans Accept Them)*. Working Paper 823–07. National Council for Eurasian and East European Research (NCEEER). http://www.nceeer.org/papers/85-to-owe-is-not-to-own-why-russians-reject-mortgages-and-why-americans-accept-them.html.

Zavisca, Jane R. 2012. *Housing the New Russia*. Ithaca: Cornell University Press.

Zelizer, Viviana A. 1994. *The Social Meaning of Money*. New York: Basic Books.

Zelizer, Viviana A. 1996. "Payments and Social Ties." *Sociological Forum* 11 (3): 481–95.

Zelizer, Viviana A. 2011. *Economic Lives: How Culture Shapes the Economy*. Princeton: Princeton University Press.

Zerubavel, Eviatar. 1979. *Patterns of Time in Hospital Life: A Sociological Perspective*. Chicago: University of Chicago Press.

Zerubavel, Eviatar. 1991. *The Fine Line: Making Distinctions in Everyday Life*. New York: Free Press.

Zerubavel, Eviatar. 1996. "Lumping and Splitting: Notes on Social Classification." *Sociological Forum* 11 (3): 421–33.

Zerubavel, Eviatar. 1997. *Social Mindscapes: An Invitation to Cognitive Sociology*. Cambridge, MA: Harvard University Press.

Zerubavel, Eviatar. 2003. *Time Maps: Collective Memory and the Social Shape of the Past*. Chicago: University of Chicago Press.

Zerubavel, Eviatar. 2006. *The Elephant in the Room: Silence and Denial in Everyday Life*. Oxford; New York: Oxford University Press.

Zerubavel, Eviatar. 2007. "Generally Speaking: The Logic and Mechanics of Social Pattern Analysis." *Sociological Forum* 22 (2): 131–45.

Zerubavel, Eviatar. 2012. *Ancestors and Relatives: Genealogy, Identity and Community*. Oxford; New York: Oxford University Press.

Zerubavel, Eviatar. 2015. *Hidden in Plain Sight: The Social Structure of Irrelevance*. New York; Oxford: Oxford University Press.

Index

211

Index

thought styles 2–3, 22, 29, 31, 34, 42, 45, 82
cognitive asymmetry 25–6, 45–6
cognitive cultures, local 12, 31, 33–41, 57, 86, 88
  occupational 31, 35–7
cognitive neuroscience 5, 7–9, 16–18, 30, 32, 98, 149, 180–1, 183–5, 189
  cognitive variation 2, 5, 12, 14, 20, 22, 24, 31, 33–5, 37, 41–9, 57, 61, 64–6, 90, 94, 102, 147, 150, 160, 164, 189–90
collective representations 5–7, 9–13, 59, 172–3, 177
cross-case, cross-context comparisons 3–4, 14, 20, 32, 37, 49, 52, 55, 57, 59–61, 64, 98, 109, 112–15, 118–20, 160, 187–91, 193
cross-domain comparisons 7, 14, 24, 69–70, 75, 86, 189–92
cross-scale comparisons 14, 41, 52, 55, 61, 70, 191, 193
cultural capital 8, 124, 132, 137, 188, 190
  black 124, 137, 188
  historical 159
  mainstream 188
  multicultural 113
  nocturnal 138
  subcultural 63, 73
cultural categories of worth 95–6
cultural codes 6, 10–13, 15, 19, 80, 124, 185, 192
cultural frames/framing 24, 45, 51, 56, 75–6, 78, 88–92, 98, 109, 160
cultural meanings, moral 44, 74–5, 86–9, 91–4, 96–8, 100–1, 110, 150, 162, 185
cultural resonance 22, 98, 103–5, 147, 156, 160, 185
cultural schemas 24, 95, 104, 156, 177, 188
cultural sociology/sociologists 1, 5, 8–11, 16–19, 24, 79, 171–2, 186
cultural toolkit tradition 8–9, 15–16, 172–3

cultural trauma 106, 157–8
cultural weighting 64–5, 70–2
culture
  cognitive 12, 31, 33–41, 57, 86, 88
  occupational 31, 35–7
  collective 5–6, 10–14, 23, 42, 46, 59, 98, 106, 147
  group-level 34–7, 40, 42, 98
  representations of 5–7, 9–13, 59, 172–3, 177
  fragmented, inconsistent 8, 15, 18, 175, 178
  in action 8, 12, 15–17, 56, 98, 171, 173, 176–8, 181–2
  strong program in 5

Daipha, Phaedra 35–6
danger, perceptions of 22, 41–8, 57, 76, 85, 104, 178, 186
Danna Lynch, Karen 82, 140–1
Davis, F. James 65–6, 86
DeGloma, Thomas 143–4
deliberate cognition 19, 22, 24, 28–33, 47, 107, 141, 143, 166, 182, 190–1
DiMaggio, Paul 21, 95, 112
disasters 29, 45–8, 55
discourse 6, 9–11, 13, 17, 19, 28, 53, 77, 89–90, 96, 98–100, 102, 104, 106, 121, 132, 150, 156, 185, 191
disruptions
  to order 55, 74, 76, 186
  to routine 29–30, 32–3, 42, 47, 52, 144
DiTomaso, Nancy 26, 187
Douglas, Mary 59, 75, 77, 85
dual-process models of cognition 17, 29, 32, 172–8, 180–1
Durkheim, Émile 4–7, 9–11, 13–15, 23, 26, 59–60, 100, 147

Eliasoph, Nina 12, 51
embodied/embodiment
  experience and cognition 6–7, 17–18, 30, 33, 83, 98–9, 121, 123, 188, 191

Index

embodied/embodiment (*cont.*)
  metaphors 98–100, 184
  perspectives on cognition 6–7, 9,
    17, 172–8
  practice 18, 33, 77, 83–4, 98–9,
    132, 188
emotion 10, 41, 82, 123, 160, 165–6,
  179–80
  emotional alignment 83
  emotional blinders 82
  emotion codes 10, 185
ethnography/ethnographic methods
  13, 19, 37–8, 82, 99–100, 116,
  127, 177, 179, 190
  interviews in 81, 116

Fine, Gary Alan 13, 73–4, 156, 164–6
Fleck, Ludwik 13, 34
fluidity 32, 38, 61–2, 67, 69, 81
Force, William 33, 122, 126, 192
frames/framing 7, 22–4, 52, 81, 88,
  147, 160
  in frame and out of frame 22–4,
    52–3, 55, 58, 78, 88, 112, 139,
    148
  media 44–5, 55–6
  narrative 89, 103–9, 177
  of meaning and interpretation 7,
    22–4, 41–7, 51–6, 63, 70, 75–6,
    78, 81, 88–98, 105–9, 126, 139,
    148, 157, 160, 163, 179, 187,
    191
  of relevance 23–4, 41–3, 46–7, 70,
    139, 148, 160
  organizational 45–7, 53–4
  social movement 7, 52–3, 88–9
frameworks, cultural
  of danger and safety 41–5, 57
  of nature 73–4, 76
  of racial classification 67
Friedman, Asia 22, 24, 49–50
Fuller, Sylvia 61–4, 75

Garroutte, Eva Marie 67, 123
general social patterns 2, 14, 55, 57,
  61, 64, 86, 98, 114, 118, 171,
  183, 189–93

generations 13, 149–53
  generational identity 153
  generational imprinting 150
Gergen, Kenneth 128
Goffman, Erving 4, 6–9, 11, 13–14,
  23–6, 38, 51–2, 81, 88, 111–12,
  136, 139–40, 142
Goodwin, Charles 53–4
Grazian, David 138–9, 142
Green, Adam Isaiah 19, 30–2
Griffin, Larry 151–3, 155
Gubrium, Jaber 128–9
gun owners, perception 43–4

habitus 8, 17–18, 22–4, 31, 47, 98–9,
  132, 175
Haidt, Jonathan 174, 180–1
Holocaust 106, 157–8
Holstein, James 128–9, 160–1, 192
Howard, Jenna 115–16, 119
Hurricane Katrina 55–6

identity
  as strategic resource 33, 112,
    116–27, 131–45
  authenticity 112, 118–27, 137, 142,
    145, 188, 190
  auxiliary characteristics of 117–27,
    137, 145–6
  class, social 85, 118, 131–2, 135
  commuters/commuting 117–18,
    125, 136, 140, 144–5
  density 117, 118, 120, 122, 124
  disputes 114, 117–27
  duration 117, 118, 120, 125, 140
  integrators/integrating 117–19,
    136–8, 140, 142
  lifestylers/lifestyling 115, 117–18,
    123, 135–6
  migration 144–6
  mobility 112, 117–20, 123, 128,
    136–46, 190
  multidimensionality 14, 112,
    118–20, 127–36, 140, 145,
    190–1
  personal/autobiographical 142–3
  racial/ethnic

Index

Index

subcultural and primary group
cognitions (*cont.*)
overeaters 98–9
perception
gun owners 43–4
subcultural authenticity claims and
disputes 121–3, 127
surveys, survey methods 17, 19, 67–8,
84, 134, 175, 177, 179, 182
Swidler, Ann 8–9, 15–16, 30, 107,
176–7
Swistun, Debora 19, 47–8
symbolic boundaries *see* boundaries,
symbolic
symbolic classification/differentiation
59, 63, 77, 79, 93, 95–6, 101
symbolic deprivation 93
symbolic indulgence 93
symbolic interactionism/interactionist
perspective 7, 9, 11–13, 172
symbols 6, 8, 10–12, 15, 42, 53, 100,
109, 126, 150, 156, 175, 183

Tavory, Iddo 82–4, 190
thought *see* cognition/thought
time
as metaphorical commodity 168
experience of 148, 163–8
event-centered 148, 163–5
jail 166
movement of 148
organizational 164–6
personal and private 164
queer 167

street 166
time work 167–8

unmarked *see* marked and unmarked

Vaisey, Stephen 16–17, 29, 68, 84,
172–7, 180, 184
Vaughan, Diane 45–7
Vila-Henninger, Luis 180–2
Vinitzky-Seroussi, Vered 142–3,
157–8
vision, collective
creative 36
influenced 42
moral 54
organizational 54
professional 35–6, 54
restricted 48
trained 36

Wherry, Frederick 91–3
Wilkins, Amy 132–3, 190
Williams, J. Patrick 123, 127
Winchester, Daniel 99
worldviews 13, 15, 27, 31, 34, 38,
73–4, 84, 99–103, 129–30,
143–5, 151, 173, 181
Wuthnow, Robert 48–9

Zavisca, Jane 93–5
Zelizer, Viviana 90–1
Zerubavel, Eviatar 2, 5, 9, 13–15,
20–1, 32–3, 55, 60–2, 158–60,
164, 172